Unfortunately there was an error
on page 45. Here is the corrected version.

Orff Schulwerk
in Diverse Cultures
An Idea That Went Round the World

A Series of Publications from the International Orff-Schulwerk Forum Salzburg

edited by Barbara Haselbach

International
Orff-Schulwerk Forum
Salzburg

Texts on Theory and Practice of Orff Schulwerk
Volume II

Orff Schulwerk in Diverse Cultures

An Idea That Went Round the World

edited by Barbara Haselbach
and Carolee Stewart

Pentatonic Press

Cover Design: Lisa Berman
Editors: Barbara Haselbach, Carolee Stewart
Maps (except cover map): Jack Neill
Design of the International Orff-Schulwerk Forum Salzburg logo tree: Hermann Regner
Book design and typesetting: Bill Holab Music
ISBN 0-9773712-7-1

Dedicated to the memory of
Hermann Regner,
who helped so much to share the Schulwerk around the world

and to
all the children and teachers
who love to sing and dance and play

Contents

PART I
TEXTS ON THEORY OF ORFF SCHULWERK

PART II
TEXTS ON PRACTICE OF ORFF SCHULWERK AROUND THE WORLD

AFRICA

NORTH AND SOUTH AMERICA

OCEANIA

Orff Schulwerk in Australia
Compiled and edited by Peta Harper and Sarah Powell
Orff Schulwerk in Aotearoa New Zealand
Linda M. Locke

APPENDIX

Foreword

I am delighted to offer my sincere congratulations on the publication of this book. This collection of articles from member associations of the International Orff-Schulwerk Forum Salzburg documents how the idea of Orff Schulwerk has gone around the world and has been developed and transformed in each country where the seed has landed. As we know very well, Orff Schulwerk in every context is influenced by and responds to different educational, artistic, social, and political developments in each country. The need for continuing development of the approach was recognized by Orff himself.

This second volume of the *Texts on Theory and Practice of Orff Schulwerk* contributes to knowledge about these developments and to the exchange of ideas. It encourages and informs mutual understanding for the different adaptations of Orff Schulwerk internationally and strengthens our communication with music and dance teachers worldwide.

I hope this book will find an extensive circle of readers.

Shirley Salmon,
President of the International Orff-Schulwerk Forum Salzburg
July 2021

Introduction

In its timelessness the elemental finds understanding all over the world.
So it was...the idea itself that went round the world. (Orff, 1978, p. 277)

...and it has now gone for more than 70 years!

How did it come about and how does an idea change over such a long time through influences from diverse cultures?

This is not the first time that an attempt has been made to survey and comment on the phenomenon of the rapid and worldwide spread of the Orff Schulwerk. A most comprehensive account was made with *Begegnungen* by Hermann Regner in 1990, but many cultural, social, and political influences have caused changes since that time. Thus, it seemed reasonable and necessary in the context of the publication series *Studientexte zu Theorie und Praxis des Orff-Schulwerks / Texts on Theory and Practice of Orff-Schulwerk* to follow the traces of this dissemination and to document the various ways of adaptation by representatives from the respective countries.

In 1948, the Orff Schulwerk, initially developed and published at the Günther-Schule für Rhythmik, Gymnastik und Tanz in Munich from 1926 to 1944, turned for the first time to a new target group, namely classes of elementary school children. Gunild Keetman, Orff's long-time collaborator, to whom much of the published material and initially all the pedagogical activities are owed, conducted school radio broadcasts at the Bayerischer Rundfunk (Hartmann, Maschat, & Regner, 2000) and in children's classes at what was then the Akademie Mozarteum in Salzburg (Grüner & Haselbach, 2011). This developed into what is now known and practiced in a wide variety of forms and languages in many countries on all continents as "Orff Schulwerk, Elemental Music and Movement/Dance Education." [1]

Was this international dissemination based on a plan, an organized procedure? Orff himself said in 1961:

> *Schulwerk did not develop from a pre-considered plan—I could never have imagined such a far-reaching one. (Orff, 1963/2011, p. 134)*

Historical development in brief

In retrospect, this wave of dissemination can be outlined thus: After the publication of the five volumes of *Musik für Kinder* (1950–54), the Schulwerk was presented to an international audience at pedagogical conferences as early as 1953; individual interested parties from abroad came to Salzburg to study with Keetman during the 1950s; in 1961, the Orff Institute was established as:

---

1 For example, see André de Quadros (Ed.), 2000, *Many Seeds, Different Flowers - The Music Education Legacy of Carl Orff*, Perth: CIRCME; Cecilia Chu Wang (Ed.), 2013, *Orff Schulwerk - Reflections and Directions,* Chicago: GIA Publications.

...a training centre in which music, movement and speech should be taught with equal emphasis, and a centre, that should catch and satisfy the interest and desire for information, that was now world-wide. (Orff, 1978, p. 241)

Its largely international student body took back to their home countries the ideas, publications, and instruments they had learned in Salzburg. Their pioneering work attracted interest from colleagues and institutions, and as a result, lecturers from the Orff Institute, and later its graduates, were invited from various countries to give seminars. Orff and Keetman themselves participated in a few conferences.

The "Special Course" or "Post Graduate University Course: Advanced Studies in Elemental Music and Dance Education–Orff-Schulwerk" was established in 1969, and it attracted many foreign educators who could not be away from their obligations for more than a year. In their countries of origin, many of them taught at universities in teacher education programs upon their return. Orff Schulwerk societies were founded, and the first levels courses were created within the larger societies, such as in the USA, Australia, Canada, and some other countries, intensifying the dissemination within each country. First Schulwerk adaptations were submitted to Orff, Keetman, and later to Hermann Regner[1] for review and comment, and soon other publications *á la* Orff Schulwerk appeared in various languages. Graduates returned to the Orff Institute with the experiences from their home countries and taught in summer courses or as guest teachers in the various courses of study. Inspiration and exchange of information very soon took place in both directions. In short, it was like when a stone is thrown into the water and new wave circles continue to emerge from it.

Different ways of adaptation

With this almost unmanageable growth of the Schulwerk, however, something arose that Orff himself called a "wildflower." Therein lies its greatness, its power to develop and adapt, but also a certain danger of unqualified use of its name and content. Orff was aware of this danger early on:

> *Every phase of Schulwerk will always provide stimulation for new independent growth; therefore it is never conclusive and settled, but always developing, always growing, always flowing. Herein of course lies a great danger, that of development in the wrong direction. Further independent growth presupposes basic specialist training and absolute familiarity with the style, the possibilities and the aims of Schulwerk. (1963/2011, p. 134)*

And so, Orff and Keetman, as artists and inspiring teachers, decided against a fixed system and in favor of the openness of inspiration for carefully trained educators in Schulwerk.

However, the development during the subsequent decades has shown that different interpretations have occurred. Initially, it often happened that what was meant as a model was used exclusively as binding material for instrumental training or for impressive children's concerts. In some countries or among some educators, even today, strict adherence to the material structure seems to be paramount. Elsewhere, the emphasis is not so much on the technical aspect, but instead it is on the pedagogical goals for "human formation" (*Menschenbildung*), in the sense of fostering creativity and independence, as well as holistic, interdisciplinary, and creative

---

1 Hermann Regner (1928–2008), composer, conductor, musicologist, pedagogue, former director of the Orff Institute, and chairman of the Carl Orff Foundation for many years started and supported adaptations of Orff Schulwerk in different cultures and languages. He gave countless lectures, seminars, and workshops all over the world.

work in the community. This may also have been reinforced by the expansion of the Schulwerk to include a variety of new target groups, involving senior citizens, inclusive education, and music-therapeutic fields of work.

Occasionally there has been talk of "cultural colonialism" in relation to the dissemination of the Orff Schulwerk. The assumption may be obvious if one disregards the fact that the intense interest has always come from individual countries, pedagogical institutions, or educators who sought information, went to study in Salzburg, or organized courses in their own environment with lecturers from the Orff Institute or other similar centers. Hermann Regner talked about this in an interview with Orff, and Orff's answer became a kind of guiding principle for all teaching activities in other cultures:

> When you work with Schulwerk abroad, you must start all over again from the experience of the local children. And the experiences of children in Africa are different from those in Hamburg or Stralsund, and again from those in Paris or Tokyo. (Regner, 1984/2011, p. 220)

Not only Western guest lecturers but also, and above all, the educators of the respective countries have increasingly sought the sources of traditional material such as songs, dances, rhymes, and games of children and thus contributed to the fact that cultural heritage is not lost. The nature of the encounter between educators from the region and guest lecturers strives for what Regner called "equality in dialogue."

Nevertheless, it must be made quite clear that the pedagogy of the Orff Schulwerk by no means serves only to preserve the cultural tradition, even if "tradition is not guarding the ashes, but kindling the fire" (Jean Jaurès). The emphasis on the experimental, the support of the creative, and the integration of artistic forms of expression points to a clear relationship with contemporary art but does not exclude the inclusion of pop culture. In this sense, the Orff Institute has certainly done pioneering work over the years. Unfortunately, most reports from other countries express little on this aspect. Perhaps much encouragement is still needed.

Part I: On the themes of dissemination and adaptation

To begin, we present a collection of articles, both reprinted and newly written, that set the scene for the topic of the dissemination of Orff Schulwerk. First is a reprint of an article by Hermann Regner originally published in English translation in 1993. Regner wrote and spoke on this theme many times. Mary Shamrock has updated a portion of her 1995 monograph in which she addressed issues concerning global dispersal of Orff Schulwerk. The article by Michael Kugler is also a reprint and a more recent discussion of intercultural aspects of Orff Schulwerk. Wolfgang Hartmann's article on the "principles" of Orff Schulwerk describes fundamental and universal concepts of the approach. The section concludes with a newly written article by Doug Goodkin on the use of world music.

Part II: On the selection of the invited countries and societies and the focus of the contributions

Not all of the nearly 50 different countries in which the Orff Schulwerk has made its home could be invited to contribute. This would have far exceeded the size of this publication. Because the focus of this collection is primarily on "diverse cultures," contributions from Asia, Africa, North and South America, and Oceania are the focus, supplemented by a few European contributions that have a special feature to show.

Thus, the Czech edition was the first one that did not include examples from the original German edition but was arranged by two young Czech composers in agreement with Orff. Greece as the country that originated the idea of *mousiké* and Spain as a country coexisting for centuries with many different cultures take a special place. Likewise, the contribution of the Nordic countries of Europe describes a pedagogical unity in the diversity of sources and materials.

It was also important to us, where available, to let more than one organization or initiative within a country speak in order not to convey a one-sided picture. This concerns especially the development of the Orff Schulwerk in China and Turkey.

The editors have tried to obtain comparable information without prescribing a narrow system. For this purpose, various topics were requested for the contributions: these included a historical overview of the development of the Orff Schulwerk in the country; the inclusion of country-specific sources (songs, texts, games, dances, instruments, etc.); the relationship with an often different musical system; the inclusion in the respective teaching system, and the difficulties of adapting to such a system; the target groups addressed, and so on.

A striking feature of many contributions was the mention of dependence on the country's political system and the emphasis on the difficulty of enforcing creative, experiential, and process-oriented learning against predetermined performance tests.

Acknowledgements

It may be characteristic for the way of communication and cooperation in dealing with the Orff Schulwerk that very few articles were written by one author alone, but in most cases by a team of specialists. On the one hand, this has prolonged the process of the book's creation and enormously extended the interesting correspondence with the individual teams and their members. On the other hand, it also ensures a varied and well-rounded picture of each contribution.

It is not possible to mention nearly seventy authors by name here, but we would like to express our heartfelt thanks to each one of them, and to all of them collectively, for their highly committed and extremely time-consuming collaboration. Our gratitude is also extended to the individuals who contributed photographs.

We also want to thank Verena Maschat, who aided in several ways during the editing process, and whose expertise with many languages was invaluable, and Jack Neill, who created the maps of each continent showing the countries that are represented in this book.

Special thanks go to our publisher and highly esteemed, dear colleague Doug Goodkin, who offered of his own accord to publish this English-language volume in his publishing house Pentatonic Press in America and who has been helpful to us in every way.

In the spirit of a "dialogue of cultures," we wish our readers a stimulating read and "journey around the world," from which perhaps many an inspiration for their own work could arise.

Barbara Haselbach,   Carolee Stewart,
Salzburg, Austria   Martha's Vineyard, USA

July 2021

PART I

Texts on theory of Orff Schulwerk

Musik für Kinder—Music for Children— Musique pour Enfants: Comments on the Adoption and Adaptation of Orff Schulwerk in Other Countries [1]

Hermann Regner

This article is a first tentative attempt to bring together comments about the history of the adoption and adaptation of Schulwerk in other countries. Through the self-destructive efforts of the Western world to dismiss everything of a permanent nature, everything that could have validity for yesterday, today, and tomorrow, there is a resultant danger that one of the most important music educational movements of this century will be forgotten and dismissed, and only because it is no longer "new"—and this before one has really got to the bottom of its possibilities.

"Start from the experience of the children"

> When you work with Schulwerk abroad, you must start all over again from the experience of the local children. And the experiences of children in Africa are different from those in Hamburg or Stralsund, and again from those in Paris or Tokyo. (Regner, 1975/2011, p. 220)

This sentence comes from an interview that I had with Orff on the occasion of his eightieth birthday. When I asked him if he could encompass an overall view of the worldwide movement that his Schulwerk had released in many branches of education and in many parts of the world, he replied:

> That is quite impossible for me to encompass, it's become like an army camp. But I can always be glad from the outside that I have made so many contacts with interesting people, people who have similar concerns—or who have perhaps unconsciously had such concerns, that, through being addressed by Schulwerk have become clear to them. This is all very gratifying, and there are bound to be outstanding people, who are working in ways that are quite different from those that I had planned. But that is the essence: if something has a living growth–if I plant a tree, I never know how big it will become . . . One remains small, another grows very tall. That depends on the soil, on the amount of sunshine and on other conditions that have to contribute. Such things cannot be planned; they can only come into being. (1975/2011, p. 220–222)

The soil seems to have been good: there are materials in many countries that owe their origins to Schulwerk. Neither the Orff Institute in Salzburg, nor the original publishers (Schott/Mainz), can guarantee that a list of editions in other countries is really complete. It is often the

1 This is a reprint of the English translation by Margaret Murray that appeared in *Orff-Schulwerk Informationen* 51, Summer 1993, pp. 11–15. This issue was dedicated to Hermann Regner on the occasion of his retirement from the Orff Institute.

case that after several years, and quite by chance, one discovers that somewhere in the world a Schulwerk edition has appeared.

The last volume of the original German edition appeared in 1954—nearly forty years ago. Only two years later the first volume of an English adaptation was published. It is informative to examine this edition in some detail.

The first edition in a foreign language

Dr. Arnold Walter, at the time Director of the Music Department of Toronto University, came to know of the work of Orff and Keetman on the occasion of an international conference for college directors in Salzburg. On his recommendation one of his pupils, Doreen Hall, came to Salzburg to study with Keetman. On her return to Toronto, she worked further on the collecting of material and on her practical experiments with children. A glance at this first edition to appear outside Germany shows the degree of circumspection with which this work was approached. A translation of Orff's Preface is followed by an Introduction by Arnold Walter. The author starts by stating that Orff is not only a celebrated composer, but also one of Europe's most remarkable music educators.

> *As such, he is no writer of learned treatises or long-winded essays: Music for Children is an eminently practical primer, a compendium of everything a child ought to be taught while being initiated into music . . . (Orff & Keetman [Hall/Walter], 1956, Introduction).*

Walter goes on to describe the then new, and to him remarkable, content of Orff Schulwerk with the following emphasis (the reader should consider the date: December 1956):

> *The primary purpose of music education, as Orff sees it, is the development of a child's creative faculty which manifests itself in the ability to improvise. This cannot be achieved by supplying ready-made and usually much too sophisticated material of the classical variety, but only by helping a child to make his own music, at his/her own level, integrated with a host of related activities. Speaking and singing, poetry and music, music and movement, playing and dancing are not yet separated in the world of children, they are essentially one and indivisible, all governed by the play instinct which is a prime mover in the development of art and ritual.*

If Arnold Walter criticizes music teaching, is this criticism only valid for Canada and the United States?

> *It has been taken out of the play-sphere, it has lost its innocence and joy, it has become a very serious business concerned with fingerings and counting beats and reading clefs and practicing, it is altogether too conscious, too technical, too mechanical.*

In our time writes Walter further, the music teacher finds no readymade foundation on which to build . . . he must begin at the beginning: which is the heart of the matter.

In this Introduction it is also established that after all these fundamental considerations it did not seem meaningful just to translate such a work. It was necessary to find analogous material from English, Canadian, and American sources.

The "first generation" of foreign language editions

It is not possible within the confines of this article to examine all the editions critically. The comments made in the Hall/Walter edition are valid—in spite of their differences—for all other adaptations that have appeared between 1956 and 1968.

The Swedish edition was the work of Daniel Helldén. In the *Singing Games* in the first part of the first volume there are 10 examples where he has freely translated the German texts; five songs to which he has fitted traditional Swedish texts, and he has added 20 songs of his own, i.e., for those folk texts that he found he has made settings of his own in the style of Schulwerk. This constitutes a markedly higher proportion of his own settings. Year by year Helldén has given courses for teachers in Sweden and Denmark and has especially developed his method for use in music education in general schools. He is an independent artistic and educational personality, to whom it came to show Orff's ideas in settings of a different kind (Gersdorf, 1975, p. 53).

An interesting indication of the relationship between original and adaptation is to be found in the introduction to Margaret Murray's 1958 English Version. Walter Jellinek writes:

> No attempt has been made in this English version to keep rigidly to the original German texts or to traditional English tunes. No apology is made for either, because a way has been sought to follow the principle of Carl Orff's theories.

With the term Orff's "theories" he can only mean that he is stressing the openness of the approach. In a speech in 1963 Carl Orff said:

> Every phase of Schulwerk will always, provide stimulation for new independent growth, therefore, it is never conclusive and settled, but always developing, always growing, always flowing. (Orff, 1964/2011, p. 134).

This is valid for children and young people who work with the Schulwerk ideas and models, for teachers who accept the challenge of such a stimulus, and for those colleagues to whom Orff entrusted the preparation of the foreign language editions. All the "first generation" editions were discussed with him and Gunild Keetman. He looked through all the settings himself and not infrequently made suggestions for changes and corrections.

Guillermo Graetzer has produced an edition for Latin-American countries. Here one can also see the discretion with which he approached the work.

> A thorough understanding of the cultural needs and possibilities was necessary if one was to introduce Schulwerk to a country in which not a few voices were raised in protest at the importing of foreign teaching methods. We based our work mainly on the children's folk material. I made use of round dances, rhymes, and songs that are basic, with minimal differences, to the whole of Latin America, by reason of hundreds of years of Spanish influence... Our excavation activities in the seminars, that were attended by perhaps some thousand teachers, were particularly fruitful in this respect, for there were many rhymes that had been almost forgotten and were no longer being used by children at play in the cities. (Gersdorf, 1975, p. 39).

We will often have indicated that it is Orff's incitement to go back to individual cultural traditions that has triggered off the search for traditional games, texts, songs, and dances in many countries. Professor Naohiro Fukui, long-time Director of the Musashino Academy in Tokyo, confirms a development along these lines in Japan. He reported in 1975 about the work of a study-group and declared that not only at the Musashino Academy, but *in practically the whole of Japan, Orff's ideas about music education are being put into practice, particularly in Kindergartens, Primary, and Middle Schools. (Gersdorf, 1975, p. 37).*

That this picture is today seen differently may lie in the fact that changes are taking place in Japan's capital city at a hardly conceivable rate, perhaps also in that touring visitors always see mainly that which they want to or should. Naohiro Fukui's report continues:

We have thereby been able to establish that 1) rhythmic education has been much promoted through the experience of movement; 2) improvisation has been fundamentally enriched through the use of simple percussion instruments. Even our children's songs and folk songs have been rediscovered and more widely distributed through their connection with Orff-Schulwerk.

Such statements seem to prove to us that it is neither missionary zeal nor some kind of cultural colonization that lies at the root of the expansion of the Schulwerk ideas over extensive parts of the world. Long before the official state cultural policy had prescribed that culture "is not a commodity to be exported, but rather: a process of meeting in partnership" (Witte, 1983, p. 37) those musicians and teachers who were concerned with Schulwerk had developed an awareness of and a sensitivity towards the independence of cultural groups and their equality of rights within the process of dialogue. It is not only a question of non-interference, but that Schulwerk's clear stipulation that it is the indigenous folk material that must be used has, in parts of the world, awakened an awareness of their own sources of folk material and a striving for cultural identity. Orff has written: "Traditional children's rhymes and songs are the natural starting point for this work" (Orff & Keetman, 1950, Preface). This statement by Orff will remind those in the know of Béla Bartók's assessment of the value of folk music:

It is my conviction that within our genuine, in the narrowest sense of the word, folk melodies, each and every one is a true example of the highest artistic perfection. (Bartok, 1957, p. 158)

The "second generation"

In the title of the Spanish edition that appeared in 1969 one can already notice a further remove from the original authors. The title *Music for Children* is included but it then continues "Spanish original version based upon the work of Carl Orff and Gunild Keetman." The authors have a close relationship with Salzburg—Montserrat Sanuy studied there—and have tried to take an original path in their edition. In the Introduction, written for teachers, one can read:

Everything is original and all exercises are intended for Spanish speaking children, their individual customs, their mentality, and most importantly, everything is founded on Spanish folklore. (Sanuy & Sarmient, 1969, p. 8)

It is characteristic for the editions of the "second generation" that they show greater independence in structure and a far-reaching tendency not to include the rhythmic and instrumental pieces from the original volumes. Another volume to appear in 1969 was that from former Czechoslovakia. Up to 1968 a strong interest had been noticeable from colleagues in this country. Again and again the Orff Institute was able to look after students from this neighboring land. Questions such as "What is this Orff Schulwerk?" and "Can we use it in our schools?" were answered in lectures and seminars. Two famous Czech composers—Ilja Hurnik and

Petr Eben—have published a tasteful and skillful collection of material that has grown into three volumes.

I can remember the occasion when Carl Orff and some of his Salzburg colleagues first handled the Czech material and listened to their recordings. Orff was in turn critical, skeptical, attentive, amazed. His final comment: quite different, but very good.

The Danish adaptation also belongs to this generation. The author, Minna Lange-Ronnefeld, student and later engaged as a teacher at the "Mozarteum" in Salzburg, worked for eight years in primary school and music school on her return to her homeland.

> *From the harvest of these experiences, the plan to work out a Danish version, whose educational construction deviated quite considerably from the German original, arose as a natural and necessary consequence. (Gersdorf, 1975, p. 54)*

In the USA Schulwerk has been a subject for discussion since the mid-nineteen-fifties. Egon Kraus introduced it at a MENC Conference in St. Louis (Gieseler 1969, p.186). In 1956/57 Doreen Hall initiated a series of training and further education courses at Toronto University that are still on offer today.

> *This was the beginning in Canada, and possibly also in the United States, of teacher training on a university level for the elementary music educator. (Gersdorf, 1975, p. 48)*

This was also confirmed by American colleagues:

> *It was the courses that were organized by Arnold Walter and Doreen Hall in Toronto that offered the first opportunity for Orff-Schulwerk training in the North American continent. (Gersdorf, 1975, p. 46).*

Konnie Koonce Saliba reported in 1975 on a questionnaire sent to 392 North American colleges and universities. They received replies from 61%:

> *38% had offered courses that included Orff principles; 28% had planned to offer courses or workshops within two years; 31% had faculty members who had some Orff training (Gersdorf, 1975, p. 46).*

Within a few years a considerable interest in the content and principles of Schulwerk seems to have arisen. Yet in 1969 Walter Gieseler stated:

> *The reverberation of Orff ideas in the relevant American journals is very sparse, in fact for all practical purposes I could say it is nil. (p. 224)*

In connection with this statement, one must also observe that it appears to be altogether a peculiarity of those educators who work with Schulwerk, that they impart information through practical work rather than through articles in relevant journals. Whoever looks around in the USA today will be impressed by the hundreds of Schulwerk summer courses at many universities all over the whole country, by the quality and intensity of the annual conferences run by the American Orff-Schulwerk Association, and by the vitality with which the American music and dance teachers work at the adaptation of Orff's stimulating ideas to the conditions in their large and multifaceted land.

The publication between 1977 and 1982 of an individual *American Edition* covering a total of 650 pages also serves this purpose. From the first glance this edition is different from all the others. The material is no longer grouped according to the nature of the exercises: Volume 1 is described as for Pre-School, Volume 2 for Primary and Volume 3 for Upper Elementary Grades. All volumes contain examples of pentatonic, diatonic, and free tonality. The incitement to play and dance through and with music is essentially more comprehensive. Brief instructions help teachers to find their way, establish an order of procedure and work through it methodically. During several years of working together, 33 authors from all regions of the USA have composed, commented, and tried out the material. Experiences from more than 20 years of practical and theoretical work with Schulwerk ideas have poured into this publication. Carl Orff looked through the manuscript of the first volume to appear with interest. The task of conception and co-ordination was given to the author of this article by the original contributors and the publisher.

Orff Schulwerk as model

On this theme Werner Thomas has indicated:

> *The term 'model' can imply a pre-sketch for something about to be created, i.e., a 'proto-type,' as well as implying a reduction of something already created, i.e., a 'copy.' It shows the baseline in a clear and comprehensible form. The model can be used for the study of substance, structure, and proportions. The model is instructive and–in the widest sense of the word–educational. It sparks off the imagination: it stirs the will to test, to change, and develop. This is exactly the situation of Schulwerk and describes the intentions of its author (Thomas, 1977, p. 20)*

The printed examples confirm this tendency to change and develop. Does this not also show an inherent danger? An ever-widening distance from the original? A loss of the actual idea of Schulwerk?

The idea of Schulwerk

When Carl Orff talked about the "idea of Schulwerk" he meant "the elemental":

> *The elemental remains a foundation that is timeless. The elemental always means a new beginning . . . The elemental is always reproductive. I am glad that I was destined to seize the reproductive spark, to accost the elemental in mankind, and to awaken the spirit that binds us together (Orff, 1978, p. 277).*

Not only Orff, but many artists have spoken about the elemental in the first half of this century. Scientists have made an effort to define the term. Still—or time after time—there are people who dismiss everything that cannot be concisely and precisely defined as vague, incomprehensible or mystical, people who–because they have not experienced it–search in vain for a verbal definition.

With the term elemental we do not mean the sphere of "elementary education," we do not mean "the simple." By Elemental Music and Dance Education is meant "the elemental event:" that experience of understanding something from the inside. It is a question of the gain from the elements of insight and activity in the realm of music and dance.

The following are characteristic of the means, no longer at all new today, but nevertheless established by Orff and his colleagues as the way towards an intensive and fundamental relationship between human beings, music and dance:

• the special relationship between music and dance,

- the special relationship between music and speech (language),
- the inclusion of elemental instruments,
- the challenge to improvise and create forms.

Even if it is not possible to comment on this list it should be emphasized that these are the constants out of which all the various different versions and adaptations are made.

In retrospect Orff wrote:

> So it was not Schulwerk, about which I have written here in order to record an idea, but the idea itself that went round the world (Orff, 1978, p. 277).

A detailed description of the effects of the impetus of Schulwerk must take into account the many complementary and supplementary volumes that have appeared. These publications fulfilled two different needs: first that of settings of songs with instrumental accompaniments (from Germany, Greece, Brazil, Bolivia, Ghana, Italy, Estonia); for the second, pieces were added and developed to enable the preoccupation with elementary instruments to be carried over to more sophisticated instruments (piano, violin, and wind instruments).

The "Orff Institute" was founded in 1961 as a branch of the "Mozarteum" College for Music and Dramatic Art [now University Mozarteum (the editor)] in Salzburg to establish an important center for the development of Schulwerk.

Salzburg turntable

Carl Orff wanted the Salzburg Institute to perform two functions. Firstly, it should take over the training and further education of teachers of elemental music and dance. In the years from 1961 to 2010[1] 1,606 students from 63 countries have completed courses lasting between one and six years. In addition, 74 special schoolteachers, social workers, and therapists have taken a one-year course in Music Therapy, and approximately 396 music and dance teachers have taken part in a Special Course for English-speaking students of one or two semesters in length. With the exception of Austrians, who are taking courses of study at the Orff Institute in increasing numbers, Salzburg has taken care of students from the following countries: Argentina, Australia, Belgium, Bolivia, Brazil, Bulgaria, Canada, Chile, China, Columbia, Croatia, Czech Republic, Denmark, Egypt, Estonia, Finland, France, Germany, Ghana, Greece, Hong Kong, Hungary, Iceland, India, Indonesia, Iran, Ireland, Israel, Italy, Japan, Latvia, Luxembourg, Netherlands Antilles, Macau, Madagascar, Malta, Mexico, Netherlands, New Zealand, Norway, Peru, Philippines, Poland, Portugal, Rumania, Russia, Scotland, Singapore, Slovakia, Slovenia, South Africa, South Korea, Spain, Sri Lanka, Sweden, Switzerland, Taiwan, Thailand, United Kingdom, Uruguay, U.S.A., Venezuela, Yugoslavia. Through these former students, most of whom have returned to their homes to work, lively relationships have been established in many parts of the world. Orff's second role for the Institute was that it should act as a center that would answer questions relating to Schulwerk and that would register the international reverberations.

Repercussions and experiences

In 32 years, the collected experiences have had an effect on the work of the Orff Institute and associated faculty. First: we have learned many games, songs and dances through the work with colleagues in other parts of the world. Through this we have come to realize the problems

---

1   The information in this article was updated by the editor.

of the different stages of an adaptation to a 'foreign' culture. We have seen how long the path from imitation to transformation is.

In many parts of the world, we find stylistic characteristics from Schulwerk that we know–pentatonic, motor expression of rhythm, the principle of ostinato, gestures–that distinguish much of the music of Schulwerk.

Of course, we did not need to introduce the drum to Brazilian children, on the contrary, they showed it to us–and it was in Latin America, Africa, and Asia that we began to feel with what variety and how powerfully a drum can speak.

Whoever is prepared to commune with other people must be ready to hold their critical yardstick and their learnt aesthetic judgements in check. We should not decide what is good, valuable, or beautiful for others. The boundaries between serious and light music, between art song and pop song, yes between kitsch and art, are flexible. Making decisions for others is unacceptable.

Our colleagues in other countries have taught us how important it is to keep feeling and intellect, heart and head in the right proportions. How important it is for our children to enjoy music and dance, not only to analyze it, write about it and take part in the most perfect possible adult-orientated performances. We have learnt how empty our talk about music is in comparison with the fulfilment of actively making music and dance.

The significance of creativity, divergent thinking, and emancipated behavior was continuously under observation through our experiences in working with people for whom different aims and ways are natural. We have seen the importance of revision, practice, constancy, contemplative reflection, and internal discipline. Also, how decisive composure and serenity are for the fostering of ability, of Art.

Translation: Margaret Murray

References

Bartók, B. (1957). Ungarische Volksmusik und neue Ungarische Musik [Hungarian folkmusic and new Hungarian music]. In B. Scabolcsi (Ed.), *Béla Bartók, Weg und Werk, Schriften und Briefe*. Kassel: Bärenreiter.

Gersdorf, L. (Ed.). (1975). Symposion Orff-Schulwerk 1975. *Informationen 16*. Salzburg: Druckhaus Biblos.

Gieseler, W. (1969). *Musikerziehung in den USA im Vergleich mit Deutschen Verhältnissen* [Music education in the USA in comparison with German conditions]. Stuttgart: E. Klett.

Orff, C. (1978). *The Schulwerk* (M. Murray, Trans.). New York: Schott. (Original work published 1976)

Orff, C. (2011). Orff-Schulwerk: Past and future (M. Murray, Trans.). In B. Haselbach (Ed.), *Texts on theory and practice of Orff-Schulwerk: Basic texts from the years 1932–2010* (pp. 134-156). Mainz: Schott. (Original work published 1964)

Orff, C., & Keetman, G. (1950). *Orff-Schulwerk Musik für Kinder: Vol. I. Pentatonik*. Mainz: Schott.

Orff, C., & Keetman, G. (1956–1961). *Orff-Schulwerk. Music for children* (Vols. 1–5) (Canadian adaptation by D. Hall & A. Walter). Mainz: Schott.

Regner, H. (1975, July 10). Carl Orff zum 80. Geburtstag [Carl Orff on the occasion of his 80th birthday]. Bayerischer Rundfunk.

Sanuy, M., & Gonzalez Sarmient, L. (1969). *Musica para niños. Versión original española basada en la obra de Carl Orff y Gunild Keetman* [Music for children. Original Spanish version based on the work of Carl Orff and Gunild Keetman]. Madrid: Unión Musical Española.

Thomas, W. (1977). *Musica Poetica, Gestalt und Funktion des Orff-Schulwerks* [Musica poetica, shape and function of the Orff-Schulwerk]. Tutzing: Schneider.

Walter, A. (1956). Introduction. In C. Orff & G. Keetman *Orff-Schulwerk. Music for children: Vol. 1. Pentatonic* (Canadian adaptation by D. Hall & A. Walter). Mainz: Schott.

Witte, B. C. (1983). Die Auswärtige Kulturpolitik der Bundesrepublik Deutschland [The foreign cultural policy of the Federal Republic of Germany]. In Deutscher Musikrat (Ed.), *Referadte Informationen 55*.

A Consideration of Cross-Cultural Adaptation of the Schulwerk Pedagogical Model [1]

Mary Shamrock

Orff Schulwerk has been with us now for nearly 100 years. Originating in 1924 with adult learners, and reconfigured for children in 1948, this idea for experiencing, understanding, and participating in music making has found its way around the world. The Orff Institute in Salzburg has hosted students from more than 70 countries, attracted by this unique approach for involving learners of any age in a humanistic process of artistic development. They in turn introduce this development in their own countries with their own students, experimenting with adaptations needed in their individual situations.

As a pedagogy for facilitating this process with children, the Schulwerk builds upon fundamental principles:

1. active participation by all learners, in a group setting, with content analysis emerging from reflection upon experience;
2. rhythm as the starting point, developed from the child's natural desire for playful activity;
3. primary learning experiences involving spoken language, singing, movement, and playing instruments;
4. improvisation and invention of original material included in all activity areas;
5. song and speech activities developed from traditional material.
6. The following discussion considers these components from a global perspective and suggests guidelines for adaptation based on relevance of the principles. It also examines social, cultural, and educational practices that impact the acceptance and development of the Schulwerk process.

Speech/Language

Orff considered spoken language to be not only a means of communication but also a powerful expressive medium and the source of musical expression. He was particularly fascinated by Latin and old Greek as representing the roots of European civilization. From spoken language he built a direct connection to rhythm, including both free expression and strongly pulse-driven patterns. Orff advocated the continuing inclusion of dramatic speech as an important component in the child's artistic development.

The Schulwerk model considers spoken language to be the basis for development of musicality because of the inherent rhythmic properties of both language and music in their most basic forms. The role of stress in European languages creates a natural rhythm that extends logically and naturally into the concurrent musical styles. In principle, any language having patterns of stressed and unstressed syllables can be used for developing rhythmic exercises in

1 Content adapted and updated from the author's monograph *Orff Schulwerk: Brief History, Description, and Issues in Global Dispersal*, American Orff-Schulwerk Association, 1995.

a manner similar to the German of the original model. English adapts easily to this purpose. In the worldwide Westernization of culture occurring throughout the past several centuries, Western languages have in certain cases been adopted by or forced upon non-Western cultures as the common medium of communication. In many situations, European languages are part of the standard school curriculum, although not used regularly in oral or written communication.

If rhythm is considered at its most basic level—as the temporal arrangement of sounds— then many languages have rhythmic characteristics of their own that may be substantively different from Western stress-based structures. One can speculate that there is an intimate connection between such natural speech rhythms and the temporal patterns of related indigenous musics. The patterns that predominate and the combinations formed vary from one culture to another, with certain features being unique. It is this intimate relationship with language that the Schulwerk model would view as "elemental" and would serve as the appropriate basis for development of rhythmic musicality in any given culture. Because initial Schulwerk development in cultures with a non-European spoken language often has been directed almost exclusively to the development of Western musicality, forming rhythmic patterns from the indigenous language requires finding word combinations that fit specific rhythmic patterns comfortably (Hoshino Yoshio, 1979).

Languages based on tonal accent, such as Japanese and those in which tonal patterns carry meaning, such as Chinese or Thai, suggest a more direct connection to melody than to rhythm. In such instances, melody could be considered a more logical starting point for Schulwerk activity. A conscious decision could be made to develop this connection first. Certainly, in singing Western-style melodies and much of present-day song repertoire globally, the characteristics of musical style dominate any consideration of the tonal qualities of language. Certain accommodations to the language are made but maintaining the melodic integrity of the spoken text is not a major issue. Nonetheless, it is possible to construct a more "natural" melody by considering the text more closely (Personal interviews—Japan, Taiwan, Thailand, 1987). One can speculate that Orff would have identified this connection between the tonality of language and related melodic structure as "elemental."

In order to honor the principle of language as the source of music, each culture needs to examine carefully the relationship between its own spoken language and the structure of rhythm and melody in the musical tradition being developed. The most natural connections need to be determined, and from these, small exercises can be devised that will lead children easily and playfully from the spoken to the musical.

Focus on traditional sources for activity development

The Schulwerk model specifies that speech and song material should connect with the play and fantasy world of children—e.g., nursery rhymes, riddles, proverbs—the rationale being that the child at a deep level needs nourishment from cultural roots rather than from current trends in popular music. In actual practice, speech material based on the current and familiar—e.g., television programming, computer games—has proven very effective in drawing children into the fascination of speech play from their own current experience. The background and character of each group of children will determine the initial material to be utilized. If traditional material has been left behind, it may be appropriate to seek out and include examples in the context of Schulwerk activity.

Ideally a suitable balance can be struck between the traditional and the modern, with the prevailing standards of good taste governing choices of either type. A very strong factor here is that students in the majority of today's classrooms represent several if not multiple cultural backgrounds. Little or no song and speech material can be considered "traditional" for all. The challenge for today's teachers is finding representative material for each culture that will be appropriate and appealing for all students as well as serving the intended artistic goals. This will likely include material that represents none of them, serving to expand their cultural perspective as well.

Movement/Dance

In the initial development of Schulwerk at the Günther-Schule, movement and dance were strong components of the work with adult students. The initial work with children involved radio broadcasts, for which movement played no role. When Gunild Keetman resumed regular class teaching, movement again took its rightful place, being equal to sound in the total expression of musical ideas. The functional and playful movements of the child—e.g., walking, jumping, skipping, hopping, swaying—provide the material for exploring musical and dramatic ideas and for developing small forms and little dances that may be integrated with musical sound or exist on their own. (These movements deserve as much teacher attention and support as the voice in singing, but no special training.) The forms invented may take on a cultural identification according to what is common in child game formations or in the gestures, attitudes, and floor patterns of folk or classical dance traditions to which the children are exposed. This may well include styles taken from other cultures. For example, Western ballet has gained much popularity in certain non-Western cultures. Training in such styles is available to children through classes that, like those for most traditional music, are generally quite separate from public education.

The use of natural movements as a means for experiencing and understanding musical structure and energy, along with the use of movement and dance as an expressive and creative medium, is definitely a "foreign" pedagogical idea in almost all cultures. In some cultures, behavioral standards require children to become increasingly reserved in outward display of emotion and in actions calling attention to themselves. This creates a conflict when the child is asked specifically to do what behavior standards dictate should not be done. It has been suggested that some societies tend to move in limited ways because of space constraints, e.g., living in crowded circumstances, they have little opportunity to "play" with space. Western observers also need to recognize that the emotional content of movement may be relative only within the parameters of a single tradition. For example, there may be as much emotional energy in the restrained arm gesture of one tradition as in the elevated leap of another (Yaginuma Teruko, personal interview, Japan, 1987). This principle is well demonstrated in Asian traditional dance forms that contain many subtleties—e.g., movements of eyes, fingers, manipulation of costume—that have little role in the much more space-oriented Western dance styles. Regardless of cultural setting, children's movement can all too easily become an optional and occasional activity rather than a vital and integrated part of the pedagogical whole. If movement in the sense of the original Schulwerk model is to be included, teachers must themselves be comfortable with it. They must be aware of children's movement capabilities at different ages, and able to motivate and guide students to experience this potential. The majority of teachers who experience this type of movement in teacher training settings come away with a very positive impression of its value. They find that exploratory and creative movement can be a decidedly beneficial experience for students, as the freeing of traditional personal boundaries may be very much needed. However, for teachers to develop sufficient skill and confidence to direct movement activities themselves usually requires training over a longer period. Lack of sufficient training and capability is still a significant issue in Schulwerk pedagogy as practiced in many cultures.

These considerations indicate that although movement must be retained as an essential component of the Schulwerk model, the type and extent of movement deserve rethinking as much as the rhythmic and tonal materials. Two issues are involved: 1) the prevailing cultural attitude toward movement, and 2) whether or not movement can be considered valuable in the total educational process. If response to the first issue indicates a conservative climate but to the second invites a change in attitude, special steps may be needed to insure that this aspect of the instruction is handled effectively, e.g., team teaching, with someone more skilled in movement in charge of that aspect. If certain cultural limitations come into play, such as interaction of boys and girls or the need for certain types of clothing, these must be honored to satisfy individual and group requirements.

Movement is not to be considered an expendable option within the Schulwerk model. Without it, a major portion of the potential for total involvement and development of the child's kinesthetic understanding and powers of fantasy is lost.

Tonal development

Before discussing singing and playing instruments, a word must be said about the tonal context in which these are developed. The original Schulwerk with children begins with sol-mi [minor third] and sol-mi-la chants and songs, extending to the complete major pentatonic and then to the diatonic scales of the Western musical system. In other cultures, different chant patterns may well be more appropriate as starting points. In Japan, for instance, the major second with the upper tone as final is very common in children's chant songs. The original model in its more advanced levels proceeds through exploration of the Western diatonic modes, which may be of little or no relevance in other cultures unless there is a specific focus on exploring them.

Music educators in each culture developing the Schulwerk model must determine the tonal goals and sequence the tonal materials accordingly. There may even be bi-musical goals—that is, the development of Western musicality as well as that of an indigenous tradition. The relative amount of time and concentration devoted to each will be determined by those responsible for guiding the instructional program in each situation.

Singing

Orff intended that the child's natural musical instrument, the singing voice, be considered the primary means of melodic expression in Schulwerk activity. Singing was notably absent in the early days at the Günther-Schule; a choral experience was soon added, but Orff felt that neither speech nor singing were given sufficient attention. He felt strongly about establishing these two components as the natural starting point when the work began with children in the late 1940s (Orff, 1976, 214).

In practice, however, singing tends to be the component most often neglected in applying the Schulwerk model; the rhythmic, movement, and instrumental aspects are so attractive that attention to good singing becomes a peripheral issue. Development of a mature vocal technique is beyond the scope of the Schulwerk, but assistance with basic features such as posture, breath support, placement, and intonation are as much needed as simple technical instruction for playing the instruments.

The child voice quality prevailing in the culture of the original model is the light, pure head voice associated with children's choirs of European tradition. This particular timbre may be unrealistic and indeed inappropriate in other cultural settings. Educators developing a Schulwerk model need to determine the natural characteristics of good singing within each set of cultural parameters. Students can then be guided in using their singing voices appropriately.

As material for singing, the Schulwerk model emphasizes children's songs from traditional heritage rather than songs composed in a childlike style. As with speech, the rationale is that children need this deep thread of continuity with their cultural roots. Here also, in actual practice, songs relating to current events and situations may better relate to the child's experience and motivate interest and participation. Because students in current classrooms represent a multiplicity of cultures, songs can be chosen as needed and appropriate for the intended artistic learning goals.

Use of instruments

Known as "Orff instruments," the unique percussion instruments developed for the Schulwerk tend to stand out as its primary attraction. This aspect has been misunderstood in situations worldwide, with children being taught to play set pieces in the manner of an elementary percussion ensemble. (In some cases, this may be a justified alternative, but it is not to be considered part of Schulwerk pedagogy.) The original Music for Children volumes contain small instrumental pieces to be played as written. Examples of the need for this are:

1. to develop sensitivity to and understanding of a new musical element, such as a rhythm or mode,
2. to accompany small movement and dance forms invented by the students, and
3. to provide ready-made music for a dramatic project under development.

Nonetheless, the primary purpose of these pieces is to serve as models for others to be worked out, through improvisation, as part of the learning process.

In each culture adapting the Schulwerk model, it is essential that the role of the Orff Instrumentarium be clearly understood. The instrumental resources are, in essence, "laboratory equipment" for creating small compositions utilizing the musical elements being explored. Students must be assisted in developing a minimal technical facility, e.g., correct use of mallets, comfortable playing positions. More advanced techniques may be needed if the overall level of musicianship warrants more sophisticated instrumental capability. All students should have opportunities to learn to play all instruments in order to experience the varied timbre possibilities and differences in playing technique.

The common tuning standard for the barred percussion instruments is the Western equal-tempered octave. However, viewing the instrumentarium as an experimental resource rather than a fixed performance medium opens possibilities for accommodating other tonal and scale systems. In some instances, cultural considerations may deter such a practice, as the use of Orff instruments to play music of indigenous tradition may be perceived as inappropriate. In some cultures, it may be more acceptable to use instruments quite different from those included in the instrumentarium, and some traditions may require few or no instruments at all. For most children, playing Orff instruments is a very appealing and motivating activity, but consideration must remain open for alternatives or for combining them with other instruments as appropriate for the culture.

Orff instruments are indeed legitimate instruments, not toys. Though music making in the Schulwerk initially is based upon play, it is play as the "serious work" of children. To honor this principle, instrument makers must be held to a high standard of excellence in sound quality and workmanship.

Improvisation

An examination of Schulwerk activity during the 1930s with adults (the Günther-Schule) reveals that the central focus of this music making was spontaneous invention, using whatever media were available and whatever technical level had been attained. New techniques and musical elements very quickly became source material for improvised invention. In the Schulwerk model, this process is considered essential for enabling learners to discover their own innate capabilities for making music, as contrasted with learning to reproduce music.

Each culture adapting Schulwerk pedagogy must recognize the importance of improvisation, and deliberately include it in the pedagogical structure. If a Western-based musicality is being developed, rhythmic improvisation can begin with simple patterns and meters and progress to more complex structures typical of Western tradition but appropriate as used in that specific culture. Although in the original model the pentatonic scale is considered the ideal structure for beginning tonal improvisation, its usefulness may be questioned in some cultures. Within Western tradition it tends to mask the strong model of more commonly heard music organized around harmonic function. However, in a culture in which pentatonic is a very common tonal structure and improvisation is not a part of traditional music making, pentatonic improvisation may seem inappropriate OR a refreshing extension of the familiar.

If an Indigenous musicality is being developed in a non-Western musical culture, the role of improvisation may be limited. Improvising within a style that normally does not include it may well antagonize traditional practitioners of the style and leave participants with a false impression of how music is made in that tradition. These limitations notwithstanding, most likely there will be some traditional components in any given culture in which improvisation will not violate music-making principles. The best potential for adaptation to the Schulwerk pedagogy lies in sensitivity to how this aspect best fits into the indigenous traditions of music making.

Student/Teacher interaction

An aspect of Schulwerk pedagogy that may be a challenge, in any culture, is the reciprocal relationship between students and teacher. Ideally, the teacher guides the direction as facilitator, and the students contribute to the developing scheme in creative, significant ways. Educational practices in Europe and America include discussion classes, facilitated by the teacher but allowing for development and exchange of ideas. Along with learning and understanding content, the goal is to develop a confidence that enables students to conduct their own discussions, with teacher assistance as needed. The aim for Schulwerk activity is similar: to bring the students to the point where they can successfully manipulate the materials at hand, with guidance rather than specific direction from the teacher. The Orff class may be regarded as a laboratory experience, with speech, singing, movement, and playing instruments as the means for exploration and development.

The type of student/teacher interaction just described can now be found in many educational settings worldwide, but the more traditional model, in which the teacher is considered the authority and the students the recipients of knowledge, may strongly persist. Therefore, practice of the Schulwerk requires a commitment to what is considered a more open social structure. Educators may well consider the interactive educational climate superior in supporting student learning. But change is difficult, especially if educators themselves have not experienced this environment as learners. A first stage can be relatively simple, e.g., having students respond to specific instructions by doing rather than merely listening, and in addition, having some freedom of choice built into the responses. The next stages take time to develop, e.g., helping students reach a level of confidence that allows them to assume leadership roles themselves.

The contrast in pedagogical style becomes even more pronounced when traditional musics are involved. The authority/recipient model has likely persisted for centuries as a means of insuring correct performance of the music according to traditional standards. To accomplish this, the student must follow the teacher's instructions exactly and without question, out of respect for the teacher and for the art form. Application of the Schulwerk pedagogy to traditional music may well be considered both unnecessary and inappropriate.

Intra- and intercultural dialogue

With its inherent flexibility, the Schulwerk model allows for a great deal of variation in teaching style and emphasis. In any culture, establishing dialogue among widely different points of view is difficult, because in order to do so, no particular variant in teaching style is to be considered the "correct" or "only" way. Instead, each must allow that something can be learned from the others, and that all may offer valid possibilities. A sense of competition rather than cooperation can also play a negative role. However, such problems do not deter individual schools and teachers from developing exemplary Schulwerk programs. Cooperative effort on a regional, national, and international scale has proven effective in establishing a wider awareness and recognition of the pedagogy and in providing appropriate teacher training.

First attempts in developing the Schulwerk model in any culture require ongoing experimentation, evaluation, and refinement. Initially, only specific activities and techniques may be introduced. A degree of success at this level is likely to stimulate consideration of long-term goals and how they might best be served by this pedagogy. A slow, continuously re-evaluated development of the Schulwerk model is likely to be much more robust than a quick, enthusiastic reception that is all flowers with no roots. Hermann Regner, longtime director of the Orff Institute, stated that any significant development of the Schulwerk in a given culture should not be expected in less than twenty-five years. He pointed out that in Western-oriented cultures, where rapid change is expected and better models in every field are constantly sought, the Schulwerk pedagogy may well be discarded as outdated before even a small portion of its potential has been realized (Regner, 1984, 784-791). Responsibility thus falls to those cultures in which the Schulwerk has persisted and developed, to attest to the wealth of potential and value to be found in the model, and to encourage and assist others in searching for the most suitable adaptations. If true to the spirit and intent of the original model, proponents of the Schulwerk pedagogy in any culture will continue this search.

References

Hoshino Y. (1979). *Theory and application of Orff Schulwerk: Starting from the Japanese language* (working translation by Mako Ueda). Tokyo: Zen-ON Gakufu Shippansha.ot, 1987.

Orff, C. (1978). *Carl Orff. Documentation: Vol. 3. The Schulwerk* (M Murray, Trans.). New York: Schott, p. 214.

Regner, H. (1984, December). "Music for Children: Observations on the reception and adaptation of Orff-Schulwerk in other countries" (M. Shamrock, Trans.), *Musik und Bildung: Zeitschrift für Musikerziehung* 16, 784–791.

Related Reading

Focus on Music and Culture. (2014, Winter). *The Orff Echo* (Quarterly Journal of the American Orff-Schulwerk Association).

Exploring Culturally Responsive Elemental Music Making. (2017, Summer). *The Orff Echo*.

Grüner, M., & Haselbach, B. (Eds.). (2015/2016). Interkulturalität in der Elementaren Musik- und Tanzerziehung I und II / Interculturality in the elemental music and dance pedagogy I and II. *Orff-Schulwerk Heute, 93 & 94*. https://www.orff-schulwerk-forum-salzburg.org/magazine-osh

Regner, H. (2011). "Musik für Kinder—Music for Children—Musique pour Enfants." Comments on the adoption and adaptation of Orff-Schulwerk in other Countries. In B. Haselbach, B. (Ed.), *Texts on theory and practice of Orff-Schulwerk: Basic texts from the years 1932–2010* (pp. 220–244). Mainz: Schott. (Original work published 1984)

Shehan Campbell, P., & Wiggins, T. (2013). *The Oxford handbook of children's musical cultures*. New York: Oxford University Press, (Paperback 2014). ISBN 978-0-19020-64133.

Intercultural Aspects of the Orff Schulwerk [1]

Michael Kugler

The intercultural reception of the Orff Schulwerk starts with a document from Greece. In 1936 the musician and musicologist Thrasybulos Georgiades (1907–1977) sent a statement of two pages to Munich that reports the application of the Orff Schulwerk concept Elemental Music Practice (predecessor of *Music for Children*) in private lessons and courses in Athens (Kugler, 2013). The Orff Schulwerk "can be used with the same success in countries with the most different musical cultures because it … grasps the primary conditions of musical expression" (p. 200). According to Georgiades it is only necessary to pick up the supplementing materials from the relevant culture. I think that this strategy is very similar to the way of the Orff-Schulwerk Forum in Salzburg. But now let us look back into the historical context of the Orff Schulwerk.

1.   The influence of non-western cultures on the Orff Schulwerk

1.1 The art of expressionism and the *Ausdruckstanz* (expressionistic dance)

The idea of the elemental and elemental music cannot be understood without the historical context of the Modern. The artistic concept of expressionism, to which Carl Orff was connected through his preference for the Ausdruckstanz and for the poetry of Franz Werfel and Bertolt Brecht, grew up at a distance from European aesthetic. The artistic idea of expressionism was that of an absolute new origin, a beginning from point zero. New roots and new sources were found in the art of the so-called primitives. Pablo Picasso formed his early cubistic picture The girls of Avignon from 1907 through the integration of African masks. The Munich artists group around Franz Marc called themselves "Germany's wild ones" and were inspired by archaic folk art, woodcuts of the Middle Ages and Japan, and sculptures of the South Pacific.

In the *Ausdruckstanz* of Mary Wigman, intercultural inspirations can already be found:

- The importance of percussion instruments for the connection between dance and music through rhythm is rediscovered. Wigman owned a collection of non-western percussion instruments and her school at Dresden possessed an extensive percussion orchestra some years before the Günther-Schule.
- The combination of dance with masks and ecstasy in the dances of Mary Wigman is linked to the reception of oriental and far eastern cultures. In her dance *Zeremonielle Gestalt* from 1925 she is using a mask of the Japanese Noh Theatre and the dance *Drehmonotonie* from 1926 is based on the sound of a Chinese gong and influenced by the dance tradition of the Sufis.

---

1   Reprinted from Kugler, M. (2015). Intercultural aspects of the Orff-Schulwerk. *Orff-Schulwerk Heute*, 93, 56–59.

1.2 Ethnomusicology: Curt Sachs

The ethnomusicologist Curt Sachs had a very extensive influence on Orff. Orff met him three times in the decisive incubation phase of his conception of "Elemental Music"—in 1921, in 1923, and in 1926. Sachs emphasizes particularly those aspects of music that shape the phenomenon of music in many cultures worldwide: The importance of percussion instruments and of dance for the creation of music. Orff was not content with the conversations with Sachs but enlarged his knowledge through further ethnomusicology books and records. His reception of ethnomusicological theory in the twenties is reflected in Orff's articles in the years 1931 to 1933, which were written down parallel to the first Schulwerk courses. They can be summarized as follows:

- The non-western musician has a physical relationship to his instrument. His attitude to music is bound to bodily movement consequently leading to the primary orientation of rhythm on bodily movement.
- In his theory of primitive or elemental instruments Orff picks up the genealogy of instruments, which begins with percussion instruments as explained by Curt Sachs in his famous books about the anthropology of musical instruments.
- The production of melody is based on pattern formation with optional improvisation. Polyphony is created only by parallel thirds, fifths, and sixths.
- The bass region is shaped by the monophonic structure of drone (bordun).

2. The crossing-borders music concept of Carl Orff

Orff's view of music history is strongly influenced by ethnomusicology. For him, the beginning of European art music in the Middle Ages is oriental music with its linear music concept, a heterophonic shaping of melody, and drone as a basis of sound. He emphasizes that the preferred instruments of that age came from Africa, the Middle and Far East and that they were used until the Renaissance and were later abandoned for a new aesthetic of sound. Orff did not want to position his music within the framework of European tradition but in the environment of world musics. Musicologist Horst Leuchtmann (1988, p. 337) therefore rightly interprets Orff's compositions as an "opting out of the contemporary music" (*"Ausstieg aus der Musik der Zeit"*). Orff's music concept from the beginning of the 20th century is about crossing borders and therefore ready for intercultural exchange. This is valid for both his compositions and his pedagogy. In my opinion the intercultural aspects are more vivid in the workshop phase of the Schulwerk during the twenties than in the fifties and also more vivid in the minimalistic dance compositions of Gunild Keetman than in those of Carl Orff.

Indeed, the following aspects of musical behavior in the Günther-Schule during the twenties were able to resolve the aesthetic norms of European art music and the "soundfog" of post-Wagnerian orchestral music:

- Preparing improvisation processes by body percussion.
- Creating music by Orff's "Conducting practice" (*"Dirigierübung"*) with improvisation and gesture.
- Learning rhythm by movement in Keetman's lectures.
- Integrating percussion instruments into choreographies by Maja Lex.

3. Intercultural aspects of the Orff Schulwerk

Intercultural aspects of the Orff Schulwerk can be found in musical instruments, musical structures, and modes of musical behavior.

3.1 The instruments

Worldwide the xylophones have become a symbol for the Orff Schulwerk. From the first appearance at the Günther-Schule, xylophones–regarded as artifacts of a different culture–have been a symbol for the foreign. Until today the sight of an Orff ensemble with xylophones and drums has an exotic effect and leads the listener from the cultural context of European art music into the world of non-western cultures. The same effect is in the percussive sound of Keetman's "Ecstatic Dance," composed in 1930. The music pedagogue Irmgard Merkt therefore suggests a didactic concept that travels virtually from the culturally well-known Orff xylophone back into the Indonesian parent culture and by this to rediscover the foreign character of the xylophone once again.

The models of the first xylophones, made by Karl Maendler in Munich, came from West Africa (one original marimba and one acculturated xylophone in the form of a box) and from Indonesia (one example in a Munich museum). Apart from some European percussion instruments, the Günther-Schule owned many non-western instruments, e.g., great frame drums, four double skin drums (Chinese model), woodblocks, a slit drum, 3 tam-tams, 2 great xylophones (Indonesian model), some metallophones.

All these artifacts had already been removed from the context of the authentic cultural meaning. A few of them had been adapted to the European music culture, e.g., the diatonic or chromatic tuning for the xylophones. Above all, these instruments were imported and used without their authentic music, instead becoming integrated into the framework of a school for gymnastics and dance that was open for exploration and improvisation. The extraordinary strategy of Orff is based on using the impulse of ethnomusicology for developing a new access to the general modes of musical behavior using foreign instruments.

3.2 Musical structures and modes of musical behavior

Now I want to summarize the features of an intercultural border crossing in the Orff Schulwerk, distinguishing between musical structures on the one hand and modes of musical behavior on the other.

3.2.1. Structures

- A general dominance of rhythm. The audible rhythm corresponds to the visible movement of the body. Rhythmic units are formed by repetitive patterns.
- The result is a reduced rhythmic-melodic structure that you can find in oriental music to this day. The preferred scales are pentatonic and modal.
- Language can be shaped metrically bound or unbound based only on percussion.
- Harmony is dominated by monophonic structures (which is not sufficiently described with the term "bordun"). Sometimes there are parallel degrees, but nonfunctional harmony.
- The construction of formal units originates from repetitive structures like patterns, series, refrains.

3.2.2 Modes of musical behavior

In my view there are three modes of musical behavior that are important for the Orff Schulwerk—motion, percussion, and improvisation—all of which are common in so many non-western music cultures.

- Motion:

The rhythmic and expressive movement of the body generates primary structures for music and dance. Looking at movement is important for generating and understanding music.

• Percussion:

The percussive mode for generating tones and sounds predominates musical practice world-wide. This is a great contrast to the western aesthetic with its affective intensification of the single note.

• Improvisation:

In the concept of Orff and Keetman, improvisation meant firstly the new possibility in the Modern to explore sounds and musical structures and, secondly the traditional concept to create music without notation on the basis of proved materials and patterns. Indeed, from the twenties (Günther-Schule) until the fifties (Musik für Kinder) making music without notation was very innovative.

3.3 The problem of orality and literacy

In these times improvising music without notation meant crossing of cultural borders. The term interculturality includes above all the crossing of boundaries and innovation through exchanging processes. Such processes took place within intracultural limits in the legendary Günther-Schule in Munich between 1924 and 1934. Orff was working with his colleagues and students and did not exchange his ideas with people of non-western cultures. He did not want to import strange and exotic material but wanted to liberate the elemental in the European individual. He did not need notation for the liberation of physical aspects of music, rhythm, melos, and the regaining of the ability to improvise.

Bringing elements from oral cultures to a literal culture was a fundamental problem for Orff's pedagogical concept. The foreign for European users consists of the newly discovered modes of musical behavior because these modes cannot be handed down by notation but only by face-to-face communication. As a connecting link between the foreign and the self, Orff had to use the problematic medium of musical notation. From that originated one great concern of Orff and Keetman: Having published the volumes of the Schulwerk they could see at once that teachers just read the notated examples literally instead of putting them into the practice of a living improvisation.

4. Transcultural effects of the Orff Schulwerk?

Let me now make a last remark on the problem of intercultural reception. We began with an example from Greece. A lot of additional material is given in the TV series With xylophone and fantasy by Werner Lütje and Hermann Regner (Kallós, 2016, 64), the collection *Begegnungen: Reports about the acceptance and development of stimuli from Orff-Schulwerk by the Orff-Schulwerk Forum* (Regner, 1990), the extensive volume of André de Quadros, *Many seeds, different flowers: The Music Education Legacy of Carl Orff* (2000), and—not to forget—the video archive of Coleman Kallós.[1]

Translation: Annette Kugler

---

1 These along with numerous other videos are housed at the Orff Institute in Salzburg, Austria.

References

de Quatros, A. (Ed.). (2000). *Many seeds, different flowers: The music education legacy of Carl Orff.* Perth: Callaway International Resource Centre for Music Education.

Kallós, C. (2016, Summer). Mit Xylophon und Fantasie [With xylophone and fantasy]. *Orff-Schulwerk Heute, 94,* 64.

Kugler, M. (Ed.). (2013). *Elemental dance–Elemental music. The Munich Günther School 1924–1944* (M. Murray, Trans.). Mainz: Schott. (Original work published 2002)

Leuchtmann, H. (1988). Carl Orff oder Der Ausstieg aus der Musik der Zeit [Carl Orff or the exit from the music of time]. *Bayer. Akademie der Schönen Künste, Jahrbuch 2*(1), 337.

Regner, H. (Ed.). (1990). *Begegnungen: Berichte Über die Aufnahme und Entwicklung von Anregungen des Orff-Schulwerks* [Encounters: Reports about the acceptance and development of stimuli from Orff-Schulwerk], Orff-Schulwerk Forum Salzburg.

The Principles of Orff Schulwerk [1]

Wolfgang Hartmann
in cooperation with Barbara Haselbach

So, what is "Orff Schulwerk" actually? It is certainly remarkable that this fundamental question arises even when one has engaged in a long intensive pursuit of the pedagogical ideas of Gunild Keetman and Carl Orff. Does the term Orff Schulwerk represent only the printed material in the five volumes of *Music for Children* (Orff & Keetman, 1950–1954; Orff & Keetman, 1957-1966)? Does it stand for a particular teaching style in music pedagogy, or in general for unconventional, creative activities with children in the area of music, dance, and speech?

With such fundamental doubts, it is not surprising that there have always been attempts to search for categories of Orff Schulwerk in order to present its characteristics in a comprehensive way.[2] We can assume that even Carl Orff himself was aware that the description of the essentials of his Schulwerk resisted a simple straightforward definition. Thus, he starts his oft-quoted lecture *Das Orff-Schulwerk: Rückblick und Ausblick* (Orff-Schulwerk: Past & Future) (Orff, 1964/2011b) in 1963 with this fundamental question, many years after his pedagogical ideas had already found their international recognition. His answer helps only indirectly and leaves room for individual interpretation. He points to the history of its origin, referring to the "prehistory" in the Günther-Schule and the practical implementation as a school radio program in 1948. In this context, he also uses his much-cited picture of the *"Wildwuchs"* (rank growth) (p. 134/135). Margaret Murray's translation as "wildflower" approaches this concept in a very euphemistic way, because the word "Wildwuchs" also includes weeds and everything that grows near fences and paths. Thus, we learn that the Schulwerk is NOT the result of a clearly thought-out didactic plan and that it can exist and be effective even without systematization.

If we try to use the word "Schulwerk" as an interpretative approach, this does not solve the problem either. "Schulwerk" was a newly coined word that can also be found in Paul Hindemith's works (*Schulwerk für Instrumentalspiel*, op. 44, 1927) and as the title of violin manuals (*Geigen-Schulwerk*, 1932–1950) by Erich and Elma Doflein. At the very least, a comparison of these shows a fundamental similarity: Rather than using simple exercises, the concepts of Orff and Keetman, Hindemith, and the Dofleins employ authentic compositions that correspond to the learner's ability.

With this in mind, it would be natural to call "Schulwerk" exclusively the published material in the famous five volumes by Orff and Keetman and the supplementary editions. But if we keep in mind that, during an international summer course with well-known experts in Orff Schulwerk, these original pieces may constitute only a fraction of the material used, along with songs and dances of different cultural origins and creations by the teachers and participants, then we realize that this definition attempt would also be too narrow.

---

1 This article initially appeared on the website of the International Orff-Schulwerk Forum Salzburg. It has been translated and printed in publications and/or websites of Orff Schulwerk associations in Spain, Argentina, Colombia, Russia, Turkey, Greece, and the United States.

2 See as an example: H. Regner (1975/2011a), Carl Orff's Educational Ideas: Utopia and Reality.

Of course, the artistic and aesthetic quality of the short music pieces created as models by Orff and Keetman is beyond any doubt. However, we have to recognize that the musical reality of our time has changed considerably and cannot any longer be represented exclusively by the musical language of Orff and Keetman. Even more important is the fact that a printed representation of dance and movement in general is very difficult. Therefore, in the volumes mentioned, dance, as one of the fundamental aspects of Orff Schulwerk, is limited to a few notes in the appendix. To summarize all these considerations, we must also recognize that the term Orff Schulwerk evades a simple definition and that it may lose itself in vagueness and can lead to misinterpretations.

In the course of the preparation and realization of the annual meetings of collaborators and members of the International Orff-Schulwerk Forum Salzburg, Barbara Haselbach and I have seen the necessity to find a description of the pedagogical concept of Carl Orff and Gunild Keetman, which could serve as a base for the cooperation with and between the national Orff Schulwerk Associations and Associated Institutions.[1] The description we propose is based on the characteristic way of teaching and other typical features that are essential to put the artistic and pedagogical spirit of the Orff Schulwerk into practice. We call these features the "Principles of Orff Schulwerk." Of course, some of these principles may also apply to other music and dance education concepts. We only speak of a working and teaching style that corresponds to the Orff Schulwerk if all these characteristics are present and are incorporated in the work process.

1. The individual is at the center

Undoubtedly other music pedagogical concepts will also claim his principle. Therefore, a more detailed explanation must be given: Carl Orff's intention is that the students experience themselves as creative persons and thereby grow in personality. Orff calls it *Menschenbildung* (the development of human character) (Orff, 1964/2011b, p. 157).[2] The objective of the Orff Schulwerk is not primarily to learn music and music theory in order to find one's own musical expression. It is rather that the students can create their own music in order to understand music. The short music pieces, dances, and songs in the five volumes are intended to inspire, to be models and examples for work in the classroom. Of course, the teacher helps in the development process so that the students can identify with "their" music. One can describe it with the following picture: The Orff Schulwerk does not want to lead the child to "great" music, but to bring music to the child. When children experience themselves as "music-makers" in the way described, one can expect that they are motivated to search for "the great world of music in its fascinating variety" over time. The concept of Orff and Keetman is learning by making music, in contrast to the traditional way of learning in order to be able to make music.

2. The social dimension

Group work is the social form of teaching best suited to the Orff Schulwerk. Everyone learns from everyone; rivalries and tendencies toward competition are to be avoided carefully. This requires corresponding conduct by the teacher, for the teacher should not be the prominent, all-important example. The teacher points the way and makes suggestions and gives the students enough room to co-determine and promote forms of cooperation. In the group, the

---

1   See the program for the Orff-Schulwerk Forum Convention Salzburg, "Orff-Schulwerk in the School," July 4–7, 2013.

2   Margaret Murray translated *Menschenbildung* as "developing the whole personality" (Orff, 2011b, p. 154).

various forms of expression during their interaction (dancing, singing, and speaking) can be experienced very well.

3. Music is an integral term

"Elemental music is never music alone but forms a unity with movement, dance and speech. It is music that one makes oneself, in which one takes part not as a listener but as a participant" (Orff, 1964/2011b, p. 144). Therefore, when, in working with the Orff Schulwerk, we speak about elemental music. It is always understood that singing, dancing, playing instruments are equal, complementary, and connected forms of expression.

Carl Orff found this interplay of the different artistic activities realized in the ancient Greek theatre where all forms of representation were summarized, from singing to declamation, dancing and instrumental playing, under the term *musike techne*. This wide-ranging musical concept of the Orff Schulwerk also invites stretching the arch further and creates bridges to other artistic forms of expression, such as to the visual arts[1] or poetry (B. Haselbach, personal communication, February 8, 2017).

> *A person sensitive to movement ... can also experience movement visually; if we give them a piece of clay ... they will be able with very little practice to create sculptures that are movement-related and spontaneous. It will be the same if we give them a pencil; the movement pictures that are drawn will relatively quickly acquire life...Above all—a sense of one's own security awakens an interest in unfamiliar forms, one sees, hears, feels in other areas and there grows a sincere interest for artistic creation that has not been imposed externally. (Günther, 1932/2011, pp. 88–90)*

4. Creativity in improvisation and composition

In the reception of Western music, creativity is usually only acknowledged in outstanding persons, for example, composers as "music creators" and musicians who improvise in a masterful way. Thus, creativity in the musical development of a person is admitted very late, as the perfection of a musician. The overwhelming majority of active musicians (apart from jazz and some folk music) are consequently only reproducing. In dance, there is a similar development in that improvisational collaboration became a recognized way of working in choreography only during the second half of the 20th century.

Orff wanted to go the opposite way: Music making should emerge from improvising. The students should be able to experience creative activity from the beginning, be it in their own improvisation with three notes on a xylophone, in finding a sequence of steps to a given melody, in a movement improvisation, or in a personal arrangement of a text.

5. Process and product—the interplay of development and artistic result

If we compare professional activities of musicians and dancers with the work in music education, we find a major difference. In the professional field, it is usually only about the preparation for the best possible performance, and the rehearsal phase is kept as short and efficient as possible. A music teacher who thinks and works in the same way makes a serious mistake. In the classroom, the developmental process is especially important because it is the phase in which learning happens. There should always be enough time for the students to contribute

---

1 Orff (1964, p. 17) says, *"Here liegen noch viele unausgeschöpfte Verbindungen zur bildenden Kunst."* (Here there are still many unexploited connections to the visual arts.)

their own ideas and also to try out some of them in order to gain personal experience. This requires the methodical skill of the teacher. The use of the term "method" in connection with the Schulwerk sometimes leads to misunderstandings. There is no official didactic procedure or normalized method for the Orff Schulwerk. Although it is correct that the Orff Schulwerk is not a method—even if so-called in some countries—it needs good methodical implementation. Each teacher is responsible for its practical implementation in the classroom.

We talk about "process-oriented teaching" in Orff Schulwerk. This means that the goal is open enough to include the suggestions and creative contributions of the students in the result. A lesson, such as learning a fixed instrumental piece in several parts or a dance form prepared by the teacher, can only be called an "Orff Schulwerk" lesson if this instructor-led unit is preceded or followed by sessions with relevant creative phases. Teaching that does not aim to engage and further the creative potential of the students can hardly be called Orff Schulwerk.

Of course, such a teaching process only makes sense if the final result is a presentation of the completed work, whether in the classroom or, on special occasions, in a performance for others (or at least this should be planned). One must understand that creativity is on the one hand the search for solutions, and on the other hand, it is also necessary to make decisions to select the final version. Work process and result—the educational path and the artistic results (corresponding to the level and ability of the students)—cannot be separated from each other in Orff Schulwerk.

6. The so-called "Orff-Instruments"

The use of small, easy-to-use percussion instruments, including the barred instruments (xylophone, metallophone, and glockenspiel) in music lessons brought a completely new approach in music pedagogy. Thus, the xylophone became the visual trademark of Orff Schulwerk. Unfortunately, some believe that the use of the percussion instruments put together by Carl Orff is already sufficient to characterize a music educational activity as Orff Schulwerk. Carl Orff was aware of this danger, saying, "Nevertheless one cannot remain silent about the disastrous nonsense perpetrated with these primitive instruments" (Orff, 1932/2011a, p. 102). In a superficial approach, an essential aspect of this "elemental instrumentarium" is ignored. These are instruments that can be easily experienced by playing due to their simple sound generation. Thus, a creative approach is possible from the beginning, and it is not necessary to overcome technical hurdles in order to experience the joy of instrumental music making. On the other hand, the use of these "movement-orientated instruments" (p. 100) represents an ideal connection to movement and dance.

7. Orff Schulwerk can be used in all areas of music and dance education

At the second birth of the Orff Schulwerk, as an educational radio program first broadcast on September 15, 1948, on *Radio München*, now *Bayerischer Rundfunk* (Bavarian Radio), the target group was precisely defined: The Orff Schulwerk should find its way into the elementary school in Orff's homeland of Bavaria. Today, the aim is no longer exclusively the primary school. The Schulwerk is firmly established in early childhood music education as well as in the fields of therapeutic work, inclusive pedagogy, and activities for seniors.

Of course, each of these areas requires an adequate selection of material and activities. The music presented in volumes four and five of *Music for Children*, as well as the numerous supplements such as *Paralipomena* (Orff & Keetman, 1977), shows clearly that working in the style of the Schulwerk can continue during the secondary school level. Orff's volumes for piano and violin show the way to the application in instrumental teaching (Orff, 1934a; 1934b).

8. As an educational practice, Orff Schulwerk can also be implemented in other cultures

Orff's and Keetman's pedagogical concept was not limited to Bavaria. The international dissemination began shortly after the first radio transmission of the Schulwerk. Music pedagogues from other countries (such as Canada, Japan, Great Britain, or Argentina) realized that Orff's and Keetman's ideas could also be applied in their countries. However, a prerequisite is that songs, dances, and texts have to be taken from the respective cultural area. Orff himself pointed out these necessary modifications in an interview with Hermann Regner: "When you work with the Schulwerk abroad, you must start all over again from the experience of the local children. And the experiences of children in Africa are different from those in Hamburg or Stralsund, and again from those in Paris or Tokyo" (Regner, 1993/2011b, p. 220).

Conclusion

Orff Schulwerk is based on change. However, any extensions, modifications, and additions must be made in a careful and conscious way. This requires knowledge and deep understanding of Carl Orff's educational work. Only in this way can the fundamental principles presented here be preserved in their entirety. Orff transferred the responsibility for further work to all those who want to include Orff Schulwerk in their teaching. Thus, we understand the conclusion of the speech "The Orff-Schulwerk - Past and Future" which has been cited here. Carl Orff concludes with the first line of a quote by Schiller: "I have done my part…" (Orff, 1964/2011b, p. 156).[1]

Translation: Verena Maschat

References

Günther, D. (2011). The rhythmic person and their education (M. Murray, Trans.). In B. Haselbach (Ed.), *Texts on theory and practice of Orff-Schulwerk: Basic texts from the years 1932–2010* (pp. 78–92). Mainz: Schott. (Original work published 1932)

Orff, C. (1934a). *Geigenübung I + II*. Mainz: Schott.

Orff, C. (1934b). *Klavierübung*. Mainz: Schott

Orff, C. (1964). Das Schulwerk—Rückblick und Ausblick [The Schulwerk—Past and Future]. In W. Thomas (Ed.), *Orff-Institut Jahrbuch 1963* (pp. 13–20). Mainz: Schott.

Orff, C. (2011a). Music out of movement (M. Murray, Trans.). In B. Haselbach (Ed.), *Texts on theory and practice of Orff-Schulwerk: Basic texts from the years 1932–2010* (pp. 94–102). Mainz: Schott. (Original work published 1932)

Orff, C. (2011b). Orff-Schulwerk: Past & Future (M. Murray, Trans.). In B. Haselbach (Ed.), *Texts on theory and practice of Orff-Schulwerk: Basic texts from the years 1932–2010* (pp. 134–156). Mainz: Schott. (Original work published 1964)

Orff, C., & Keetman, G. (1950-1954). *Orff-Schulwerk: Musik für Kinder* (Vols. 1–5). Mainz: Schott.

Orff, C., & Keetman, G. (1957-1966). *Orff-Schulwerk: Music for children* (Vols. 1–5). (English adaptation M. Murray). London: Schott.

Orff, C., & Keetman, G. (1977). *Paralipomena*. Mainz: Schott.

---

1 "…Now do yours," ends Schiller's play *Don Carlos*.

Orff-Schulwerk Forum Convention Salzburg 2013. (2013, Winter). *Orff-Schulwerk Informationen*, 89, 81.

Regner, H. (2011a). Carl Orff's educational ideas: Utopia and reality (M. Murray, Trans.). In B. Haselbach (Ed.), *Texts on theory and practice of Orff-Schulwerk: Basic texts from the years 1932–2010* (pp. 168–192). Mainz: Schott. (Original work published 1975)

Regner, H. (2011b). Musik für Kinder—Music for Children—Musique pour Enfants: Comments on the adoption and adaptation of Orff-Schulwerk in other countries (M. Murray, Trans.). In B. Haselbach (Ed.), *Texts on theory and practice of Orff-Schulwerk: Basic texts from the years 1932–2010* (pp. 220–244). Mainz: Schott. (Original work published 1984)

Something Old, Something New
World Music in the Orff Schulwerk

Doug Goodkin

The years after the First World War…was a time of re-orientation, a time for seeking new themes in Arts and Education, the awakening of a new body awareness, an emancipation from internal and external shackles—a time when close contacts were being made with exotic culture, their art, their dances and their music. For the first time one saw Indonesian dances and shadow plays and the accompanying Gamelan orchestras, as well as African dances and their accompaniment by rhythm instruments (shakers, drums and rattles) and songs. (Keetman, 1978/2011, p. 44)

It is often in the windstorm of social upheaval that great art and sweeping cultural shifts begin to emerge. 1924, the year the Günther-Schule opened and the decade that followed, was the beginning of a radical re-orientation that echoed down the century to our very doorstep today. As Keetman notes, one of the new possibilities that helped re-shape European culture, emancipated it from "its internal and external shackles," was exposure to new ways of considering what the body can do, what the ear can hear, what the heart can feel, what the mind can imagine. To the receptive mind ready for change, the music and dance of Africa and Asia opened new vistas, affirmed new intuitions of a world beyond the known. And so these visionary artists—Dorothee Günther, Carl Orff, Gunild Keetman, Maja Lex, and others—felt their ideas enlarged by these, at that time "exotic," art forms. Without trying to replicate them, they instead created a new language influenced by them.

Fast-forward some 40 years and here we enter another period of great upheaval and turmoil, particularly in the United States. The cry for long-denied Civil Rights for Black Americans grew to a roar, unchecked capitalism, the role of women, the goals of education, the tenets of religion, and more were all called into question. When Orff, Keetman, Wilhelm Keller, Lotte Flach, and Barbara Haselbach arrived in Toronto from the Orff Institute in 1962 to offer their radical re-envisioning of music education, the ground was fertile and ready to receive the seed. That same year, the San Francisco Zen Center opened, and various Indian gurus were attracting followers, showing new possibilities for spiritual seekers beyond the established Christian and Jewish norms. The Nigerian drummer Babatunde Olatunji had performed and recorded many albums in the U.S. and Mantle Hood had begun the first gamelan group in an American university, UCLA. Change was in the air.

By 2020, what was once rare and "exotic" in 1924 is now commonplace. Folks in just about any city worldwide might go to a yoga class, then out to a Mexican restaurant, and then bring their djembe to an evening drum circle. Go to any Orff workshop and you might play a Brazilian agogo bell, a Middle Eastern *dumbek*, a Cuban conga, and Chinese temple blocks. You might do a folk dance from Bulgaria, Israel, or Japan, sing choral songs from South Africa, Iceland, or Argentina, play games from Chile, Thailand, or Ghana, perform body percussion from Austria, Indonesia, or the U.S. The world once shrunk to a global village through plane travel, television, radio, and movies is now shrunk smaller yet, interconnected through Facebook, e-mail, or Zoom. What once had to be painstakingly described in language or musical notation is now instantly viewable, hearable, and accessible with a quick click on the YouTube button. Add to all the above the massive movements of immigrants or refuges and the norm of homogenous cultures is rapidly shifting to the new norm of heterogenous ones, a diverse mix of language, religion, cuisine, ethnic heritages, and art forms.

This changes everything. Not only in the world of music performance, but in the field of music education. The narrow spectrum of traditional music education limited to a Eurocentric repertoire on traditional European instruments following traditional European methods of transmission through written scores, private lessons, and solitary practice is necessarily called into question. In response to the times, "World Music" [1] is finding its way into music classrooms, workshops, and conferences.

Yet without a vision of what this all means, what's important to transmit to children, and how and why, we run the danger of simply shopping at the World Market, grabbing things off the shelf that attract our eye or ear without any knowledge of where it came from and what it means to its creators, without any idea of where it might go and what it might mean to the next generation we share it with. Where might we find some guidance as we move forward?

Enter Orff Schulwerk. Though neither Orff nor Keetman had any intention of creating anything resembling a "World Music" curriculum, my own experience with over four decades working with children and adults has revealed the Schulwerk as a strong foundation from which one can investigate further many of the world's diverse music and dance traditions. As Keetman testifies in the opening quote, such diversity was already present at the inception of this experimental work.

Now the question remains how to adapt this broader framework to music for children. What does it mean to a young child to play, sing, or dance a piece that may come from a completely different cultural background, but because they experience it at a young age, it simply becomes part of their repertoire and mindset? What does it mean for a teacher trained in European methods and experiencing music from that particular definition to widen their practice and perspective? What does World Music contribute to the further development of the Schulwerk? What does the Schulwerk contribute to a growing diversity found in the music classroom? What connects it to various folk—and even some classical traditions—worldwide? In no particular order, here are five such connecting points.

1. Instrumental ensemble

We made ourselves strung rattles that could be worn on wrist, knees or ankles and we used exotic models, mostly African, that could be found in every folklore museum. (Orff, 1976/1978, p. 18)

As Orff (1978, p. 70) notes in *The Schulwerk*, among the first instruments used in his experimental work in the Günther-Schule were Chinese tom-toms, Spanish castanets, Turkish cymbals, Middle Eastern tambourines, West African-inspired rattles, and German glockenspiels. He tells the story of the West African xylophone gifted to him and his exposure to Indonesian

---

1   Louis Armstrong once famously said, "All music is folk music. I ain't never heard no horse sing a song." We can likewise say that "All music is World Music. I ain't never heard no Martian sing a song." But for the sake of convenience, we'll use the term as the recording industry does, to identify most folk music from outside the European classical tradition, the American jazz tradition or the world pop culture.

gamelan that inspired the creation of the first "Orff instruments" still used today—xylophones and metallophones. Thus, from the very beginning, his unique conception of elemental composition was realized on an instrumental ensemble drawn from various corners of the world.

Thanks to increased contact with other cultures, these foundational ensembles are yet further augmented in contemporary classrooms filled with Brazilian surdos, Cuban congas, Senegalese *djembes*, Middle Eastern *dumbeks*, Cajun washboards, Turkish or Russian spoons, Chinese gongs and temple blocks, Indonesian angklung, Finnish kanteles, Hawaiian ukuleles, and yet more. Instruments that have never met each other before sit together in the same music room and new families of sound are created. It's a whole new world.

Not only does this allow for new compositions and improvisations with a new mix of techniques and timbres, it also invites completing a circle by playing music from those cultures. In the San Francisco School where I taught for 45 years, we have an extensive collection of musical instruments that we use in two ways:

1. A springboard to improvisations and compositions by children using combinations of instruments that traditionally have not played together; *djembes, dumbeks,* and *bombos* meet and create an entirely new musical drum conversation. This idea follows the spirit of Orff and Keetman's early experiments in elemental music.
2. An opportunity to teach traditional cultural styles using traditional instruments. We have arranged traditional xylophone music from Ghana, Uganda, Zimbabwe, Thailand, Bali, Nicaragua, and Mexico on the Orff xylophone; Javanese gamelan on metallophones; music from the Andes on recorders—often with the authentic instruments from those cultures either joining with the Orff ensemble or, when the tuning is a challenge, playing an introduction. When adapting traditional music in this way, something is necessarily lost in timbre and tuning—the shimmering quality of the gamelan with instrumental pairs tuned slightly apart, the buzz of the Ghana xylophone, the different tuning of the Thai xylophone, the breathiness of the Andean *tarkas*—thus, whenever possible, we do strive to integrate the original instruments.

Here we enter the territory Orff and Keetman rarely traveled. In adapting diverse musical styles in this way, the original cultural context is radically changed, the accompanying dance is sometimes too difficult to adapt, the tempos are changed to accommodate the children's skill levels. Yet the connection of the Orff ensemble with these instruments from diverse cultures makes it possible to approximate the sound and style in a way that gives children a foundation for future exploration on the authentic instruments, further investigation of the dance and cultural context.

San Francisco School orchestra. Photo: Doug Goodkin

2. Play, sing, & dance

> *Elemental music is never music alone but forms a unity with movement, dance, and speech. (Orff, 1963/2011, p. 144)*

Orff's well-known quote describes the expanded definition of music that most world cultures understand. It is noteworthy that one of the first photographs in his book *The Schulwerk* is of Nubian female dancers drumming, dancing, and singing (1978, p. 16). The specialization in Western classical music that separated playing, singing, and dancing as distinct art forms from which the aspiring artist had to choose is the anomaly more than the norm in many of the world's folk cultures.

In a folk music and dance course my colleague Sofia Lopez-Ibor and I once attended in Bulgaria, most people chose between the dance class, the singing class, or the instrumental class. As Orff Schulwerk teachers, we were the only ones who took all three. The other attending students were still in the grips of a specialist mentality. Yet the Bulgarian teachers themselves certainly knew the dances they played for, the songs they danced to.

In Kofi Gbolonyo's Orff-Afrique Course in Ghana, it is well understood that drumming, singing, and dancing are not electives, that each is necessary to the other. How can you dance if you don't drum? How can you drum if you don't dance? How can you do either without singing? The Schulwerk is a contemporary reincarnation of this old understanding that music, dance, and song are of one piece.

3. Participatory versus presentational

> *It is music that one makes oneself, in which one takes part not only as a listener but as a participant. (Orff, 1963/2011, p. 144)*

In his book *Music as Social Life*, author Thomas Turino (2008) makes a useful distinction between participatory musical culture and presentational music culture. Each carries particular assumptions and aims for different results. Western music, be it classical, jazz, or some pop, and by extension, most Western music education, leans heavily toward the presentational model—performers on a stage entertaining seated and attentive audiences. Participatory musical cultures are community-centered, invite all to join in playing, singing, and/or dancing. As such, they proceed from the assumption that everyone is musical and capable of adding their voice and body to the occasion.

Much of the world's music is like this—in festivals like *Carnaval* in Brazil, Bolivia, or Cuba, in Saturday night dances in the rural barn or the city dance club, in neighborhood caroling at Christmas, Mexican posadas, Puerto Rican *aguinaldos*, in synagogues, temples, and churches worldwide, people gather to sing and dance together. Much "World Music" exists within a participatory social context, its purpose and meaning as much (if not more) to forge and sustain human community as to artistically shape sounds and gestures.

Naturally, the two modes—participatory and presentational—are rarely mutually exclusive. But in the Orff Schulwerk classroom, the circle is the preferred formation for learning, all equally represented, all included and a space in the middle for those moments of individual expression, often echoed back by the group. The accent is on direct participation, on the way music and dance help children connect with each other, the way music and dance can frame and enliven the school's calendar of ceremony and celebration. In my school this includes the re-creation of various celebrations from diverse musical cultures—a Samba Contest, Chinese Lion Dance, English Sword Dance, and St. George play, amongst others.[1]

Because music and dance are also performing arts, the work generated in the participatory classroom will then be brought to the presentational stage in the school concert. By beginning with the discovery of each child's innate musical and kinesthetic gifts, finding a place for them in the group ensemble, and then sharing with the public, we avoid the trap of the "star syndrome" and "putting on a show" for mere entertainment. Again, we find the conscious shift from the assumptions of a Eurocentric music education to a more universal model.

4. The body, voice, and ear

… the making of music comes first, then the writing and setting down of one's own music, and later, after this, the interpretation of the music of others. (Orff, 1963/2011, p. 144)

Most of the world's music outside the European classical tradition is transmitted directly without the intermediary of written notation. This oral/ aural/ body-based learning is notably different from the literate/ visual/ deciphering symbol-based approach of traditional Western music education and creates a different kind of musician entirely.

Starting with music's connection to dance in the Günther-Schule, it is no surprise that Orff's work favored the direct expression of music without the interference of printed scores. The musicians accompanying dance needed to watch the dancers in order to both respond to and lead their movements. The dancers accompanying themselves musically naturally could not play or move freely while looking at sheets of paper. The xylophones that became the center of the instrumental work were difficult instruments to play looking at scores, as the mallets were not as tactically connected as fingers and often required looking at the bars.

Once the work was re-imagined with young children, the child's natural development had to be taken into account. Just as children learn to speak before they read and write, so should music education put sound before symbol, "speaking" music directly with rhymes, songs, body percussion, and dance. When imitating given music, as in imitating given speech, the ear must immediately process the sounds and patterns and translate them to the voice, hands, and body. Echo patterns, improvised questions and answers, singing what you hear, and playing what you sing are all common practices in Orff Schulwerk classes.

Yet again, the connection with various World Music traditions is clear. I can personally testify that having studied a little bit of Brazilian samba, Bulgarian bagpipe, Balinese gamelan, South Indian drumming, Ghanaian xylophone, all was learned by rote—the teacher plays a phrase, I repeat and begin to build the piece phrase-by-phrase. In this way, they become etched into my memory in a distinctly different process than learning a piece by reading the score and then memorizing it. It "sticks to the ribs," attaches to the muscle memory, connects to the ear. If there is a dance connected to the piece, it drives it all home yet deeper. (In 1978, I learned a long, complex piece on a South Indian drum called the *maddalam*. Thirty years later, I returned to meet my teacher, sat down, and having hardly ever played that piece in all those intervening years, was able to remember the opening part.)

---

[1] I have written in more detail about these celebrations in two of my books: *Play, Sing and Dance* (Schott) and *Teach Like It's Music* (Pentatonic Press).

5. Elemental composition

I encouraged the activation of the students by the playing of their own music, that is through improvising and composing it themselves. (Orff, 1963/2011, p. 136)

[Elemental composition] is unsophisticated, employs no big forms and no big architectural structures, and it uses small sequence forms, ostinato and rondo. Elemental music is near the earth, natural, physical, within the range of everyone to learn it and to experience it, and suitable for the child. (p. 144)

Carl Orff was first and foremost a composer and it is striking that his ideas of music education should accent composition—and the spontaneous composition known as improvisation—at the beginning of the whole matter. Most Western approaches emphasize instrumental technique, mastery of repertoire, musical literacy and only then consider that one is prepared to compose something new. Yet Orff suggests that from their very first music lesson, children are capable of simple composition and improvisation, especially if one finds the right child-size structure to house their creative impulses. Starting with rhythms on the body, sounds in the voice, expressive movement, the Schulwerk teacher guides the students to simple (but musical) structures of what Orff calls "elemental composition," arriving at music in the Orff ensemble using the universal elements of drones, ostinato, pentatonic and modal scales.

Orff and Keetman worked relentlessly to present models of such compositions in their five-volume series *Music for Children* (1950–1954). These models were meant to be adapted, simplified, extended as means to further explorations—children improvising within the pieces or composing new sections or composing whole pieces based on the models. And further yet, to children creating dances or performing the pieces in the context of a story or play.

One of the greatest gifts of incorporating World Music in today's curriculum is the opportunity to show how these elements of drones and ostinati and pentatonic/modal/diatonic scales present themselves in other styles markedly different from Orff and Keetman's. By expanding the range of compositional models, the child's very definition of music enlarges and their ideas about how to compose or improvise new sounds increases their colorful palette of possibilities. Compositional techniques rarely found in Western music can be introduced through exposure to particular musical cultures and then incorporated into the children's further improvisations and compositions. A few examples:

- The interlocking parts (*kotekan*) of Balinese gamelan.
- The beat/offbeat hocketing of Uganda *amadinda* xylophone music.
- The 3 against 2 polyrhythms of Ghanaian drumming and xylophones.
- The parallel 4ths of the Andean *tarka* music.
- The minor pentatonic scale (blues scale) over the I^7–IV^7–V^7 harmonies in American blues.

Amidst all the social reasons to consider expanding one's repertoire beyond the often-Eurocentric model, this stands out—to increase each child's capacity for larger musical thought and invention.

In the same way, exposure to the world's dance traditions enlarges the number of ways the body can express itself—its relationship to gravity, its use of previously unused muscles, its relationship to the various planes, its rhythmic vitality. Likewise with the human voice, discovering where in the body the vibration will sing out best and what phonemes will create new melodic shapes and colors. The hills will be yet more "alive with the sound of music" when the musical sounds themselves emerge from the mountains and valleys of the world's diverse landscapes.

Conclusion

> *"Something old, something new*
> *Something borrowed, something blue."*

In England of former times, the bride-to-be followed this rhyme when putting together her wedding dress. Its purpose was to ward off the evil eye and bring good luck to the marriage. In the marriage between Orff Schulwerk and diverse world music traditions, between innovation and tradition, between our past and our future, this little rhyme holds valuable instruction for us as well.

"Something old" is the legacy our musical ancestors bequeathed to us—including the *Music for Children* volumes within our almost 100-year-old Orff history. It asks us to consider keeping the old rhymes, children's games, songs, dances, instrumental pieces, stories alive as we pass them on to the children. It affirms that the present is enlarged if it keeps the past alive within it, helps us feel part of a continuum, part of a legacy that passes us the baton and urges us forward.

"Something new" suggests that we meet the gifts of the old with the understandings of the new. Just as jazz musicians are still re-inventing tunes composed a century ago, so can we bring our new and contemporary perspective to each piece of material. The question "How else can we do this?" that drives good teaching invites students to adapt and adopt and extend and change—create new dances to pieces, new music to dances, add sections, subtract parts, change words, play old pieces on new instruments, and more. Such freedoms, done responsibly with good intention and artistic integrity, bring a vitality and freshness to each activity, keep things perpetually moving forward.

"Something borrowed" is the sharing of repertoire from the world's glorious musical cultures. Artists have always used the material at hand for their personal and collective expression, whether it be using bamboo to make instruments, imitating the calls of the local frogs or birds or bringing to life the story their grandmother told them. What's "at hand"—through travel, contact with diverse people, recordings, YouTube—has changed dramatically, yet still serves the same purpose—to ignite the imagination and enlarge the craft of making music and dance and art and drama. And like good neighbors, it is always proper to return what you've borrowed. That can take the form of sharing one's own music, offering some kind of payment to the culture bearers, committing to teach the children about our shared humanity.

And "something blue?" Many of the amulets fashioned to ward off the evil eye are colored blue. Blue also is often associated with the sky, with water, with calmness, peace, harmony, happiness. And then there's the blues, that vibrant art form that came from the blending of diverse cultures, born from suffering but rising as a healing balm. Blue certainly deserves its proper place at the wedding of the old and new, the far and the near, the particular and the universal.

It is in the mix of the old, the new, the borrowed, and the blue that the vibrant music education of the present—and thus, the future—lies. In the world of the Orff Schulwerk yet to come, may this be our new mantra.

References

Keetman, G. (2011). Memories of the Günther-Schule (M. Murray, Trans.). In B. Haselbach (Ed.), *Texts on theory and practice of Orff-Schulwerk: Basic texts from the years 1932–2010* (pp. 4464). Mainz: Schott. (Original work published 1978)

Orff, C. (1978). *The Schulwerk* (M. Murray, Trans.). New York: Schott. (Original work published 1976)

Orff, C. (2011). Orff-Schulwerk: Past and future (M. Murray, Trans.). In B. Haselbach (Ed.), *Texts on theory and practice of Orff-Schulwerk: Basic texts from the years 1932–2010* (pp. 134–156). Mainz: Schott. (Original work published 1963)

Orff, C., & Keetman, G. (1950-1954). *Orff-Schulwerk: Musik für Kinder* (Vols. 1–5). Mainz: Schott.

Turino, T. (2008). *Music as social life: The politics of participation.* Chicago: University of Chicago Press.

PART II

Texts on practice of Orff Schulwerk around the world

AFRICA

Ghana

South Africa

The World to My Village, My Village to the World
Orff Schulwerk in Ghana

Kofi Gbolonyo interviewed by Doug Goodkin

Editor's comment: We begin the series of international contributions with one that is in many respects an exception. First of all, it is not a report but an interview between two musicians, music educators, and friends who have learned one from the other and continue to strive to do so. Furthermore, it represents a country that does not (yet) have an Orff Schulwerk society, but in which the ideas of Orff Schulwerk have been as alive as one could wish for centuries, so they do not really need the Schulwerk. Or do they? The text speaks of how learning from each other and teaching each other complement and mutually enrich each other. Therefore, it opens the following series of contributions.

DOUG: When I first went to Ghana in 1999, I was visiting the University of Legon and heard some fantastic music. I found a class with students doing some powerful drumming, singing, and dancing, and outside the class this sign: "Silence. Lecture in Progress."

And there it was—the yawning gap between the European idea of education and the African traditional idea where a "lecture" meant receiving the information directly into the body, voice, heart, and mind.

You have lived in both worlds and have also been trained in a third musical culture: the Orff Schulwerk. How you think of each and how you imagine their intersection might open up understanding and possibilities in each of them. But let's start with the first—your musical upbringing in the village of Dzodze in eastern Ghana.

KOFI: From very early childhood, music was everywhere around me from dawn to dusk and even all through the night. Just hearing the music and watching my family members regularly participating was already music education. Even before I was old enough to walk, I was carried on my mother's back, felt her singing and the vibrations of the bell she played. I was absorbing the music in my whole body.

When I got to walk, I remember that the first thing I was encouraged to do was dance. Every adult invites you to dance to see if you can keep the rhythm and have the right feeling. Then came singing. We were already singing along in the house with the music we heard around us, before we even came to a performance. For those who were curious and eager to play, instrumental playing came next. As young children—between 4 and 12 years old—we would go to the community center where the drums were stored and volunteer to bring them out to the adult drummers. While we waited for the adults to come tune the drums, we would start playing them ourselves. We hoped they would come late so we could play longer! We would try to imitate the exact rhythms we heard the grown-ups play.

Now if you didn't play the parts right, the adults would take the drum away from you and let the other kids keep playing. So you were motivated to really learn them and do your best! But it all came from just listening and imitating—there were no formal lessons or an expectation that you would practice. You simply joined the musical community.

We also made our own musical instruments as kids, using anything that was around us. And we played many traditional children's games. The more you play those games, the better you are at dancing, singing, and playing.

We also sang in the local Catholic Church. The choir director could read Western notation, but both the choir and the congregation learned everything by ear—there were no hymnbooks.

In the schools, music just happened when it had to happen. There's always singing every morning, with a mixture of Western percussion, bass, and snare drum, and traditional drums like the talking drum all combined together. You sing and march to your classroom, the national anthem, and things like that. Most of these songs are in English and follow the Western hymn style. But we also sang traditional music during the day in each classroom. The teacher would just decide when it was a good time to sing a song.

But I remember there also was a period just for music and the teacher might teach a new song or a student would share a song. Some teachers who had this kind of background did a little solfege training. There also was an annual music and dance competition and kids could volunteer to create and practice a particular traditional repertoire, sometimes with adults helping, sometimes just by ourselves for over a three-month period. These competitions included Western style choral singing, poetry recital, talking drum language interpreting a poem, traditional drumming, and dancing.

DOUG: I'm feeling so many parallels with the Orff Schulwerk in everything you describe. The biggest difference, of course, is that Orff Schulwerk teachers are doing all these things formally in a scheduled music time in a scheduled music room. There's one adult and 15 to 40 children and, if we're lucky, twice a week for 45 minutes. The constant presence of music and dance you describe, the full participation of people of all ages, all the adults taking interest in what the children are doing, leisure time for kids to play (without adults) children's games—this is all something the Orff Schulwerk teacher can only envy.

KOFI: Of course, growing up, this didn't feel like anything special. I imagined this was just the way all people in the world participated in music like a home language.

DOUG: In that first trip to Ghana, the two kinds of tourists I encountered were missionaries who wanted to change traditional culture and religion and ethnomusicologists/anthropologists who wanted to preserve it like a museum piece. Meanwhile, the Ghanaian musicians I met were clear about the value of their extraordinary musical legacy while always keeping open to new ideas. When I asked one musician if new styles were emerging, he said: "Innovation is the tradition of Africa." I loved that. But in places where change is slow and the old ways still alive and vibrant, it seems that those innovations are small and carefully considered, always existing within the context of the established styles.

And this brings us to the role of improvisation in traditional music. When you talk about adults seeing if you danced well, you imply that there is a particular established style that's "correct" and that you can't just move any way you want. What is the role of improvisation and creativity inside of these structures and styles passed down?

KOFI: It exists in everything. Yes, there is a certain dance style, but within that structure there is a lot of room for creativity, to introduce your own particular way of doing it and these are welcomed by the community. Those are the things that help the style thrive, to live on. The children who grow to be master musicians, dancers, culture bearers, are those who have made a discipline of improvisation and refined their personal expression.

DOUG: Something I admire greatly in my limited experience with your musical culture is this idea of the freedom of personal expression housed within the responsibility of community harmony. That feels like the beautiful elusive balance that I think the world needs today—and has always needed.

KOFI: That's exactly it! There is room for you to express who you are, but you should be concerned about the overall well-being of the community and/or the musical practice. You don't introduce your personality in a way that it destroys the style.

Western music education

DOUG: From this foundation, you began to experience other kinds of music and ways to learn it. When did that begin?

KOFI: I went to a teacher-training college. Some form of music education was required for all teachers of all subjects at that time. This was where I was introduced to Western music notation, going from solfege to written notes. This particular school was founded by German missionaries who brought their brass instruments with them. We had ten of these instruments at the school—tuba, trombone, trumpet, French horn, euphonium. Nobody knew much about how to play them, so my friends and I started experimenting on our own. I started on the trombone. One of the guys knew a little something about reading and another knew a little something about blowing technique. So they became the "teachers."

DOUG: And here we hit on one of the great connections between Orff Schulwerk and oral-based music cultures. Orff took up the old idea that the ear preceded the eye, that we learn to speak before we learn to read, that children can make fantastic music without having to decipher a complicated notational system. I love that you played these brass instruments by ear, making the written repertoire of church hymns new and vibrant and personal through taking the traditional approach.

KOFI: Yes, and it worked! People liked us and we played at various festivals and gatherings.

I went to study music education at the University of Winnebah in Ghana and there I got more practice in Western notation. That's where I actually first heard of Carl Orff! We had a course in which we were introduced to Orff, Kodály, Dalcroze, and Suzuki, but it was only academic.

In that program, we were studying mostly Western classical music—harmonic theory, studying piano, composing in Western styles from Baroque to 20th century. I loved the composition classes, especially Baroque, because I recognized the harmonies that I knew from church music.

Since independence, traditional music became part of the University in Winnebah, we had two courses per semester with playing traditional musics and also music theory of these styles. There's a descriptive theory that analyzes common types of melody and harmony within the different styles of various ethnic groups. Again, to show that you understand the theoretical basis of these styles, you had to try to compose in a given style.

In your final year, you have to compose a piece and you have the choice of a Western style, a West African style or a blend of the two. I chose to transpose traditional drum patterns to the brass instruments. This piece actually was performed in California, directed by a Ghanaian teacher teaching there!

DOUG: I know your lifelong curiosity about music and culture led you to apply for the Master's and then PhD program in ethnomusicology at the University of Pittsburgh. What was your biggest challenge and success in this program?

KOFI: I was so excited about getting accepted and getting a scholarship and starting this next step in my journey; when they gave me a course to teach as a TA, it was piano! My sight-reading on piano was horrible! Later I found out that they often gave African students the piano class because the course was for non-music majors and they knew that while our piano technique skills might be low, our musicianship was very high.

On the positive side, the lecture class was a completely different experience from Ghana. The professor expected me to challenge him, question him, talk about the article I read. In Ghana, you listen. They tell you; you listen! But here, the professor would say: "Come on, let's hear what you think!"

DOUG: Once you got used to this discipline of critical thought, did you appreciate it?

KOFI: Absolutely! I became the biggest critic and when I read articles about music of Africa, I found there was a lot to critique!

DOUG: In the West you may have found a big contrast to the Indigenous way of learning, not just in Africa, but in folk cultures throughout the world. Did you feel the enormous gaps between these two worldviews? Did you feel the Western way as wrong?

KOFI: Yes, in the sense that my freedom to play music outside of that piece of paper was being limited and I felt that there's so much I could do with this piece of music that could make it sound better. And some professors would make sure that you don't add anything, that you stick to the written notes in a rigid way and that was too much for me to take.

But no, because all music has a clear structure and within that structure, you can add your own flavor to it, especially as a composer. In my traditional music, there is a clear structure as well. The bell player cannot start improvising, for example! But certain parts, particularly the master drummer, has some freedom to interpret—but again, not like a rock drummer playing whatever he or she wants. It has to make sense within the context of the particular piece. So in the West, that freedom comes mostly in composition instead of improvisation (with the exception of jazz, an African-inspired music) and I appreciate that.

DOUG: European classical music began with a healthy respect for improvisation. Bach was a master improvisor, as were Mozart and Beethoven.

Still though it's worth noting that improvisation in the European classical world is an individual affair and doesn't have the collective community qualities found in the African diaspora where many people are improvising at once. And then there's the matter of dance. Getting the music in the whole body and improvising while dancing adds a whole other element.

KOFI: Yes! Until I got to the U.S., I never realized that there are incredible musicians who have music in their head and their fingers, but not in their whole body.

This is where I see Orff Schulwerk being important to people in my country, the place where it could bring in a bridge between the good in my traditional culture's way of music-making and the good in the Western approach and how we can make the two together and give that to children.

DOUG: And there you've hit on the essence of this conversation! And so, let's go to your first exposure to Orff Schulwerk, your first impressions and the way this dream began to take shape in the Nunya Academy project and the Orff-Afrique course.

KOFI: It began in 2001 when I was assisting in my cousin Paschal's summer course teaching Ghanaian music to Westerners. I was intrigued by two of the students—Sofía López-Ibor and Judith Cook Tucker. They wanted to know how I learned what I knew, and how I taught it, and why I was interested in teaching them.

DOUG: And why did you want to teach them?

KOFI: Because I wanted to share my traditional culture with anyone who was interested. And I was also curious about how other people learned what we have done so naturally.

DOUG: Were you surprised that what seemed simple to you seemed so difficult for them?

KOFI: Yes, I was surprised that some could not get simple things no matter how much we tried to break it down and make it understandable. The fact that they kept persisting made me think that there must be something very valuable in this music and dance I grew up with. This was not their culture. What was the value in making such an effort?

I was also surprised because these were Western music teachers and musicians who were having such trouble. What was missing in their education? Certainly dance. It was hilarious to see all these music teachers who couldn't move to rhythms the way that we felt it.

DOUG: Sofía often tells the story about how she spent every moment she could with the children who gathered around. Did you notice that?

KOFI: Oh yes, I was in charge of counting the people before they got on the bus and Sofía was often missing! I always found her and Judith off to the side with the children! That gave me a new perspective on how children learn our music. Before, I never paid attention to these games the children played as something important. Sofía and Judith's interest in that really opened my eyes.

DOUG: And what do you think Sofía saw in you that attracted her interest?

KOFI: I think it was that while I was teaching them, I was also explaining a lot about what I was teaching. She noticed the way I could connect it with the greater Ewe culture.

DOUG: And that's precisely why I feel so connected to you! Many Orff Schulwerk teachers are content to just teach good music and dance in a fun and effective way and that's great, but I'm always looking to go further and connect it with the greater culture and consider what it might mean to both affirm who we are and consider who we could be.

KOFI: Yes!

DOUG: Now we get to the Summer Course at the Orff Institute in Salzburg. Do you remember your first impressions of that experience?

KOFI: To be honest, the first few days I had great doubts: Why am I here? Why would music teachers come here and spend so much money to do something so simple, something our children could do so easily? I have to admit, I was so bored in your first class—you had me playing a simple drone! But when you began to talk about the how and why of what we were doing far beyond the music itself. And when you asked us how else we could do it and we had some freedom to improvise, then things got interesting. And the same thing in Barbara Haselbach's class, as I began to understand the philosophy behind the activities.

DOUG: After that experience, you went on to begin your master's degree in Pittsburgh and we invited you to visit James [Harding], Sofía, and me at The San Francisco School. What was that experience like?

KOFI: Coming to your school, I was impressed by the atmosphere of the community. It was very casual with the students calling teachers by their first names, but it was clear that they respected you because you respected them. Watching the three of you teach, it became clear why you were teaching the way you were teaching, why people came to Salzburg to learn how to teach in this way. And then having the opportunity for the first time to teach Western kids in a Western classroom. That was the moment that I realized that this thing called Orff Schulwerk—I needed it. The children in Ghana need it.

DOUG: And what precisely is the "it" you felt was so valuable?

KOFI: To teach in a way that is fun and effective. To be playful. Now I realized that what we did in our villages was essential to our musical development. And also, the way you explained what you were doing to the students, to ask them what they thought they were doing so they were involved in thinking about how they learned what they learned. Again, we don't do that in Ghana. This seemed like a fascinating possibility of bringing something new to teaching music of any style.

Remember, before I came to the U.S. I was already learning Western music and even teaching it. I was teaching from the paper and was very strict about getting it right the first time. But I didn't see you do that, and yet, the students were playing very well and enjoying it too. That made me realize that there was a Western way of teaching music and then there was Orff Schulwerk.

DOUG: And this is why I value your perspective so much. You've experience three very different but related worlds—your oral musical upbringing in the village, your formal Western music learning in universities in both Ghana and the U.S. and now Orff Schulwerk.

So let's fast forward to a few years ago when the SF School students did a benefit concert for your Nunya Academy project. By now, the kids had worked with you many times and learned some of the repertoire Sofía, James, and I learned from you. How did that feel?

KOFI: So good! The students played and danced well, but they also understood what they were doing and knew where it comes from and respected the people who created that music.

And before that concert, I was involved in the play about the West African story Sundiata that James and Sofía did with the kids. That was wonderful to see the blend of traditional West African music and materials with Orff Schulwerk on stage. That really impressed me.

DOUG: I'm curious about what your levels training experience in the San Francisco International Orff Course meant to you.

KOFI: Of course, I learned a lot. The dance part was very confusing to me at the beginning, so different from my background of dance as always connected to strong rhythms I had no idea of modern dance before working with Christa Coogan. But eventually, what began as strange to me grew to something that I ended up enjoying a lot.

DOUG: Were there other parts of the Schulwerk that didn't resonate with your Ewe culture and others that clearly did, even if in a new form?

KOFI: The part that both have in common is the perception of the child as a consummate musician, a creator, not to be treated as a blank sheet of paper. Also this idea that children can be teachers of other children and this resonates with my Ewe upbringing—that the teacher is not the only one who teaches. What I see the Schulwerk bringing that is new and valuable is that the child is given the tools of analysis and learns how to talk about what he or she is doing. The teacher gives the child the opportunity to express verbally or in written form what they're thinking about what they're doing. We don't do that in Ghana. It's not in our traditional culture. Also interesting is that the student can be teacher to the teacher—in our culture, no! This is a valuable new idea for both the students and the teachers in my culture. Also interesting is the idea that every culture has value. Orff Schulwerk helped me learn how to appreciate it and share it.

DOUG: That's interesting to me, because traditionally Ewe children learn Ewe music. But in today's world, university students come from different regions of Ghana and encounter new music and musical styles—like the xylophones in the north that were not known in the south. In the Orff-Afrique course, you bought many xylophones, and this can now be part of the musical education of the kids in Nunya Academy. Why does this feel valuable to you?

KOFI: It's important that the kids know that music isn't only what they perceive it to be, that it can be played, approached, and understood in different ways. In other words, the challenges you have trying to understand other's music will be the same challenges others have trying to learn your music.

DOUG: Beautiful. And none of this exploration outside one's inheritance negates that inheritance, but amplifies it, enlarges you as a person.

KOFI: Exactly. And that is the great gift of the Orff-Afrique course we created. We bring music teachers from all around the world to my village and hope they leave with a new perspective on my culture, not only learning the music, songs, dances, and games, but living the context of the music for two intense weeks. Going to traditional religious ceremonies, Western churches, festivals, visiting weaving villages, playing games with the children in Nunya Academy,[1] drinking palm wine, and so on. And the children get to meet so many new people, and share their games and music, and learn some new games and songs, and maybe become a little bit prouder when they see how people come so far to learn about their culture. This is so valuable. I am **bringing my village to the world and bringing the world to my village.**

DOUG: And the world is richer for it. Thank you so much.

Practice for a future Ghanaian drummer
Photo: Sofía López-Ibor Aliño

---

1 www.nunyaacademy.com

Orff Schulwerk in South Africa

Compiled and edited by Janice Klette Evans [1]

Introduction

The Orff-Schulwerk Society of South Africa (OSSSA) is a small, vibrant organization, run by an enthusiastic committee of volunteers who meet regularly and organize workshops and levels courses in various centers across the country, predominantly for the benefit of schoolteachers. Approximately 100 members pay a small annual membership fee, benefitting from the support of the committee and fellow members of the Society, and enjoying the website, which offers lesson plans, teaching ideas, and access to resources.

When OSSSA was formed, systemic racism was legislated across all facets of social, political, and economic life in apartheid South Africa. Black people could neither vote nor enjoy access to many of the privileges granted only to Whites. Education and teacher training of the majority of the population, namely people of color, was significantly under-resourced and inadequate. The system of "Bantu Education" for Blacks was particularly oppressive in ensuring that Black people had little access to subject knowledge or skills development other than preparation for menial labor. School infrastructure was sub-standard, most schools being without running water, electricity, and sanitation. There was very little formal arts or music education in government schools (except those in White areas), with most music education taking place in informal, community contexts, where music making has always been a vital part of South Africa's cultural life.

A history of our society

Hazel Walker Cunnington and Janet Hudson formed the Orff-Schulwerk Society of South Africa in 1972, after having completed courses at the Orff Institute, Salzburg. They developed primary school Orff Schulwerk courses and set up a core committee that met monthly in Johannesburg. Soon other branches around the country, such as Pretoria and (for only a short time) Cape Town, were started. Biennial general meetings were held in different centers, where both Cunnington and Hudson conducted workshops. Eventually levels courses were established and attended by teachers from Johannesburg and surrounding areas. The OSSSA also developed a pre-primary course that was attended by many preschool teachers. Rhodes University made levels courses compulsory for music education students (though this is no longer the case). Lecturers from the US, Austria, UK, Ghana, Australia, and Canada were invited to teach well-attended workshops at the major centers around South Africa.

Membership of the Orff-Schulwerk Society was never limited by race. Slowly a small number of Black teachers became interested in Orff Schulwerk and attended early levels courses, though they faced the challenge of teaching in environments with very little support and minimal

---

1   With kind support of Miriam Schiff, Margriet van Zyl, Colleen Hart, Bronwyn Pieters, Adeyemi Oladiran, Diana Cowen, and Susan Harrop-Allin.

resources. By the late 1990s, several workshops and short courses were held for these teachers in townships like Soweto.

In April 1994, South Africa elected its first democratic government. As the country transformed from apartheid to democracy, OSSSA committee members decided to rewrite the levels courses to better reflect South African content and context.

Since 2008, in preparation for restructuring our levels courses, several members of the OS-SSA have attended levels courses in San Francisco and Australia. Experienced international Orff Schulwerk teachers (Doug Goodkin, James Harding, Sofía López-Ibor, Verena Maschat, and Susie Davies-Splitter) have travelled to South Africa. OSSSA chose to adopt the model of four one-week levels courses, similar to those in Australia and better suited to our Southern Hemisphere school schedules.

In 2017, Gerard van de Geer of Tasmania, Australia, offered invaluable assistance with the launch of the new Level 1 in Cape Town, compiled and presented by Janice Evans, Hastings Nyirenda, Adeyemi Oladiran, and Colleen Hart, and presented again in Johannesburg in 2018. Level 2 was launched in Cape Town in 2019, with Tersia Harley taking over from Colleen Hart, and repeated in 2020 in Johannesburg. We are hoping to introduce Levels 3 and 4 in the coming years.

There have been many teachers of diverse backgrounds attending these courses. It has been a long process of integrating South African music, language, and cultural expression into the philosophy and approach of Orff Schulwerk. We firmly believe that the current offerings are far more suited to our cultural and linguistic context and the diversity of our teachers, classrooms, and learners.

Teacher training and curricula

Apartheid has resulted in a very divided society. In 1994, the first democratically elected government proclaimed 11 official South African languages—English, isiZulu, isiXhosa, Sepedi (Northern Sotho), Setswana, Sesotho (Southern Sotho), isiNdebele, Siswati, Tshivenda, Xitsonga and Afrikaans—all having equal legal status.[1] It is extremely difficult to incorporate all these official languages into the national music curriculum. Children living in rural areas often speak only a local language and learn songs specific to a particular region. Songs in unfamiliar languages can be fun to learn but are often difficult for teachers to access. Many thousands of teachers in rural and outlying schools have no formal music education and are struggling with overcrowded and under-resourced classrooms.

Teacher training

Lecturers in teacher education at certain prominent universities, such as at the University of the Witwatersrand (Wits), have recognized the importance of the Orff Schulwerk approach in music teaching programs and have helped to promote it at tertiary education level. Between 2004-2008, a large-scale teacher training course (The Advanced Certificate in Education–Arts and Culture), reaching thousands of teachers in the country, was developed and run by Wits and the University of Cape Town (UCT). The music components of these courses were largely based on an adapted Orff Schulwerk approach and implemented by teachers in a wide range of schools. Teacher training courses, such as the Post Graduate Certificate in Education (PGCE), further utilize and teach Orff Schulwerk philosophy and teaching practice, which students adapt to their own contexts. In a Community Music program at Wits, community musicians

---

1   https://www.gov.za/about-sa/south-africas-people

and teacher trainees are introduced to, and encouraged to work with, Orff Schulwerk principles in community music settings (taking music education into urban and rural communities).

The University of Pretoria includes aspects of Orff Schulwerk in the module "Music Education." Caroline van Niekerk's work is well known, as is that of Dorette Vermeulen and Riekie Van Aswegen, who co-wrote *Junior Collage* (1999) and *African Collage* (2009), both well-known examples of Schulwerk-based South African music teaching materials. Student teachers at both Pretoria and Wits Universities are encouraged to attend workshops and levels courses run by OSSSA.

School curriculum

During apartheid, government spending on music education—and Orff Schulwerk—was reserved exclusively for schools in White privileged areas. In 1994 the new government, in its effort to improve the mathematics and science skills of learners, focused school budgets on these subjects. Spending on music was cut and in most government schools music teaching posts were discontinued. As a result, the Orff Schulwerk learning in those schools disappeared and many instruments were unused and fell into a state of disrepair. The government then allowed schools, based mainly on the wealth of their communities, to choose from fully subsidized, semi-funded, or private funding models, creating tiers of financial dependence on government. Semi-funded and privatized schools were able to choose to continue with music as an integral part of the curriculum, and many of these schools continue to produce a high standard of music education. Many private schools with the will and resources to keep Orff Schulwerk and music teaching going consider it a point of pride—and a part of their marketing strategy—that they offer their students a rich music and Schulwerk-based experience.

Orff Schulwerk principles were again incorporated into the National Schools Curriculum 2005-2012 (cf MacMillan's publications *Arts and Culture for All*, Grades 4–9).[1] In 2012, however, the curriculum again changed to the Curriculum and Assessment Policy Statement (CAPS) and the time dedicated to music teaching was reduced.

Teachers working with younger children, namely preschool to grade 3, can easily incorporate Orff Schulwerk techniques into the national curriculum. In the higher grades, however, the CAPS curriculum is very content heavy, and teachers find it difficult to cover all the work while employing an inclusive, creative, experiential, and improvisatory approach. Often teachers simply move away from the national curriculum if they feel unable to follow it, and—depending on the demands made by their particular school—they create their own curriculum. In the private school system, teachers have more freedom in curriculum design and implementation than those in government schools. Those who have been exposed to Orff Schulwerk will follow its approach.

Orff Schulwerk training

A South African challenge is that many music teachers are without formal qualifications. Some schools are happy to employ music teachers based only on their performance abilities. However, in some private schools, Orff Schulwerk is known as a successful approach, and teachers applying for music jobs are asked to provide evidence of Schulwerk training. Orff Schulwerk

---

1   The MacMillan publications were produced as a series of text books for use by school teachers, and endorsed by government education authorities. The activities presented in these books are in line with what was then the National Schools Curriculum. The MacMillan books are no longer officially in use and our Society aims to provide help for teachers in our training workshops and courses.

has proved to be the ideal way to instruct teachers, based on the body and voice as resources, making instruments and using language to generate rhythm.

Teacher training course
Photo: Suzy Rodriques

Elements of South Africa's own cultural heritage in relation to Orff Schulwerk

Historically, Western colonial influences on South African education have been very strong, and the vast majority of material used in past Orff Schulwerk training was in English. African Indigenous music intrinsically contains elements central to Orff Schulwerk, with song, dance, improvisation, and rhythm inherently interwoven into the cultural fabric of its various communities. It is well known that the playing of instruments—both non-melodic and tuned percussion—are an integral part of African music. Adapting Orff Schulwerk teaching to include material from our country's Indigenous cultural heritage began slowly many years ago but has notably accelerated since the restructuring of the levels courses in 2017.

In many underprivileged South African communities, children often spend time outdoors, singing traditional folk songs, dancing, and skipping. Games are often developed using items from the natural environment, e.g., stone games and songs, played by children and adults alike. These traditions are being incorporated into Orff Schulwerk teaching.

South Africa also has a long tradition of choral singing. Solfa (using fixed *do*, as opposed to solfège, which has a moving *do*) has been fairly widely taught, and solfa notation [1] is the main method of teaching choral music. It is very common for South African singers to add harmonies by ear. A lot of the choral singing is based on gospel music—evidence of the strong influence of missionaries—and a lot of the music contains I–IV–V harmonies. Choral singing in the largest church—the ZCC (Zionist Christian Church)—is based on traditional dance-music forms.

A wide range of scales and harmonic systems can be found in traditional South African folk music, including pentatonic in certain contexts, though in other contexts it is not a familiar

---

1 https://www.singsolfa.com/about/methodology/

sound. Familiarity with the pentatonic scale and solfa are advantages when introducing Orff Schulwerk.

Indigenous Southern African songs, dances, and music traditionally performed on instruments like the *mbira* (a Zimbabwean instrument also known as a thumb piano[1]), *phalaphala* (Kudu horn[2]), and *uhadi* (a bowed string attached to a resonator, usually a calabash[3]) have been adapted to be played on instruments associated with Orff Schulwerk. Marimbas (large, resonant xylophones derived from a number of African traditions) are popularly used in Orff Schulwerk classrooms.

African music is typically based around repeated motifs. The concept of the bordun is therefore familiar, and much marimba playing employs borduns. Marimba playing has grown in popularity in many schools, with courses for teachers and children offered by non-government organizations such as Education Africa, which bases its marimba teaching on Orff Schulwerk principles. Each year, the Education Africa International Marimba and Steelpan Festival brings groups from around Africa and elsewhere to play and compete together. Performers on Orff instruments and Orff ensembles are encouraged to participate. In a formal school context, the Orff Schulwerk approach is useful for helping marimba students to understand the elements and structure of the music, rather than simply playing learned patterns by rote.

Another strongly South African tradition exists in the Afrikaans cultural heritage. The Afrikaans population originated from Dutch, German, and French settlers. As the settlers lost their ties with Holland and Europe in general, the Afrikaans language (somewhat close to Dutch) developed into a unique language of its own, and the community has maintained a rich and proud heritage that includes many folk songs and dances.

Playing marimbas and xylophones
Photo: Miriam Schiff

Orff Schulwerk in relation to music and movement/dance education

South Africa's history has demonstrated the strength and tenacity of the human spirit, as well as the human need for singing and dancing in order to keep that spirit strong. There are many forms of South African traditional dance, some of which are being informally incorporated into education, dependent on the educators in any given situation.

Isicathulo (known popularly as gumboot dancing[4]) is an example of a South African urban dance form that developed in a very specific socio-political situation in Johannesburg's gold

---

1 https://en.wikipedia.org/wiki/Mbira
2 https://digitalcollections.lib.uct.ac.za/islandora/object/islandora%3A20259/print_object
3 https://en.wikipedia.org/wiki/Uhadi_musical_bow
4 https://en.wikipedia.org/wiki/Gumboot_dance

mines. Black mine workers deep underground in gold mines developed sores on their feet and legs from constantly wading through underground water. The mine bosses provided thick rubber boots (gumboots) as a solution to this problem. Mineworkers underground began to develop a system of communication among themselves, involving stamping and slapping rhythmic patterns on the gumboots. This dancing also helped to boost morale.[1]

Gumboot dancing is being taught in our Orff Schulwerk levels courses, and some teachers are teaching it in schools. It provides students with an enjoyable physical workout as well as performing rhythmically challenging patterns and keeping a steady beat. Traditionally, gumboot dancing was performed by men, but it has become popular among all ages and genders and is now part of government-sponsored school competitions all over the country.

Improvisation and creativity, and integration of music and dance in the education system

Many of the Orff Schulwerk practitioners who grew up during the apartheid era attended well-resourced government schools and were themselves exposed to Orff Schulwerk. Its influence has been profound on them, and many are motivated to pass on their knowledge. Improvisation and creativity—and integrating music and dance into formal education—depend very much on the individual teacher in an institution and the time available. In situations where there is little guidance by a music teacher, most of what takes place is student led, and is then dependent on the background and motivation of those students. When a formally appointed music teacher is present, it still depends on that particular teacher's training and approach.

In public schools, music tuition is incorporated into the subjects "Life Skills" or "Creative Arts," and a teacher without any music experience could be expected to teach music. The results are varied. Some teachers who have a formal classical music training tend towards a Western-orientated, theoretical form of music teaching. Other teachers who are more inspired (and particularly those who have been exposed to Orff Schulwerk) favor a more creative, playful approach in which improvisation plays an important role.

Class meeting outside
Photo: Jessica Androliakos

There are many music teachers (mostly instrumental) who have an open and critical interest in Western pedagogical ideas, and many South African students are enthusiastically learning to play classical music. However, there also exists a desire (particularly in certain university liberal arts programs) to move away from Western approaches and to explore the African aesthetic as being of paramount importance. This may involve a rejection of anything "Eurocentric," rather than a combining of ideas. Fortunately, within the schooling system—and particularly

---

1   https://www.southafrica.net/za/en/travel/article/the-fascinating-story-behind-the-birth-of-gumboot-dancing

among Orff Schulwerk practitioners—there is a wide-ranging desire to share, collaborate, and learn.

Conclusion

The Orff-Schulwerk Society of South Africa has seen many changes since 1972. In 2021 we continue to reach out to a wider audience. Plans for a 2022 international conference to celebrate 50 years are in place and many internationally based Orff Schulwerk practitioners have already committed to attending. As more teachers of color participate in and are trained to facilitate Orff Schulwerk levels courses and workshops, we are better able to draw on a wider base of musical knowledge and experience to create a richer, more authentic, and relevant outcome. Orff levels course presenters constantly try new ways of engaging with local materials and including traditional songs and dances in their presentations, as well as looking beyond South Africa with the intention of including neighboring African countries.

A South African Orff Schulwerk levels course is a deeply enriching experience for teachers, and their students are delightfully receptive to the new learning. Teachers from different races and cultures within South Africa are taught a wider variety of music materials and display growing confidence to adapt these materials to their own classrooms. Improvisation is encouraged at every stage. There is great enthusiasm among teachers to source more Indigenous music, and a joyful motivation to be inclusive, share ideas and resources, and to learn from one another.

References

Arts and culture for all (Grades 4–9). (2004). Manzini: Macmillan.

Van Aswegen, R., & Vermeulen, D. (1999). *Junior Collage: Music Activities for Tiny Tots*. Pretoria.

Vermeulen, D., & Van Aswegen, R. (2009). *African Collage: Book & CD with Music Activities for the Class Room*! Pretoria.

Additional relevant South African publications

Marimba Music Volumes 1 and 2: compiled by Colleen Hart (self-published) first edition 2004. (Volume 3 is to be released soon)

Marimba Magic Books 1, 2 and 3 by Joan Lithgow (self-published) www.marimbaworkshop.co.za

33 Marimba Arrangements Celebrating South Africa's 11 Official Languages by Joan Lithgow (self-published) www.marimbaworkshop.co.za

Shaya Marimba by Bradley Lithgow (self-published) www.marimbaworkshop.co.za

The Talking Drum published by the Pan African Society of Music Educators. http://www.disa.ukzn.ac.za/TALKING_DRUM

Periodical

The Orff Beat: Journals published by the Orff-Schulwerk Society, originally quarterly, later annually, and—since 2013—replaced by website articles. *The Orff Beat* included articles from Orff Schulwerk Associations world-wide, and articles by South African Orff Schulwerk practitioners, writing about adapting the Orff Schulwerk approach to the South African context. Our website includes content intended to support our local teachers, giving lesson ideas and making known our local content around the world. https://www.orff.co.za

NORTH & SOUTH AMERICA

The Development of Orff Schulwerk in Argentina

Compiled and edited by Nacho Propato [1]

Brief history of the development of Orff Schulwerk in Argentina

The beginnings of Orff Schulwerk in Argentina are closely related to the figure of Guillermo Graetzer (1914–1993). Of Austrian origin, Graetzer arrived in Argentina in 1939 with a solid musical background and a devotion to composition and music pedagogy.

In 1946, Graetzer founded the Collegium Musicum in Buenos Aires. In this institution, he set out to promote the teaching of music based on progressive ideas that encouraged the possibility for all persons to access musical knowledge through a wide range of experiences.

In 1948, the Collegium Musicum introduced its first music education courses for children, which sparked an interest in exploring music pedagogy for childhood. This marked the adoption of European methodologies that teachers at the institution started to study and apply in their classes.

In 1957, the Collegium Musicum started experimenting with Orff Schulwerk. Graetzer probably learned about it through his correspondence with Carl Orff. Moreover, he surely found several points in common with his own conception of music pedagogy: learning music through experience, singing, playing, dancing, and composing in a group setting. He was also very enthusiastic about the use of barred percussion instruments. Children studying at the Collegium Musicum had already been using percussion instruments including claves, tambourines, cymbals, and triangles.

Courses for teachers followed. In subsequent years, new collaborators joined in, especially Antonio Yepes, a pedagogue and excellent percussionist, as well as Elisa Alcolumbre (music pedagogue) and Patricia Stokoe (dance pedagogue, who presented dance groups with percussion instruments for the first time here).

In Rosario (province of Santa Fe), the Orff Schulwerk was introduced by Christian Hernández-Larguía (conductor and founder of the well-known early music group Pro Música Rosario) and Isolda Mostny (choreographer of Austrian origin).

In later years, the training courses with foreign teachers such as Barbara Haselbach, Verena Maschat, José Posada, Siegfried Lehmann, or Daniel Basi were of great impact.

In the 1960s, the pedagogical work with music teachers was particularly intense, especially through the Barry publishing company (Buenos Aires), which published the first edition of the Orff Schulwerk (*Música para Niños*, 1963) and organized numerous annual courses in which essential elements were passed on to hundreds of educators. There were also performances, lectures, courses, and radio and television broadcasts within Argentina and in other South and Central American countries (by A. Yepes and G. Graetzer).

1 With thanks to the following members of *Asociación Orff-Schulwerk Argentina* (AAOrff) for their helpful contributions to this article: Dina Poch, María Cristina Castro, Eliana Seinturia, Carla Grosso, Fernanda García Thieme, Tamara Figueroa.

As time went by, percussion arrangements of English origin appeared in the courses, and later the teaching methods of Jaques-Dalcroze, Martenot, Willems, and Kodály were introduced. It was not until the late 1960s that elements of the Orff Schulwerk were included in primary school curricula.

The general political and economic situation has always exerted a very decisive influence on cultural and educational movements and, as the country has been (and still is) frequently shaken by cyclical political changes, our music education and its planning cannot show a straight-line development.

Although—at the national level—the Orff Schulwerk has never been fully incorporated into the curriculum of music education in compulsory education, there are several aspects of it that have had (and still have) an important influence. Several German schools in Argentina have continued over the years to apply Schulwerk concepts, in some cases with a clear inclination towards instrumental practice (because they have the instruments). In addition to the work of the Collegium Musicum, we can also mention the Pestalozzi Schule in Buenos Aires, which has a specific extra-curricular program based on the Orff Schulwerk.

In public schools the Orff Schulwerk is used occasionally, depending on the training and experience of the teacher. Adaptations of native rhymes and rhythms associated with movement, body percussion, and percussion instruments, are practiced mostly at the initial and primary level, although this is currently extending to the first years of secondary level, where we can also observe interesting adaptations of contemporary music.

Argentine traditional music and its adaptation in the Orff Schulwerk

Argentine folk music has its roots in the multiplicity of original Indigenous cultures. Four major historical-cultural events have shaped it: 1) Spanish colonization and 2) forced African immigration caused by the slave trade during Spanish rule (16th-18th centuries); 3) the great wave of European immigration (1880-1950), and 4) a major domestic migration (1930-1980). There are testimonies of all of them, especially in the music we share with young children, alongside the rich material of Indigenous children.

The legacy of the traditional world of children's play came to our land from Spain by direct transmission, as is the case with popular wisdom in general. In the Americas, it was the conquerors—especially the missionaries—who played the role of teachers. They wanted to reach the spirit of the Indigenous populations, and to achieve this, they learned the native languages. Like any schoolteacher today, missionaries made use of various didactic resources available to them: European games, tunes, and poems translated into the native languages. The individual characteristics of different ethnic groups and oral transmission then added special nuances. Today, one may find songs with similar lyrics with small or big differences, stretching from Mexico to Argentina, all stemming from the same Spanish roots. A great variety of songs that are popular in kindergartens and primary schools are often sung in ignorance of their provenance.

Scholars of folk music, aware that modernity could obliterate this cultural heritage, undertook the titanic task of compiling verses, chants, romances, songs, Christmas carols, rhymes, and even single stanzas that still lingered in the memory of ancient settlers across valleys, hills, ranches, and villages. Thanks to the work of Carlos Vega, Juan Alfonso Carrizo, Isabel Aretz, Leda Valladares, and Violeta H. de Gainza, among other specialists, this heritage has been preserved for the world to enjoy.

In 1963, Guillermo Graetzer completed the first Latin American Spanish adaptation of the work of Carl Orff and Gunild Keetman: *Orff Schulwerk, Música para niños.* Names, proclamations, and calls come with inseparable expression and rhythm. The rhythm that is born from language and slowly becomes musicalized is also conveyed to the body and to instruments. The "elemental" nature of music in the concept of Orff and Keetman is present and safeguarded in this work.

By following this path, there is much that a music teacher can discover. Words, rhythm, body percussion, instruments, songs, movement—these are all elements that, combined with the students' own contributions, will lead to the joint discovery of a world that is as ephemeral as it is solid: the world of music.

In Argentine culture, we find certain characteristics that have led to an excellent amalgamation with the ideas of Orff Schulwerk, especially the Andean music of northwest Argentina, whose rhythmic and melodic components are close to the elemental principles of the Schulwerk. Reference is made to the use of the pentatonic scale, bimodality, the basic time signature with simple rhythmic cells, or more complex ones such as syncopation. Wind and percussion instruments, typical of this style, are also very well used in didactic transpositions of works from the folklore repertoire. Dances like the *Carnavalito* lend themselves well to improvisation and collective creation in movement. Singing with the *caja*, a very characteristic musical manifestation of this region, is an improvised form of singing, in which feelings, announcements, and complaints are expressed in a very simple way. It is performed by singing over the sounds of a chord, accompanied by a drum known as *caja chayera*, and improvising texts, called *coplas* (couplets). In this sense, we find an important meeting point with the pedagogical ideas of the Orff Schulwerk, in relation to improvisation and collective creation.

Other regions of Argentina present more complex rhythms, where simple measures are juxtaposed with compound ones, generating a polymeter, so characteristic of Argentine and Latin American traditional music. The great rhythmic richness of dance forms like the *Chacarera, Gato,* and *Zamba* offers a variety of possibilities for working with the rhythm of words, body and instrumental percussion, and basic harmonic functions.

In general, these are dances with pre-established choreographies. Due to their particularities, they are suitable for facilitating the assimilation—through movement and active listening—of different elements of music, formal structures, melodic and rhythmic turns and twists, and harmonic cadences, among other features. Many of the melodies are also sung, and their lyrics refer to the socio-cultural context, including, for instance, elements of nature, places, legends, traditions, customs and beliefs of different peoples, regional words, typical food and drink, etc.

A special mention is made here to the culture of the native peoples of South America, whose artistic manifestations present us with a wide range of resources to address elemental music. Its main features include rituals involving their clothing, their dances, group singing, indigenous instruments, and the most elemental sounds produced using the body and the voice.

In view of the above, we find an excellent communion between the pedagogical ideas of Orff Schulwerk and local artistic manifestations. Argentina has come a long way to treasure its culture, but there is still a lot of work to be done, and the Orff Schulwerk pedagogical proposal certainly presents a great opportunity in this respect.

Argentine instruments
Photo: private collection

The Orff Schulwerk Argentina Association

Orff Schulwerk Argentina (*Asociación Orff-Schulwerk Argentina*,[1] AAOrff) was established in 2009 after several years of preparation.

Any reference to the early days of the AAOrff must consider the foundations on which it was built. During the 2000s, Verena Maschat and Sofía López-Ibor offered summer courses in Buenos Aires for those interested in Orff Schulwerk, jointly invited by the Pestalozzi Schule and the Collegium Musicum Buenos Aires. These courses were very well attended, were extremely enlightening, and left an important pedagogical impact and a great impression on the attendees. This aroused in teachers/musicians an enormous interest in this new way of teaching music and movement, which was for many of them totally revealing.

Thanks to the encouragement of the aforementioned guest professors, there were several teachers from Argentina who took the initiative to travel abroad to continue their training in different instances, such as summer courses in Madrid and Salzburg or level courses in San Francisco. All of this led to the formation of a working group that comprised members who were already experienced in Orff Schulwerk, working side-by-side with others who were just being introduced to its practices. Encouraged by Verena Maschat's advice, this group decided to take a step forward and—with great effort—start an Orff Schulwerk association in Argentina.

Since 2009, the Orff Schulwerk Argentina Association has carried out countless actions and initiatives, aimed at spreading the pedagogical principles of Carl Orff and Gunild Keetman. It has continued with the organization of International Summer Courses (on a bi-annual basis), inviting teachers with extensive experience in Orff Schulwerk, such as the aforementioned Verena Maschat and Sofía López-Ibor, as well as Barbara Haselbach, James Harding, Doug Goodkin, Wolfgang Hartmann, Polo Vallejo, and Soili Perkiö, among others.

Additionally, AAOrff started organizing monthly meetings for its members, which continue to this day, in which the acquired experiences are shared, and new educational activities related to the different aspects of Orff Schulwerk are offered. These meetings last three hours and cover topics such as music and movement/dance, recorder, integration of the arts, vocal-instrumental arrangements, Argentine folk music and dance, etc. At the same time, some teachers already trained in Orff Schulwerk began to give courses and workshops in the interior of Argentina and in neighboring countries. All these actions gradually increased the interest of the participants to delve into Orff Schulwerk and to learn a little more about this approach. Furthermore, experiences in improvisation and creative work in general can/should also lead to an understanding of contemporary manifestations of the arts (music, dance, literature, visual arts, etc.)

---

1 https://www.aaorff.com/

The Orff Schulwerk Argentina Association publishes its annual magazine *Música y Movimiento*, featuring a wide variety of articles of interest and covering events from the beginning of Orff Schulwerk in Argentina to the present.

Since 2018, the Escuela de Artes Pestalozzi[1] (Buenos Aires) is a member of the international network of Associated Schools and Institutions of the International Orff-Schulwerk Forum Salzburg (IOSFS). An extra-curricular artistic offering for pupils of the Pestalozzi Schule, it includes a wide range of artistic workshops for children in kindergarten, primary, and secondary school. As an institution, it encourages the inclusion of all students who wish to participate, providing a space for artistic education. All activities are carried out in a framework of respect, dignity, and solidarity towards others and the different artistic manifestations expressed through various disciplines, including music, dance, visual arts, and theater, seeking a high standard of aesthetic quality. Thus, the Art School focuses on the goals of the Pestalozzi Schule, i.e., education as a driver of peace and as a meeting point for different cultures. It puts the students at the center of all its activities, taking into account their social, family, and cultural situation, and leveraging and developing their artistic and humanistic skills and capabilities, both individually and as a group.

In 2019, AAOrff organized—in conjunction with the Asociación Jacques-Dalcroze Argentina and the Asociación Kodály Argentina—a meeting of music education methodologies/philosophies, offering attendees a very interesting range of principles from each approach, their differences and commonalities.

The Asociación Orff-Schulwerk Argentina has been a member of the IOSFS since 2012 and it maintains an active interchange with other Orff Schulwerk Associations in Latin America. During 2020, meetings continued to be held virtually due to the pandemic.

As a result of conversations at the roundtables of the annual 2020 Convention organized by the IOSFS, the Orff Associations of Colombia, Argentina, and Brazil held their first joint meeting in December 2020. It was a great opportunity to share didactic experiences, highlighting the different cultures of these countries, with the aims to continue expanding the network and to bring the Orff Schulwerk to more Latin American countries in the future. It was an unprecedented event in the history of Orff Schulwerk in Latin America and a great step towards the future.

The most widely used sources for working with the Orff Schulwerk in Argentina

Carrizo, J. A. (1996). *Rimas y juegos infantiles* [Children's rhymes and games]. Instituto de Literatura Española (I.L.E.). Facultad de Filosofía y Letras. Universidad Nacional de Tucumán.

Gainza, V. H. de (1963). *Ritmo musical y banda de percusión en la escuela primaria* [Musical rhythm and percussion band in elementary school]. La escuela en el tiempo. Buenos Aires: Eudeba.

Gainza, V. H. de (1977). *La iniciación musical del niño* [The musical initiation of the child]. Buenos Aires: Ricordi.

Graetzer, G. (1963). *Orff Schulwerk. Música para niños*. Adaptación Castellana para Latino-América (Ciclo I – IV y una Introducción en colaboración con A. Yepes) [Orff Schulwerk. Music for children. Spanish adaptation for Latin America (Cycle I - IV and an introduction in collaboration with A. Yepes]. Buenos Aires: Barry.

Graetzer, G. (1968). *Murales de Educación Musical*. (Partituras murales de canciones infantiles con acompañamientos para instrumentos Orff). [Music education posters. (Scores of children's songs with accompaniments for Orff instruments)]. Buenos Aires: Barry.

---

1   The Pestalozzi School of the Arts.
https://www.pestalozzi.edu.ar/de/padagogisches-projekt/extracurriculare-angebote/schule-der-kunste.html

Graetzer, G. (1983). *Orff Schulwerk. Música para niños.* Adaptación en español para Latinoamérica (Cuadernos I – III y una Guía en colaboración con A. Yepes) [Orff Schulwerk. Music for children. Spanish adaptation for Latin America (Notebooks I - III and a guide in collaboration with A. Yepes)]. Buenos Aires: Ricordi.

Graetzer, G. (1985). *Altindianische Tänze e Indo-Amerikanische Tänze.* Arreglos para instrumentos Orff. [Ancient Indian dances and Indo-American dances. Arrangements for Orff instruments]. Buenos Aires: Ricordi (subedición de Schott Mainz).

Graetzer, G. (1990). Aufnahme und Entwicklung des Orff-Schulwerks in Argentinien [Acceptance and development of Orff-Schulwerk in Argentina]. In H. Regner (Ed.), *Begegungen: Reports about the acceptance and development of stimuli from Orff-Schulwerk* (pp. 11–14). Orff-Schulwerk Forum Salzburg.

Haselbach, B., Maschat, V., & Sastre, F. (Eds.). (2013). *Textos sobre Teoría y Práctica del Orff-Schulwerk. Textos Básicos de los Años 1932–2010* [Texts on theory and practice of Orff-Schulwerk: Basic texts from the years 1932-2010]. Vitoria-Gasteiz: Agruparte. (Original work published 2011)

Propato, N. (2014). *Ejemplos musicales sobre modos antiguos, para instrumental Orff* [Musical examples on ancient modes, for Orff instruments]. Buenos Aires: Autoedición.

Audio-visual sources

Regner, H. (coord.). (1977). *Das Orff-Schulwerk in Argentinien* [Orff-Schulwerk in Argentina] [Film]. Documentary for the series "Das Orff-Schulwerk in aller Welt" [Orff-Schulwerk around the world] for the German Television ZDF (W. Lütje producer).

Yepes, A. (1986). *Educación Musical según el Orff Schulwerk en la provincia de Misiones* [Musical education according to Orff Schulwerk in the province of Misiones] [Film series with educational materials]. Buenos Aires: Sipted.

Periodical

Música y Movimiento [Music and Movement]. Magazine of the Orff-Schulwerk Association of Argentina, 2010-2018.

The Orff Approach in the Brazilian Creative Environment

Maristela Mosca, Magda Pucci, Lucilene Silva

In this chapter we reflect about the different Brazilian musics and the musical practices adapted to the Orff Schulwerk approach.

Brazil is marked by varied socio-cultural realities and by a great cultural diversity due to the presence of different human groups from different parts of the world that have created and still provide a pronounced melting pot of cultural references. People in each locality in Brazil communicate with a characteristic accent. The various musical genres represent different ways of expressing oneself musically. There are living and improvisational cultures in which adaptability and creative capacity are responsible for an infinite number of artistic expressions that integrate music, dance, theater, poetry, clothing, and scenery.

Even though this diversity is rich and extensive, music teachers have been guided almost exclusively by the European classical repertoire, ignoring the musical potential of Brazilian traditions. Since the 1990s, the hegemonic Eurocentric model generated by the colonial process has been questioned, and the myth of "racial democracy" in Brazilian culture, which tends to mask the differences between groups and realities, has been rethought. According to the Portuguese sociologist Boaventura de Souza Santos (2006),

> It is necessary to understand that the right to be equal when this difference makes us inferior and to be different so as not to mischaracterize ourselves must be premises. Hence the need for an equality that recognizes the differences and a difference that does not nourish or reproduce inequalities.

The attempt to credit Brazil for "mestizo" as a characteristic covered up the particularities of the various groups living here, trying to equalize them in a "national" idea of European bias brought by the colonizer, where the whole range of cultural diversity that we have here does not fit, causing an erasure of these cultures (Candau, 2010).

With more than 250 Indigenous Peoples living in Brazil, their musical expressions are practically unknown by a large part of Brazilian society, including teachers who unfortunately did not have any reference in their training about the music and cultures of these people. Just as Afro-Brazilian cultural expressions present captivating dance movements, rhythms, and melodies loaded with symbolism, there are still many Brazilians who ignore or disregard these ways of acting culturally, considering them "primitive," causing systematic destruction of important and fundamental Indigenous knowledge in the establishment of our country's identity.

In the face of strong structural racism, there is a constant lack of awareness of Indigenous and Afro-Brazilian cultures, which are almost always denied their role and representation. To this resistance to opening up to these traditions that form our culture, we credit an education and training that is still colonialist and tends to create space only for Western European expressions as a synonym for refinement and universal beauty that little corresponds to the different *Brasis* in this country.

In this sense, the creation of a multifaceted, interdisciplinary, and intercultural approach to our musical education is a great challenge that involves the recognition and appreciation of a curricular path that decolonizes knowledge in schools. Proposing a revision of the curriculum does not mean erasing European knowledge or replacing it but enabling other knowledge to be included in the school curriculum, contemplating various perspectives on the world (Nunes, 2019).

Brief overview of music education in Brazil

Although it is not our goal to address the complexity of music education in Brazil, we understand that it is important to keep in mind the context in which this subject area is inserted, because being a country of continental dimensions, with different educational processes, we still suffer the impact of the absence of music in schools for nearly 40 years.

On this path towards legitimizing the teaching of music in Brazilian basic education, there have been many difficulties, such as 1) the figure of a multipurpose arts teacher, who has to deal with all languages, without having a broad and interdisciplinary preparation; 2) the conception of classical music as the only one "of value" linked to teaching in the conservatory and technical model; and 3) the little appreciation for traditional Brazilian and contemporary music.

It was only in 2008, after a strong campaign by musicians and music educators, that a new law was enacted that defined the compulsory teaching of music in basic education, representing a great achievement for the area. The issue faced since that time has been the training of specialized teachers for music education. Universities do not graduate enough music educators to supply the demand of a public network with 50 million students. Thus, music has not yet been legitimized as a formal subject or specific official discipline in all schools, but rather, it is a content area that can be taught by teachers not specialized in music.

Orff Schulwerk approach in Brazil

Brazil does not have courses for certification of teachers in the Orff Schulwerk approach. The training of Brazilian teachers who have embraced the Schulwerk has intensified since 2000, driven by the actions of the Orff Schulwerk Association Brazil (ABRAORF, founded in 2004). Brazil currently has 22 teachers who have completed their training in San Francisco and who develop activities related to ABRAORFF. This includes Mayumi Takai, Maristela Mosca, Estêvão Marques, Cassiano Lima, Kaike Falabella, Dafne Michellepis, Patrícia Cavicchioli, Gabriela Abdalla, among others. We highlight Helder Parente, who was the first Brazilian teacher to graduate from the Orff Institute in Salzburg, Austria, bringing contributions of great value to music education, teacher training, and ABRAORFF.

Orff Schulwerk activities are centered in city of São Paulo, but the international courses promoted by ABRAORFF provide the opportunity to open this range of options and expand the approach to different Brazilian cities, such as Natal/Rio Grande do Norte, Recife/Pernambuco, Caxias do Sul/Rio Grande do Sul. We also see that most teachers who use the Orff Schulwerk approach in their music teaching work with children in private basic education schools. Cultural centers also occupy a significant dimension in the application of the Schulwerk approach.

Historical development of the Orff Schulwerk approach in Brazil

The first experiences and dialogues about Orff Schulwerk in Brazil began in 1963 at the Pró-Arte in Teresópolis (Rio de Janeiro), with Hermann Regner and Barbara Haselbach as teachers.

Two decades later the first Orff Schulwerk Summer Course was held at Santo Américo School in São Paulo, taught by Verena Maschat. Since 2001, the international courses have gained almost annual regularity, becoming a reference point in Brazilian music education. Until 2009, the activities were basically concentrated in São Paulo, but from 2009 on, states such as Rio Grande do Norte and Rio Grande do Sul began to host some meetings, always with the presence of internationally recognized teachers, such as Barbara Haselbach, Verena Maschat, Sofía López-Ibor, Doug Goodkin, and James Harding, as well as renowned Brazilian guests in music education.

By the year 2020, ABRAORFF had promoted, in addition to ten Orff Schulwerk International Courses in Brazil, three International Symposia, which sought to present and reflect on the paths of Orff Schulwerk in Brazil, its development in different educational spheres, and the progress of music education in an inclusive way within schools, cultural movements, and other experiences.

The actions promoted by ABRAORFF are more than points of intersection or dynamics of a network that has been progressively expanding despite adversities. These actions have been building a dialogue between music education and Brazilian cultural diversity, with its different influences, with music producing bodies within a society in constant transformation that creatively adapts the processes of making, sharing, learning, and teaching music.

Adaptation of Orff Schulwerk in Brazil

The progression of adapting Orff Schulwerk throughout Brazil occurs through continuous dialogue with the International Orff-Schulwerk Forum Salzburg (IOSFS) and its reverberations in the ABRAORFF summer courses, monthly study meetings, internal publications of the Association, and expansion to studies and publications of articles and theses on the Orff Schulwerk approach and the education of children, youth, and adults in Brazil, in different spaces and contexts. Such adaptations embrace the fundamental principles highlighted by Hartmann (2018) such as: the individual as the center of the Orff approach; the social dimension, the importance of music-making and dancing collectively; the broadening of the conception of music, since elemental music is never music alone; creativity in improvisation and composition, valuing the improvisational processes as principles of musical creation; the focus on the process and not on the final product; the research, the adaptation, and use of different musical instruments that promote, especially, the expansion of body movement and its possibilities; the opening of musical experience to different contexts and, especially, the possibility of implementation in different cultures, highlighting evolution and change as characteristics of the approach.

Music, movement, and language as main elements come together for the purpose of learning and teaching music and the music-pedagogical actions that permeate this approach through body games, hand and finger games, body percussion, rhythmic and melodic creation based especially on the resources of Brazilian musical cultures.

Interest in Indigenous and Afro-Brazilian repertoire has been increasing at Orff Schulwerk symposia, a fact that encourages teachers to develop contextualized activities that connect music to different forms of expression such as movement, mythical narratives, body painting, rituals and popular celebrations, and literature, creating empathy with these other ways of seeing the world, to make them respected in their culture and diversity (Almeida & Pucci, 2017).

Games and improvisations

Children's games also combine body movement, poetry, creation, and improvisation with the participation of children using their toys in different ways (Silva, 2016) and connecting with the idea of spoken language as a basis for the development of musicality (Shamrock, 1995).

The rhythm of the word is the starting point for making music. The Brazilian identity begins with the rhythmic and sung games used in the musical education of our children, who "make use of the word and constitute natural ways of language conquest: the mother tongue and the 'musical mother tongue'" (Silva, 2014).

The word as a source of music comes into Brazilian culture through rhythmic games, games with words, nursery rhymes, lullabies, hand games, circle dances from European and African heritage. The Brazilian Indigenous heritage is also marked by the declaimed tone, especially in the spoken song, onomatopoeias, and extreme rhythmic flexibility of mythical narratives based on strong orality (Pucci and Almeida, 2017).

The spoken word is linked to movement and melody, based on Brazil's traditional sounds, the cultural attitudes towards movement and dance, in creative music making. The pentatonic melody is adapted to Brazilian rhymes and nursery rhymes, configuring itself as elemental music.

With regard to tonal melodic tradition, the melodies of childhood are marked by a music that plays with the word, recites everyday life, and translates the relationship of different cultures with the world (Silva, 2014). The modal constants of traditional music, especially in the northeast region of Brazil, are unmistakable and are part of music-pedagogical practices as we can adapt the pedagogical ideas of Carl Orff and Gunild Keetman, the use of modal melodies and instrumental accompaniments.

In this way, we experience the approach first in the way of perceiving the group and its characteristics of age, regionality, diversity, and what creative elements can come from this encounter. These sessions are not completely closed, but planned in an integrated way with other areas of knowledge, conceived from a beginning, middle, and end, where the music making seeks to maintain this creative and active energy of the participants, of sharing and, especially, of musical growth of each person.

Movement

With an initial focus on the movements and dances of the childhood tradition, the adaptation of the Orff Schulwerk in Brazil seeks to demystify the movement/dance concepts of a school culture that favors dance routines that have music of little artistic value. In the beginning, we seek movement as a vital part of music-pedagogical actions, as a form of expression and understanding of musical structure and energy (Shamrock, 1995).

Dance, like the movement of music, adapts to the conceptions of Brazilian culture, especially in traditional dances. This action seeks to regard the body as a musical instrument, to work movements that go from the simple to the complex, to contextualize the actions of movement. In this process, imitation extends the repertoire of movements so that the students can create in unison and in groups. From the intuitive relationship, they can seek ways to reflect and record what has been experienced, thus going from the sensory-kinetic experience to the construction and understanding of the concept. We also consider it essential to guarantee space/time for the student to establish intimate contact with the object or theme worked on and, only in another phase, to present precise details of the journey.

Children accompanying their dance playing shekeres
Photo: Rinaldo Martinucci

Singing

A characteristic of the Orff Schulwerk approach in Brazil is the use of singing and the appreciation of children's songs of traditional heritage: in unison, with vocal drones, with instrumental accompaniments, with two voices. A widely used practice is improvisation in vocal processes, seeking to explore the body/movement from the possibilities, in solfège practices, exercises for the development of auditory and rhythmic perception, and in creative interpretation processes.

From the students' repertoires we can expand and give new significance to their music making and the world. As Shamrock (1995) states, the appreciation of cultural roots and songs that relate to events and/or situations of certain social groups is satisfactorily intertwined with the musical experiences promoted by the Orff Schulwerk approach.

In this movement, the repertoire expands, and new sounds can be experienced, created, and given new significance. The experimentation of different types of sound marks the contemporary compositions presented in the classroom with the primary purpose of new ways of listening, contextualizing, and making music. The different textures, timbres, and sound impressions are transferred to movement, to body percussion, to instrumental experimentation, and to creation.

We observe an interdisciplinary attitude in artistic languages, especially the visual arts. We contemplate and dialogue about different contemporary works: paintings, prints, statues, and installations—one of the possibilities to explore ways of perceiving reality and to create sounds over it.

Thus, we seek with contemporary music and with the music of different peoples to embrace different aesthetics, thereby constituting critical thinking in the processes of appreciating, making, and understanding music, as well as dialoguing about different ways of dealing with the sound element.

Creativity in the use of sound instruments

In Brazil, there is a shortage of musical instruments, as well as suitable facilities for music teaching. Several schools need to adapt their spaces to accommodate the practice of music, and class is often held in the middle of tables and chairs, with few resources for instrument use and inadequate space for movement. There are emerging initiatives of teachers who encourage their students to build their own instruments, which will become more frequent in the future.

In schools and cultural centers, where an instrumental ensemble is accessible, it is used especially as an experimental resource for musical creation and not only for instrument teaching. Children's traditional sounding toys, everyday objects, and musical instruments are used in a continuum of time and space, as a repertoire expansion, always thought out on the basis of students' ages, the subjects being developed, and the technical possibilities.

Free play with instruments
Photo: Rinaldo Martinucci

Dialogue and attention to musical diversity

Orff Schulwerk teachers in Brazil consider themselves mediators of music-pedagogical actions, and not as conductors of musical activity. There is always the dialogue, the eye to eye, the formation in a circle before the activities. Singing, dancing, playing, and group dramatization, maintaining the circle as a place for dialogue, peeking into and calling on other areas of knowledge whenever necessary to deepen the knowledge about the subjects under study are some of the characteristics of the processes of learning and teaching music.

The Brazilian socio-cultural reality still presents many structural limitations with regard to inadequate educational spaces and lack of tools for all students. On the other hand, the use of voice and body and the construction of instruments and sound objects from alternative materials are increasing in a creative way.

In this context of absolute musical richness and diversity, the Orff Schulwerk approach in Brazil connects its base in the appreciation of traditional sources for the development of musical praxis. Intercultural dialogue, the use of singing, dancing, movement, and improvisation, confirms the importance of an active music education that respects and values all this diversity and creative capacity.

References

Almeida, M. B., & Pucci, M. D. (2017). *Cantos da Floresta - iniciação ao universo musical indígena* [Songs of the forest—initiation into the indigenous musical universe]. São Paulo: Editora Peirópolis.

Candau, V., & Oliveira, L. F. (January 1, 2010). Pedagogia Decolonial e Educação Antirracista e Intercultural no Brasil [Decolonial pedagogy and anti-racist and intercultural education in Brazil]. *Educacao Em Revista, 26* (1), 15-40.

Hartmann, W. (Fall 2018). The Principles of Orff Schulwerk. *The Orff Echo, 52* (1), 8–12.

Nunes, M. (2019). *Descolonização: por que estudamos um lado só da história?* [Decolonization: why do we study only one side of history?]. Lunetas. https://lunetas.com.br/descolonizacao/

Santos, B. S. (2006). *A gramática do tempo: Para uma nova cultura política* [The grammar of time: Towards a new political culture]. São Paulo: Cortez.

Shamrock, M. E. (2007). *Orff Schulwerk: Brief history, description and issues in global dispersal.* Cleveland: American Orff-Schulwerk Association.

Silva, L. (2014). *Eu vi as três meninas: música tradicional da infância na Aldeia de Carapicuíba* [I saw the three girls: traditional childhood music in Aldeia de Carapicuíba]. Carapicuíba, São Paulo: Zerinho ou Um.

Periodical

Uma informativo da Associação Orff Brasil. Newsletter of the Brasilian Orff Schulwerk Association. 2006–2016.

Voyage of Discovery: Orff Schulwerk in Canada 1954–2021

James Jackson, Catherine West, Françoise Grenier,
Julie Mongeon-Ferré

*Speaking and singing, poetry and music, music and movement, playing and dancing
are not yet separated in the world of children, they are essentially one and indivisible,
all governed by the play-instinct which is a prime mover in the development of art and
ritual.* (Walter, 1956, introduction)

Carl Orff Canada's historical development

Carl Orff Canada (COC) is proud to have the longest standing international relationship with
the Orff Schulwerk including a number of firsts in our shared history.

In 1954, at the request of Arnold Walter, director of the Faculty of Music at the University of
Toronto, Doreen Hall became the first English-speaking student to study at the Mozarteum
with Carl Orff and Gunild Keetman. Upon her return to Toronto in 1955, Hall established
introductory Orff Schulwerk classes for children at the Royal Conservatory of Music. Later she
taught music education courses at the University of Toronto. She and Walter also co-authored
the first English adaptation of the *Music for Children* volumes (1954–1961). Hall began giving
workshops across Canada and the United States. By the end of the decade, local Toronto school
boards began to embrace this approach, led by Scarborough Schools music supervisor Keith
Bissell. Orff Schulwerk spread to French speaking Canada during the early sixties, notably in
the Québec Education Program and largely through the influence of Sr. Marcelle Corneille
who first trained with Doreen Hall in 1957.

The sixties saw the flowering of many Orff Schulwerk seeds throughout Canada. The first
International Conference on Elementary[1] Music Education-Orff Schulwerk was held in Toronto,
July 1962. Orff, Keetman, and other colleagues from the Orff Institute, Salzburg offered 167
participants several workshops. As the decade progressed, the Orff Schulwerk profile grew with
some national television exposure and ongoing workshops across North America. Hall developed a three-year sequential summer training program that attracted teachers from Canada
and the United States. Her courses became the model for subsequent North American Orff
Schulwerk levels courses. Since then, the Schulwerk has influenced university music education
courses across the nation.

The seventies brought in more formalized organizations. In 1974, the Orff Schulwerk Society of Canada was officially established along with the first two regional chapters in Ontario
and British Columbia.[2] In 1975, the Society's name was changed to Music for Children, Carl

---

1 "Elementary" here refers to school years encompassing ages five to twelve years. This should not be confused with
'elemental music education,' which Orff uses to describe his Schulwerk.
2 Due to the vast size of Canada, Orff Schulwerk teachers formed smaller groups (chapters) throughout the country,
where regular meetings and workshops are held.

Orff Canada, Musique pour Enfants in recognition of our bilingual nation. During that same year the first newsletter was published, and our first National Conference was held with Orff Institute director Hermann Regner and Barbara Haselbach in attendance.

From the eighties onward, we have continued to see growth in our national organization, our programs, and our network of regional chapters. In 1981, the Orff Schulwerk Québec chapter of Carl Orff Canada was founded to offer workshops throughout the year and levels courses in the French language. Since then, Sr. Marcelle Corneille, Miriam Samuelson, Françoise Grenier, Jos Wuytack, and his students Anne-Marie Grosser, Guylaine Myre, and Chantal Dubois, have served as faculty in these courses. Jos Wuytack has had the greatest influence on French-Canadian Orff Schulwerk teachers; in fact, the Orff Schulwerk approach in Québec is most often associated with his teaching and that of his students named above.

The organization of Carl Orff Canada (COC)

Carl Orff Canada is a two-tiered volunteer organization. It is made up of a National Board as well as regional chapters. We are a bilingual organization, and we try to ensure that our communications are in both official languages: French and English.

The COC National Board is currently made up of fourteen members who oversee many programs and committees. The National Board also includes an advisory board, honorary patrons, and honorary lifetime members. The Board provides support to the regional chapters; holds a bi-annual national conference; produces a professional journal, *Ostinato*; manages a website; offers scholarship support and research grants; and administers governance over Orff Schulwerk teacher professional development programs, especially levels courses.

Carl Orff Canada now boasts ten regional chapters stretching from coast to coast. Their local communication network is vital to the national organization. Regional chapters provide workshops, libraries, scholarships, and extracurricular opportunities for children or children's groups to perform and experience Orff Schulwerk beyond their schools and classrooms. Most chapters liaise with their provincial music education counterparts and provide input into their regional conferences. Many now sponsor Carl Orff Canada's levels courses in their region or provide support to the local course offered through a tertiary institution. Chapters take turns hosting our bi-annual national conference, with smaller chapters sometimes banding together to serve this function. Increasingly chapters provide support to teachers through websites and social media.

Outside of Québec, music teachers working in French join local chapters with the English-speaking majority. A particular desire to serve the Orff Schulwerk community in French is increasingly present in Manitoba, where teachers from Québec go to deliver workshops and courses. The Manitoba chapter's board also organizes events in French for teachers and their students, e.g., *Children's Orff Days* for Francophone and French Immersion students. In the rest of the country, workshops regularly feature and/or focus on French and bilingual content because many teachers work in French language settings. Carl Orff Canada encourages chapters to recruit a Francophone liaison who can connect with their Francophone members and respond to their needs.

Teacher education programs

Carl Orff Canada maintains levels course guidelines independent of universities or provincial education departments. Courses that are approved for accreditation add the COC name, logo, and seal to their own Orff Schulwerk course certificates. The focus is on elemental music pedagogy for ages five to twelve, the years during which music is compulsory. Our teacher education curriculum outlines three levels of Orff Schulwerk courses, 60 hours per level. This is usually scheduled as a two-week intensive program with the following four strands: Basic Orff Pedagogy, Choral, Movement, and Recorder. Additionally, we endorse an introductory level that provides a holistic overview of the pedagogy—usually covered in 30 hours. The courses are available in both French and English, depending on the region.

In several provinces, teachers receive official recognition or professional upgrades for having Orff Schulwerk credentials. Courses offered through universities sometimes grant academic credit, usually at the undergraduate level. Teachers who complete Orff Schulwerk Level III through an accredited course are allowed to refer to themselves as Orff Schulwerk Specialists. Undergraduates in most university Bachelor of Music Education programs usually take an elementary music methods course that combines Orff, Kodály, Dalcroze, Gordon, etc., in one course. These courses are not accredited by COC and contain quite diluted introductions to Orff Schulwerk as a pedagogical approach.

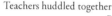
Teachers huddled together   Teachers dancing
Photos: Royal Conservatory of Music

Orff Schulwerk and the Canadian education system

Canada's education system is a provincial rather than a national responsibility. Canada has ten provinces and three territories, each with their own programs and curricula. The delivery of music and dance programs thus varies greatly between provinces and territories. The Orff Schulwerk approach has influenced the development of these curricula strongly, along with the pedagogical approaches of Kodály and, to a lesser extent, Dalcroze.

Most elementary (ages five to twelve) music curricula focus on the musical elements with little mention of dance or movement. At the same time, most teachers embrace the frequent use of movement, singing games, and dances when working with the children. Newer provincial music curricula include more references to movement as an important component of differentiated instruction. There is general recognition that all children process learning more deeply if material is presented through visual, auditory, and kinesthetic media. Improvisation and creativity are emphasized in these documents, reflecting the view that elementary music programs should be focused on the creative process more than public performance. In the Orff Schulwerk classroom, this has resulted in a de-emphasis on learning big, layered orchestrations, and an increased emphasis on creative work. Increasingly, educational trends in Canada emphasize the role of the teacher as a collaborator and coach, who co-creates knowledge by participating in an inquiry process with students.

We are very fortunate in Canada to be one of a handful of countries that have music education embedded in our public education system, at least in theory. The majority of students have access to some form of music instruction from kindergarten through grade eight, and optional access from grades nine to twelve. Up to age twelve music is typically scheduled for either one or two sessions per week. Many music teachers provide additional extra-curricular opportunities such as Orff Schulwerk ensemble, recorder ensemble, choir, ukulele, and so on. Chapters and individual teachers sometimes enrich the music programs with creative partnerships, for example, working with a local symphony for public performances involving student created music and movement.

However, the distribution of trained music specialists and program support is very uneven across the country, so COC has an important role in advocating for stronger programs and addressing the professional development gap. In some jurisdictions, teachers do not need any prior training in music to be assigned a music position, whereas in other places, teachers must have university level preparation. As a result, our courses attract teachers with a wide range of preparation. Maintaining standards of excellence while also meeting local needs is a continuing challenge for most of our courses.

Carl Orff Canada has maintained relevance and currency by changing focus along with emerging educational priorities. At the outset, bilingualism drove much of the agenda. Later multiculturalism, differentiated instruction, higher order thinking, and authentic assessment emerged as important trends. Currently teachers are mandated to address social justice, diversity, equity, and cultural competence along with subject-specific concepts. In some jurisdictions, educational trends emphasize the concepts of creativity, inclusion, play, competencies (invent, perform, and appreciate), and essential knowledge (musical language and structures, instrumental techniques, repertoire, information technology, etc.). Across the country many Orff Schulwerk practitioners incorporate twenty-first century technology into their programs in creative and stimulating ways.

Joyful movement
Photo: Royal Conservatory of Music

Enjoying making music
Photo: Nicola Betts

Highly engaged young musicians
Photos: Royal Conservatory of Music

The Canadian social context

Historically, Canada has long been a multicultural country. Our Indigenous Peoples witnessed the arrival of the French and the English throughout the 1600s. Other British Isles explorers and immigrants soon followed. African Americans and British Loyalists settled in Canada during the American War for Independence. Migration from many European and Eastern European countries grew rapidly from the late 1800s onward, with the opening up of the west. Canada became a haven for immigrants and refugees from around the world during the twentieth and twenty-first centuries.

Until recently, our French and English heritage tended to dominate our institutions and the majority of our cultural practices, including our education system. Canada has been slow to acknowledge the contributions of our Indigenous Peoples, but together through calls for action from the *Truth and Reconciliation Commission of Canada* (2015) music teachers are learning to integrate Indigenous perspectives in their classrooms. Furthermore, as Canada continues to become more culturally diverse, we are engaged in embracing all peoples more equitably in our institutions and our education systems. Carl Orff Canada has established a Diversity Committee to help teachers identify best practices and appropriate materials as we strive to decolonize our attitudes, classrooms, and repertoire.

As a national educational organization, Carl Orff Canada works within this mosaic of provincial and territorial educational structures, curricula, and initiatives. As pedagogical leaders we stay up to date with educational initiatives and have them reflected in our courses, workshops, and conferences. Our members work with provincial and national music teaching associations as recognized leaders and contributors. As individual members, we are responsible for aligning our Orff Schulwerk philosophy with our own provincial curricula.

Repertoire

Levels courses in Canada make extensive use of the Music for Children volumes adapted by Margaret Murray (1957–1966), especially as springboards for creative work. Doreen Hall and Arnold Walter's (1956–1961) five-volume adaptation of Music for Children is sometimes used as a source for songs, but not as course texts. Individual course instructors have the flexibility to choose texts and materials to fit their own context. Traditional Canadian folk songs (mostly from British and French cultures) are used extensively as course materials and classroom repertoire and were the focus of many of the early Canadian Orff Schulwerk publications. This repertoire is mostly characteristic of western European traditions, being largely diatonic (with significant exceptions, especially for music from Irish and Scottish cultures), and having a strong historical basis in the community life and celebrations of colonial times. The three-volume *Music for Children* adapted in French by Jos Wuytack is no longer published.

Today, however, teachers draw extensively on a much wider repertoire from global and Indigenous cultures as well as popular music in order to address mandates on social justice, equity, diversity, and democracy. Regional chapters host workshops on African drumming and dancing, Indonesian gamelan, Indigenous songs and dances, Chinese folk songs, South American folk dances, African American songs of freedom, South Asian songs and drumming, South African gum-boot dancing, and more.

There is much active discussion about cultural competence and cultural appropriation as Orff Schulwerk teachers identify ways to explore global music with a genuinely creative Orff Schulwerk lens while still respecting cultural integrity. Indigenous (First Nations, Métis, Inuit) music and dance presents a special challenge, firstly because it is so important that teachers include an Indigenous perspective in their teaching, and secondly because the issues around appropriate practice are very controversial, even amongst Indigenous practitioners. It is generally accepted that Indigenous music collected by earlier generations of ethno-musicologists and widely included in school music textbooks may have been transcribed without sufficient knowledge or permission and published without cultural and social contextual information (origin, use, translation, recording, etc.) that would allow for appropriate use.

Indigenous songs that are social songs and have been shared with teachers by culture-bearers may be shared with students, along with the full context of the song. However, adding accompaniments or manipulating a song in a creative way is usually not appropriate, which challenges the Orff Schulwerk teacher to both teach this important repertoire, and provide creative learning experiences inspired by it without disrespect. Indigenous songs are owned by individuals in some cultures and can only be performed by that owner or with their permission. Additionally, some songs are sacred and should not be performed outside of a particular ceremony within the culture. Cree-Dene Orff Schulwerk Specialist Sherryl Sewepagaham has provided exceptional leadership to our community by writing and composing materials intended for classroom use (see references) and presenting courses and workshops on Indigenous music.

Publication now tends to happen less formally through online platforms, rather than through hard copy productions. This vibrant process of development and sharing is producing valuable new approaches and identifying repertoire from a wide variety of times and cultures, but the challenges remain real.

In conclusion

Navigating the waters in an ever-evolving education system is the true measure of any pedagogical approach. Carl Orff Canada continues to steer a steady course through sometimes unpredictable seas, recognizing the winds and trusting in the vessel. Moving forward, as we view our practice with a more critical eye, we must consistently remember to reflect on and retain Orff's humanistic, play-centered, creative approach.

References

Government of Canada. (2015). Delivering on Truth and Reconciliation Commission Calls to Action. (2015). https://www.rcaanc-cirnac.gc.ca/eng/1524494530110/1557511412801

https://www.rcaanc-cirnac.gc.ca/fra/1524494530110/1557511412801

Orff, C., & Keetman, G. (1956–1961). *Orff-Schulwerk. Music for children* (Vols. 1–5) (English adaptation by D. Hall & A. Walter). Mainz: Schott.

Orff, C., & Keetman, G. (1957–1966). *Orff-Schulwerk. Music for children* (Vols. 1–5) (English adaptation by M. Murray). London: Schott.

Sewpagaham, S. (2015) *All my relations,* Ottawa: National Arts Centre.
http://artsalive.ca/pdf/mus/map/music-alive-program-teacher-guide-en.pdf;
http://artsalive.ca/pdf/mus/map/music-alive-program-teacher-guide-fr.pdf

Sewpagaham, S., & O. Tailfeathers. (n.d.) *Celebrating Canada's Indigenous Peoples through song and dance.*
http://artsalive.ca/pdf/mus/map/Indigenous-Teacher_Guide_en.pdf;

http://artsalive.ca/pdf/mus/map/Indigenous-Teacher_Guide_fr.pdf

Sewpagaham, S., & N. Schutz. *Nitohta: Listen to earthsounds.* (n.d.) Ottawa: National Arts Centre.
http://artsalive.ca/pdf/mus/map/nitohta_guide_en.pdf;
http://artsalive.ca/pdf/mus/map/nitohta_guide_fr.pdf

Walter, A. (1956). Introduction. In C. Orff & G. Keetman *Orff-Schulwerk. Music for children: Vol. 1.* Pentatonic (English adaptation by D. Hall & A. Walter). Mainz: Schott.

Periodical

Ostinato. Magazine of Carl Orff Canada published 3 times a year. For further information, see www.orffcanada.ca.

Additional Resources

Birkenshaw-Fleming, L., (Ed.). (1996). *An Orff mosaic from Canada.* Toronto: Schott.

Hall, D. (1992). *Orff Schulwerk in Canada: A collection of articles and lectures from the early years (1954–1962).* Toronto: Schott.

Linklater, J., & Morrow, M. J., (Eds.). (2014) The first forty years. Carl Orff Canada Special Publication.

Orff Schulwerk teachers in Canada make use of many Canadian publications as well as international texts. The following list is of authors whose works are frequently used by Canadian Orff Schulwerk teachers.

J. Berarducci and B. Kulich	G. Myre
L. Birkenshaw-Fleming	J. Reeve
M. Corneille	Rousseau
C. Dubois	S. Sewepagaham
D. Ladendecker	J. Sills
M. Moody	C. West

In addition, teachers rely on collections of folk songs, dances, and approaches to movement that provide outstanding source materials for exploration through an Orff Schulwerk lens. As they are not Orff Schulwerk publications, they are not included here.

Orff Schulwerk in Colombia

Catherine Correa Lopera, Beatriz Serna Mejía [1]

Introduction

In the middle of the 20th century, an exchange began between several Colombian music teachers and the Orff Institute in Salzburg, thus sowing the seeds for what is today the Orff Schulwerk in Colombia. The principles of this approach have been well received and assimilated by the educational and artistic community. This is due to several characteristics of our Colombian culture that we will discuss in this article, emphasizing their relationship to the philosophy of education through music and movement proposed by Carl Orff and Gunild Keetman. One of the particularities of the Schulwerk is that its pedagogical ideas can be adapted to diverse socio-cultural contexts that resonate in a country full of heterogeneous traditions as are found in Colombia.

General considerations on Colombia's cultural traditions

Our country—consisting of six regions: Amazon, Andean, Orinoco, Pacific, Caribbean, and Insular—presents very distinctive natural, ethnic, and cultural characteristics that reflect the very history of our country. Colombia was a Spanish colony for more than three centuries. With their conquest, the Spanish left us all the African tradition from the people they brought to work as slaves in our land and the European tradition they brought themselves, making Colombia a completely *mestizo* country. Today, the African legacy is lived mainly in the Pacific and Atlantic regions; the Spanish/European influence is more rooted in the Andean and Orinoco regions.

The Amazon region has been perhaps the only one that has remained outside these influences and has preserved the cultural traditions of its Indigenous communities, for example the *Uitoto* ethnic group. As a fundamental part, these traditions have music, dance, and stories in their own languages, which are transmitted orally, and are mostly linked to rituals (Ribeiro, 2012, p. 57).

Thus, with the exception of the Amazon, our country is a great mixture of traditions that combine the Indigenous with European and African cultures. Consequently, in Colombia we find musical practices within socio-cultural contexts with great differences between them. Those of us who are working towards the application of the Orff Schulwerk have been able to take its concepts, tools, and pedagogical processes to teach through them our own traditional repertoires.

---

1 Special thanks to all our colleagues who helped collecting information for this article.

Pacific Region [1]

One of the regions whose culture has more elements related to the Schulwerk is the Pacific, rich in dances, games, responsorial songs, and instrumental music. The typical ensemble of this region is made up of a variety of drums such as the *cununo*, shakers with seeds, and its main representative, the *chonta marimba*. This barred instrument, a descendant from Africa built from the chontaduro palm, is our Colombian version of a xylophone, which is similar to the African type in both form and technique. The marimba can be played by one or two people. The use of drones in the low register of the instrument and melodic improvisation in the high register stand out in its playing.

Pacific songs have texts expressing religious themes, everyday life, with some that are framed in funeral rituals. These are usually responsorial, with a leader soloing and a group responding. The dances are energetic, in loose couples and with choreographies that narrate events in the lives of Afro-Colombians. The main genres of the Pacific are: *arrullo, currulao, alabao,* and *abozao*, among others. This entire musical tradition of the Pacific was named Intangible Cultural Heritage of Humanity by UNESCO in 2015.[2]

These elements that make up the traditions of the Pacific region have been brought to the classroom in all of Colombia. The rhythm of the *currulao*, with an overlay of ternary and binary meter, appears frequently in music programs, because it is representative of Colombia but also because it helps to develop advanced rhythmic skills in children. The melodies of the songs have also been adapted to children's games of passing objects as well as clapping games. Finally, the dances are performed in schools and dance academies by children and adults.

For teachers who apply Schulwerk principles in our classrooms, all this traditional Pacific material represents a diamond in the rough. Marimba music, with its drones and improvisational melodies, lends itself naturally to developing teaching processes in which students can compose, make their own arrangements, and improvise on a harmonic base given by the drones.

The songs, with their stories of ancestral rituals, are a source for narrative creation, dramatic and corporal expression. Finally, the dances and games, typical of this region, are wonderful excuses to get closer to our cultural legacy, strengthen community ties, and develop socio-affective skills, while learning musical concepts of form, dynamics, texture, rhythm, and melody.

Andean Region [3]

In the pedagogical field, the music, dances, and texts of the Andean region are also akin to the pedagogical principles of Orff Schulwerk, permeating the educational practices in the classroom, thanks in part to the specific characteristics of the music of this region.

---

1 Pacífico Sur: https://mincultura.gov.co/proyectoeditorial/Pages/Cartilla-de-iniciaci%C3%B3n-musical-Pacifi-co-sur-que-te-pasa-vo-!!!.aspx
Pacífico Norte: https://mincultura.gov.co/proyectoeditorial/Pages/Cartilla-de-iniciaci%C3%B3n-musi-cal-Pac%C3%ADfico-norte-%E2%80%9CAl-son-que-me-toquen-canto-y-bailo.aspx
2 https://ich.unesco.org/en/RL/marimba-music-traditional-chants-and-dances-from-the-colombia-south-pacif-ic-region-and-esmeraldas-province-of-ecuador-01099#identification
3 Andina occidental: https://mincultura.gov.co/proyectoeditorial/Pages/Cartilla-de-iniciaci%C3%B3n-musi-cal,-M%C3%BAsica-andina-occidental-entre-pasillos-y-bambucos%E2%80%9D.aspx
Andina central y oriental: https://mincultura.gov.co/proyectoeditorial/Pages/Cartilla-de-iniciaci%C3%B3n-mu-sical-M%C3%BAsicas-andina-centro-oriente--viva-quien-toca-.aspx

The harmony is tonal and predictable, which facilitates its teaching for the youngest students. Its instrumental formats are varied, showing a beautiful amalgam of European melodic/harmonic instruments and the local contribution of folkloric percussion instruments. The melodies and structures are simple, and the texts are of vital importance for the understanding of the context, rich in narrative and humor.

This last element points to the development of language, which is one of the pillars of the pedagogical approach of Carl Orff and Gunild Keetman. In Andean music we find a compositional style called *trova* that has its roots in the European tradition. Although its melodies are basic and repetitive, it contains a great richness in the texts, which are improvised by the singer in assonant rhyme (only the vowels coincide). The character of the *trovas* is generally mischievous and jocular and based on daily, political, or social situations. This oral tradition remains alive through festivals, contests, and family life. For this reason, it is easy to transfer this practice to the classroom, offering students a space for creation and improvisation through language.

The predominant meter in Andean music is ternary. Among its most common rhythmic patterns are those that contain syncopations and upbeats. Some of the most representative genres of the region come from the dances that originated and developed as a result of the intermixing of cultures. Examples of these dances are the *bambuco*, the *guabina*, the *pasillo* and the *torbellino* genres performed mainly with groups of plucked strings and with beautiful texts that narrate the life of Colombian peasants.

In terms of the application of Orff Schulwerk principles, the music of this region, thanks to its clear structure, lends itself to the creation and interpretation of arrangements rich in elements of color, melodic ostinati, instrumental interludes, improvisation of texts, and the understanding of musical forms through dance.

The role of the Orff Association Colombia

The Orff Association Colombia - ACOLORFF[1] has played a fundamental role in the dissemination of the Schulwerk through courses and workshops open to the general public, taught by international and local teachers. The creation of ACOLORFF was the result of the work of many people over several decades. The ideas of Orff Schulwerk in Colombia arrived in 1966 when a three-week course was organized at the *Universidad Pedagógica Nacional* and taught by Hermann Regner and Barbara Haselbach. Following this, several people started to go to the Orff Institute in Salzburg, bringing back to Colombia new ideas about music and movement education and applying them in schools, academies, and universities. Several decades later, in 2007, Verena Maschat helped to work towards the formation of an association in collaboration with Carmenza Botero, Pilar Posada, and the Carl Orff Foundation. Finally, in 2014, ACOLORFF was officially founded by Carmenza Botero, Beatriz Serna, and Sandra Salcedo.

Each year, ACOLORFF offers five or six short workshops in which the members of our Association meet in Bogota or Medellin, around a specific theme developed by a member of the board or by a special guest from Colombia or a neighboring country. In these workshops we study musical materials from Colombian regions taught through processes that include movement, creation, language, group work, and play, always in the spirit of the Schulwerk. Significant experiences that members of the Association have had in other Orff associations around the world, such as Spain, Brazil, United States, and even New Zealand, are also shared.

---

1 www.acolorff.org

Thanks to the support of the Carl Orff Foundation, the Colombian Association has offered longer international courses during the months of June or July given by internationally known experts in Orff Schulwerk such as Verena Maschat, Wolfgang Hartmann, Doug Goodkin, Andrea Ostertag, and Nacho Propato, among others. In these courses, also held in Bogota and some in Medellin, artists with various profiles have participated, from teachers with many years of experience to young people finishing their undergraduate studies, instrumental musicians, musicologists, cultural managers, dancers, physical education teachers, experts in the Dalcroze and Kodály methods, people with no knowledge of Orff Schulwerk and, of course, members of the Association who have already been trained in other workshops.

One of the most significant achievements of these courses has been to disseminate to many people the principles that Orff and Keetman left us as a legacy of their artistic and educational work. In each of these courses, the different teachers have shown us how the Schulwerk can be a way to bring new generations closer to different artistic expressions and contemporary art. In schools this gives us the possibility to exploit the creative potential of children and to work on different themes and areas of knowledge, opening an important space for personal and collective expression with a view to the future.

Another important achievement has been the formation of a network of teachers that strengthens and grows in each of these courses, increasing the family of educators who share the same vision and passion for our work. Finally, these international courses have left us with benchmarks of excellence in our profession, stimulating reflection on our educational work, as well as highlighting the magnitude of the transformative power of music and art and the responsibility we have as educators.

Orff Schulwerk in higher education

Several decades ago, universities and conservatories offered mainly performance and composition programs following the traditional European conservatory model, with the exception of some public university music degree programs. These programs in turn focused on performance, learning Colombian music, and music theory, with a general study of 20th century musical pedagogical approaches.

As the work of the music teacher has become more important in educational institutions, it has become necessary to train musicians in music education pedagogies, and in this context, the Orff Schulwerk has played a very important role.

In Colombia, the Pontificia Universidad Javeriana (PUJ) has been a leader in the implementation of Orff Schulwerk teaching thanks to its certified teachers such as Gustavo Velandia, graduate of the Special Course of the Orff Institute and current secretary of ACOLORFF. In this university, the basics of the Orff Schulwerk are a central part of the pedagogical training of undergraduate music education students.

Additionally, the PUJ and the Universidad del Norte (in the city of Barranquilla) have been offering for some years now master's and diploma programs in music with emphasis in education, aimed mainly at musicians who have not had any training in pedagogy, but who work as music teachers. This profile of teachers—generally performing musicians without any notion of education—is quite common in Colombia, and for them the Orff Schulwerk is a revelation and a "life saver."

Publications and pedagogical practices related to the Orff Schulwerk approach

In Colombia there are public and private institutions that have published materials with compilations of games, melodies, children's songs, rhymes, and dances from all regions of the country. For teachers, it is possible to find repertoire for classroom work that covers the entire country, including Indigenous communities, coastal and inland communities, and minorities such as the *Rrom* (Roma) gypsies. This material is a great advance from the ethnomusicological point of view and an important resource for teachers. Most of these texts are limited to being a collection of materials, sometimes with instructions for teaching them, but whose purpose does not go beyond the interpretation of such music, leaving aside the creative component.

Although the principles of Orff Schulwerk are being increasingly disseminated and applied in schools and academies, the publication or systematization of these practices is still developing. For this reason, it is important to mention the work done by Pilar Posada, who holds a degree in Elemental Education in Music and Movement from the Orff Institute in Salzburg, where she studied between 1981 and 1984. Posada, author of several books on music education,[1] has an extensive reputation in children's education and teacher training, not only in her hometown Medellin, but throughout Colombia. Her work as a pedagogue and author gives her an important place in the history of the dissemination and implementation of the Orff Schulwerk in Colombia.

The Fundación Nacional Batuta[2] includes in its educational program the use of Orff instruments, for which they have publications containing arrangements of Colombian music that are not necessarily framed within Orff and Keetman's compositional style. Their processes include activities related to the principles of Orff Schulwerk such as movement, play, and the instruments themselves; however, the foundation affirms that its pedagogical application combines multiple influences of musical training methods.

On the other hand, the Network of Music Schools of Envigado[3] includes in its musical initiation program some of the pedagogical principles of Orff Schulwerk, promoting the training of its teachers within the workshops programmed annually by ACOLORFF. Finally, it is the teachers who are members of ACOLORFF in different parts of the country, who in their educational and artistic work (schools, early childhood, inclusion programs, programs with social minorities, immigrants, choirs, etc.) are committed to the application, experimentation, and development of educational processes based on the Schulwerk. These practices will continue to grow as more teachers continue their training in programs such as those offered by the Orff Institute, the San Francisco International Orff Course, ACOLORFF, and other sister associations.

The next step for Orff Schulwerk in Colombia

Given that most of our music presents a great rhythmic-melodic richness, it is easy to fall into the trap that the objective for our students is only to master the interpretation of it. It

---

1 Most of its texts are based on fundamental Schulwerk principles and contain arrangements for voices and Orff instruments.
2 The Fundación Nacional Batuta (National Batuta Foundation) is an institution with coverage throughout Colombia that "contributes to improving the quality of life of children, adolescents and young people in Colombia, through musical education of excellence, focused on collective practice, from a perspective of social inclusion, rights and cultural diversity" (Batuta, 2021).
3 Envigado Music Schools Network https://www.redmusicaenvigado.com

is important to emphasize that in Colombia we have a strong tradition of music and dance that is lived in homes, festivals, carnivals, and social life. That said, in music classrooms this tradition is replicated to a certain extent, but in most cases, it is limited to the interpretation of songs and dances.

In this sense, the pedagogical idea of Orff Schulwerk concerning students' creativity opens the door to many possibilities that go beyond interpretation and mechanical repetition. The Schulwerk invites us to question ourselves in the face of traditional musical material, to extend its possibilities, and to turn a song, a game, a rhyme, or a traditional dance into a creative experience. Thus, a challenge for all teachers who are applying the principles of the Schulwerk through our Colombian music is to expand the musical heritage we have received and give it to the children not as a "fixed sound object" that they must reproduce, but rather as precious raw material from which new meanings and artistic experiences can be created.

Another important step is to continue with the production of literature that makes use of the numerous compilations of musical material that already exist but make a contribution in terms of teaching processes from the Orff Schulwerk approach. At present, it is easy to find pedagogical proposals that employ resources common to those of Orff Schulwerk, such as body percussion, small percussion, and barred instruments, accompaniments based on rhythmic and melodic ostinati, mentioned above. However, there are few publications that explicitly present all the Orff Schulwerk principles developed through pedagogical processes that integrate traditional Colombian materials. In addition, such literature focused on the process and not on the repertoire would have a broader scope, because it would allow its application in different social and educational contexts.

Similarly, it is necessary to document and share all teaching practices based on the Orff Schulwerk that are being carried out at the moment. We know that members of our Association apply and develop Schulwerk principles in their teaching practice in schools, universities, academies, cultural centers, and even in non-governmental organizations working with vulnerable populations, but so far these practices have not been documented.

Finally, it will be an objective for ACOLORFF to continue working towards the decentralization of Orff Schulwerk training activities. Although several important courses have already been held in the cities of Medellin and Barranquilla, there is still a need to involve more institutions in various cities to support the efforts of the Association and be allies in the mission of disseminating the principles of the Schulwerk.

In a country like Colombia, where diversity is the norm and unifying training processes is impossible, the Orff Schulwerk presents itself as a wonderful tool, because it allows us to enrich and shape the pedagogical work, respecting the differences and particularities of each region. This is then our greatest challenge: to continue spreading the principles of Orff and Keetman throughout the country while preserving the cultural traditions that identify us as Colombians.

References

Convers, L., Hernandez, O., Ochoa, J. S. (2014). *Arrullos y currulaos: Material para abordar el estudio de la música tradicional del Pacífico sur colombiano* [Lullabies and currulaos: Material for the study of traditional music from the Colombian South Pacific]. Bogotá: Editorial Pontificia Universidad Javeriana.

Duque, A., Sánchez, H. F., & Tascón, H. J. (2009). *¡Que te pasa vo!: Canto de piel, semilla y chonta* [What's up vo !: Song of skin, seed and chonta]. Bogotá: Ministerio de Cultura.
https://www.mincultura.gov.co/proyectoeditorial/Documentos%20Publicaciones/Que%20te%20pasa%20a%20vo/Que%20te%20pasa%20a%20vo.pdf

Franco, L. (2005). *Música Andina Occidental: entre pasillos y bambucos. Cartilla de iniciación musical* [Western Andean Music: Between corridors and bamboo trees. Musical initiation booklet]. Bogotá, D.C: Ministerio de Cultura. https://www.mincultura.gov.co/proyectoeditorial/Pages/Cartilla-de-iniciación-musical,-Música-andina-occidental-entre-pasillos-y-bambucos".aspx

Fundación Nacional Batuta. (2021). *Quiénes Somos* [About us]. https://www.fundacionbatuta.org/c.php?id=44

García López, M. et al. (2015). *Sudamérica y sus mundos audibles: Cosmologías y prácticas sonoras de sus pueblos indígenas* [South America and its audible worlds: Cosmologies and sound practices of its Indigenous Peoples]. Berlin: Ibero-Amerikanisches Institut. http://biblioteca.clacso.edu.ar/Alemania/iai/20161116053824/pdf_1108.pdf

Instituto Colombiano de Bienestar Familiar ICBF. (2011). *Tiki Tiki Tai.* Bogotá.

https://www.icbf.gov.co/sites/default/files/procesos/document6.pdf

Leonidas, V. (2009). *Al son que me toquen bailo y canto* [I dance and sing to the music they play for me]. Bogotá: Ministerio de Cultura. https://www.mincultura.gov.co/proyectoeditorial/Pages/Cartilla-de-iniciación-musical-Pacífico-norte- "Al-son-que-me-toquen-canto-y-bailo.aspx

Posada Saldarriaga, P. (2012). *Cantar, tocar y jugar. Juegos musicales para niños* [Sing, play instruments and games. Musical games for children] (includes CD). Universidad de Antioquia.

Ribeiro, A. D. (2012). ¡¡Egua ...: la música suena boníiito, mano!! *Músicas populares tradicionales del trapecio amazónico colombiano: Cartilla de iniciación* [Egua ...: the music sounds nice, man!! Traditional folk music of the Colombian Amazonian trapeze: Beginner's booklet]. Bogotá: Ministerio de Cultura.

Serna, B. (2015, Winter): ACOLORFF - The New Orff Schulwerk Association of Colombia. *Orff-Schulwerk Heute,* (93), 93–94.

Orff Schulwerk in the United States: Always Developing

Carolee Stewart [1]

The United States and its diversity

The United States is inhabited by a diverse population of more than 330 million people. Native Americans, Alaskan Natives, and Hawaiian Natives were the first occupants of this land and everyone else is an immigrant or descended from immigrants. The first immigrants arrived from Europe during the early 1600s, and the colonial territories were part of the British Empire until 1776. Africans were brought by force by our European ancestors and enslaved from 1619 to 1865. More recent immigrants have come from Asia and Latin America.

The influence of multiple immigrant groups results in a great diversity in religion and language. All major religions of the world are practiced. While most Americans speak English, many other languages are commonly used. Another important demographic is race. In 2019 the racial/ethnic distribution was: 60.1% White, 18.5% Hispanic or Latino, 13.4% African American or Black, 5.9% Asian, and 1.3% Native American (U.S. Census, n.d.). Differences are also seen in the distribution of wealth. In 2016, 77.1% of the total wealth in the United States was held by the top 10% of income earners, while the lower half of the population held only 1.2% of the total wealth (Statista, n.d.).

American culture originated with our European ancestors and has been influenced by the cultures of African Americans, Native Americans, Latin Americans, Asians, and Pacific Islanders. Our cultural diversity can be seen in regional dialects, cuisines, folklore, festivals, art, traditional music and dance, and other characteristics. More than 500 Native American tribal nations practice traditions that have survived for hundreds of years.

There is no place where diversity is more evident than in the public schools, which serve about 87% of American children, with about 10% in private schools and 3–4% homeschooled. Public education in the United States is decentralized, meaning that the federal government is not largely involved in determining curricula or standards. This responsibility lies with each of the 50 individual states and thousands of local districts. Most school funding is determined by state and local governments, with some coming from the federal government. Schools are expected to comply with civil rights laws, special education regulations, and testing mandates, among other requirements, and whether these obligations are met is used in regulating government funds to individual states and localities.

Each state determines at what age a child must begin school and at what age or grade level they may leave. Some states do not require kindergarten; some states do not provide free access to pre-kindergarten/preschool. Multiple variables influence the quality of education that children receive. Because people with more education tend to achieve higher economic status

1   With grateful thanks to the following who have contributed by reading, editing, or supplying information: Carrie Barnette, Karen Benson, Judy Bond, Judith Cole, Tiffany English.

and social standing, one can see that at least a portion of wealth inequality can be traced to unequal access to education.

Within this structure are individual music curricula. The National Association for Music Education (formerly Music Educators National Conference) has developed *Music Standards* (NAfME, 2014) as a framework for curriculum writing. However, what and how a music educator teaches is generally up to the individual. Therefore, the lack of a unified national music curriculum makes it favorable for Orff Schulwerk teachers to develop their programs.

Development of Orff Schulwerk in the United States

The arrival of Orff Schulwerk in the United States during the 1950s can be traced to Arnold Walter, a German music educator and visionary working in Canada. Walter became familiar with the Schulwerk while attending a conference in Salzburg, and he returned to Toronto with the conviction to adapt and spread Orff's educational ideas throughout North America. He engaged Doreen Hall as collaborator and co-author in introducing the ideas of Schulwerk in Canada.[1] In 1956 Walter gave a lecture about Orff Schulwerk at a convention of the Music Educators National Conference (now National Association for Music Education) in St. Louis, Missouri. The lecture was combined with a demonstration involving local children taught by German educator Egon Kraus. Following this introduction were invitations to Doreen Hall to teach workshops in the United States during the late 1950s and early 1960s.

Most people point to the 1962 summer conference at the University of Toronto as the real spark that kindled the development and expansion of Orff Schulwerk throughout North America. Faculty included Carl Orff, Gunild Keetman, and teachers from the Orff Institute. Several Americans attended, and among them were individuals who became influential in the advancement of Orff Schulwerk in the United States: Isabel Carley, Barbara Grenoble, Ruth Hamm, Grace Nash, Jacobeth Postl, Joe Matthesius, and Lillian Yaross.[2] The Toronto courses continued for many summers and became a model for teacher education courses that developed later in the States.

During the mid 1960s several U.S. school districts received government grants to support curriculum projects promoting creativity in work with children, and the Orff Schulwerk approach was implemented for this purpose. Worth mentioning is the project "Orff-Schulwerk: Design for Creativity" in the Bellflower Unified Schools (California), led by Martha Maybury Wampler with co-teachers Gertrud Orff and Margit Cronmüller Smith. From 1967 to 1969, the Bellflower project hosted three symposia, which drew people from across the country and strongly impacted the dispersal of Orff Schulwerk in the United States.

American Orff-Schulwerk Association (AOSA)

In the spring of 1968, Arnold Burkart—who had attended the Toronto course in 1963 and recently joined the faculty at Ball State University (Indiana)—invited colleagues to meet and discuss organizing a conference. That meeting resulted in the formation of the Orff-Schulwerk Association,[3] with the selection of officers to include Burkart as president. They developed a

---

1   See the article in this volume by our Canadian colleagues.
2   Isabel Carley was the first editor of *The Orff Echo*; Ruth Hamm, Jacobeth Postl, Joe Matthesius, and Lillian Yaross all served terms as President of the American Orff-Schulwerk Association; Barbara Grenoble and Grace Nash were board members.
3   In 1970 the name changed to American Orff-Schulwerk Association.

plan for a conference the following spring and a newsletter, *The Orff Echo*, which was first published in November 1968 with Isabel Carley serving as editor until 1983.

Conferences have occurred every year since 1969. These three-day events are held in different locations, based on a rotation that attempts to engage people from the various regions of the country. Each year offers a new theme, with workshops by national and international presenters.

The Orff Echo evolved from a four-page bulletin to a full-color quarterly peer-reviewed journal with a salaried editor and editorial board. Each issue has a special focus. In 1995 a second quarterly publication, *Reverberations*, appeared as an insert to *The Orff Echo*, with news items and lesson ideas. Now it is issued weekly online as *Reverberations: Teachers Teaching Teachers*, offering suggestions for the classroom. In 2021, AOSA introduced a series of podcasts that focus on the history, programs, and initiatives of the association.

AOSA had ten founding members in 1968, and in 2019 (its 51st year) there were nearly 4,000 members.[1] In addition to the activity of the national association, further Orff Schulwerk activity occurs through local chapters. In 2021 there are 95 chapters distributed throughout all regions of the country—including Alaska and Hawaii. AOSA provides a wide range of support for chapter leaders, and chapters offer professional development workshops.

Another important aspect of AOSA is its music industry members, who provide educational materials, books, and equipment. There is a very robust business of publishing Orff Schulwerk teaching materials in the United States, and Orff instruments varying in quality are available from many different manufacturers.

Map of the United States showing the distribution of the 95 AOSA chapters
Map: Jack Neill

---

1 Membership has decreased from nearly 5,000 in the late 1990s.

American Edition of Music for Children

In the earliest applications of the Schulwerk in the United States, teachers drew from folk songs, dances, and games from all regions of the country, from our British Isles heritage, and from African American, Hispanic, and Latin American traditions. Because North American music has roots in Western European music, it was an easy step to use materials from the adaptations of *Music for Children* by Doreen Hall and Arnold Walter in Canada and by Margaret Murray in the United Kingdom.

Between 1977 and 1982 Hermann Regner coordinated the publication of the American Edition of *Music for Children*. This edition is different from previous adaptations not only in its larger format, but also in the number of contributors and in the organization of the books (Frazee, 2010; Maschat, 2011).

> *Volume 1 is described as for preschool, Volume 2 for primary, and Volume 3 for upper elementary grades. All volumes contain examples of pentatonic, diatonic, and free tonality…33 authors from all regions of the USA have composed, commented, and tried out the material.* (Regner, 1984/2011, pp. 234–236)

The contents of the three volumes are representative of American folk traditions and include some original compositions. There are ideas to inspire improvisation and composition in both music and movement. More than 40 supplements have followed. Increased interest in the inclusion of world music in American classrooms has resulted in a few supplements presenting African, Latin American, Jewish, and Hebrew materials.

Music education in the United States

Vocal music instruction was first included as a part of public education during the mid-19th century, and in the late 19th century instrumental music was introduced into schools. Today, "general music" classes are where one is likely to find the Orff Schulwerk approach in practice. A recent study found that 98% of U.S. public elementary schools offered general music (Give A Note Foundation, 2017, p. 11), meaning that nearly all children who attend public elementary schools in the United States are offered music instruction. In addition, choirs, bands, and sometimes orchestras are important aspects of many elementary and secondary school programs. Due to the decentralized nature of American schools, decisions about hiring a music teacher and funding the necessary resources for music instruction may be left to each school's principal or to the local school district.

Evidence that Orff Schulwerk is part of mainstream music education in the United States is found in the national Music Standards (NAfME, 2014), which emphasize behaviors that involve creating, performing, and responding, as described in these overarching statements:

- Students need to have experience in creating, to be successful musicians and to be successful 21st century citizens.
- Students need to perform—as singers, as instrumentalists, and in their lives and careers.
- Students need to respond to music, as well as to their culture, their community, and their colleagues.

Further signs of the influences of Orff Schulwerk in U.S. music education can be seen in the two major music textbook series. McGraw-Hill's *Spotlight on Music* contains "Orff orchestrations for grades 1–6" (McGraw-Hill, n.d.). *Interactive MUSIC powered by Silver Burdett with*

Alfred, a digital program, supports "different music specializations and pedagogies" (Savvas, n.d.). Both publishers employ experienced Orff Schulwerk teachers as authors.

In addition to public and private elementary school music programs, the Orff Schulwerk approach is sometimes included in classes with middle school students, senior citizens, toddlers, and preschool children, as well in music therapy settings and some community music schools.

Pre-service and in-service teacher education

In music teacher preparation at the undergraduate level, most pre-service teachers receive a basic introduction to Orff Schulwerk, Dalcroze Eurythmics, the Kodály Method, and the Music Learning Theory of Edwin Gordon. To promote the teaching of these four pedagogies in undergraduate education, the Alliance for Active Music Making (AAMM, n.d.) was established in 2004. AOSA is an affiliated member of AAMM with the Organization of American Kodály Educators, the Dalcroze Society of America, and the Gordon Institute for Music Learning. Due to their collaborative work, there is more emphasis on incorporating active music making approaches in many general music teacher education courses.

Another way to connect university students with the ideas of Orff Schulwerk is through individual AOSA chapters. Chapter members are sometimes guest teachers in teacher education classes, and students are invited (frequently for no fee) to Saturday workshops. The national association offers to undergraduate and graduate students free online membership, which includes access to resources such as lesson ideas, videos, articles, as well as professional development offerings and opportunities to apply for scholarships and grants. For a small annual fee, student membership includes the quarterly journal, *The Orff Echo*. Students are also engaged as volunteers to work at the annual conference.

AOSA offers several professional development opportunities that are available to all members—including students. In addition to the annual conference, members can access events and independent study units offered through the website. Professional Learning Networks are online events that offer certificates for continuing education hours and cover several sessions that give educators the opportunity to participate in live presentations and discussions around specific topics in Orff Schulwerk. Virtual Events are single sessions that cover relevant themes. The website lists Independent Study Units that include videos, articles, and lesson ideas, for which there are graduate credit options.

At the graduate level, eight universities currently offer master's degrees with an emphasis in Orff Schulwerk. Among the required courses for these programs are three levels of AOSA-approved Orff Schulwerk Teacher Education Courses.

AOSA Orff Schulwerk teacher education courses

One-week summer courses were offered in several locations during the mid-to-late 1960s. By 1976 AOSA had published its first *Guidelines for Level I Certification* followed in 1980 with *Guidelines for Teacher Training Courses Levels I–III*. The current *Teacher Education Curriculum* developed in 2012 is routinely discussed and revised.

AOSA-approved Teacher Education Courses are comprehensive three-level curriculum-based programs comprised of classes in Orff Schulwerk pedagogy, recorder, and movement, designed to develop musicianship, creativity, and teaching strategies. AOSA approves Orff Schulwerk courses that meet its current criteria and follow the *AOSA Teacher Education Curriculum*. A Certificate of Completion is awarded to individuals who meet requirements of an AOSA-approved level III course.

Typically, some 50–60 courses take place over two weeks during the summer months, with a few programs occurring during the school year. In addition to levels I, II, and III, other course offerings might include introduction to Orff Schulwerk, masterclasses, and other supplemental classes.

For people who have completed at least one level and had a minimum of one year teaching there is the possibility to participate in AOSA's Digital Mentorship program. This pairs experienced Orff Schulwerk teachers with newly trained Orff Schulwerk teachers or university teacher educators for the purpose of improving the practice of those who request mentorship. Discussions occur primarily through e-mail, online chatting, video conferencing, digital video recordings, and the like. If feasible, live observations occur.

Over many years, AOSA has developed a thorough process of overseeing courses to ensure their quality and consistency throughout the country. While each program is responsible for designing its own course, the *AOSA Teacher Education Curriculum* must be followed. There are expectations for equipment, space for classes, scheduling, the number of minutes of instruction, staffing, minimum enrollment, completion of course evaluations. All instructors must be AOSA Approved Teacher Educators.

For individuals who want to become AOSA Approved Teacher Educators, there is an apprenticeship program. This is available to AOSA members who have completed level 3 and taught for a minimum of five years. It is a rigorous procedure that involves observing and teaching under the supervision of an approved teacher educator during a level I course and submitting required materials and evaluations.[1]

AOSA employs a Professional Development Director who oversees all aspects of AOSA-sanctioned Orff Schulwerk teacher education. This individual works closely with the Curriculum Oversight and Review Subcommittee and the Curriculum and Instruction Committee of the AOSA Board to manage all aspects of teacher education.

Resources used in teacher education courses

An informal survey was sent to directors of AOSA-approved courses requesting information about required and recommended materials. Of those that responded, every course requires students to have the Murray adaptation of Orff and Keetman's *Music for Children*. Volume I is required for level I, volumes I, II, and IV are required for level II, and volumes I–V are required for level III. This reflects the theory, source materials, and examples in the *AOSA Teacher Education Curriculum*, which after many years of discussion and debate establishes the melodic and rhythmic sequence that introduces hexatonic and diatonic modes in level II and functional harmony in level III.[2] Most courses require Keetman's *Elementaria* and *Rhythmische Übung* as well as some of her xylophone books. Other sources that are listed more than five times in the responses are *Play, Sing, and Dance: An Introduction to Orff Schulwerk* by Doug Goodkin and *The Elemental Style* by Paul Cribari and Richard Layton. All courses require an assortment of collections of American folk songs and children's games, along with a variety of recorder and dance/movement books.

In the survey responses there are a few resources that connect with the cultural diversity described at the beginning of this article. African American children's games and songs are included in some of the collections. Several of the folk-dance books and recordings contain dances from around the world.

---

1 Apprenticeships are also available for individuals who wish to be approved recorder or movement teachers.
2 See Clayburn (2019) for a discussion on this topic.

Experiencing space with a frame   Recorder improvisation

Diversity, equity, and inclusion (DEI)

This brings us to an issue that is now being raised very frequently in the United States: That the cultures of non-white Americans are not recognized and celebrated in schools and in our society in general in proportion to their presence in the population. To support teachers, there are publications and workshops/courses on such topics as spirituals, gospel, jazz, Native American music, and world musics, and *The Orff Echo* as well as AOSA conferences have regularly incorporated these topics.

Currently AOSA is in the process of addressing this problem through multiple efforts that include sessions about culture and diversity in the Orff Schulwerk classroom, discussions about DEI within the AOSA structure, appointments of DEI vice-presidents to the Board, review of the Teacher Education Program through a DEI lens, and many other initiatives. Currently, an ad hoc committee is discussing recommendations for re-structuring the AOSA Board to ensure a culture of belonging in which its leadership is better representative of the range of demographics and characteristics of its members—and potential members.

Playing with sticks

Critical issues in Orff Schulwerk

Orff Schulwerk in the United States is not without its critics. Among several themes found in a review of literature, Carlos Abril (2013) summarized critical issues that force us to think about the relevance of Orff Schulwerk in today's world. He raises questions regarding the weakness of the recapitulation theory, a pedagogy that is overly simplistic and disconnected from contemporary childhood, the use of pedagogical songs composed solely for the purpose of teaching concepts, and the potential for the approach to become a method. Abril suggests that these criticisms should urge us "to continually challenge ourselves and question our actions in the classroom" (p. 21).

…always developing…

At this point in time—more than 65 years after Orff Schulwerk was introduced in the United States—it is appropriate to look beyond the classroom and examine Orff Schulwerk's place in the broader context of society. Americans are facing the realities of our long and complex history of systemic racism. AOSA leadership's multilayered and intense self-examination is involving members in re-making the organization to stay relevant and to keep the Schulwerk growing and flowing in the United States.

Reflecting on a rhythmic task

Trying out spatial axes
Photos: Sofía López-Ibor Aliño

References and additional sources

Abril, C. R. (2013). Critical issues in Orff Schulwerk. In C. C. Wang, & D. G. Springer (Eds.), *Orff Schulwerk: Reflections and directions* (pp. 11–25). Chicago: GIA Publications, Inc.

Alliance for Active Music Making. (n.d.). *AAMM goals*. Retrieved May 22, 2021, from https://www.allianceamm.org

Clayburn, T. L. (2019, Winter). Varieties of the Orff Schulwerk wildflower in North America. *The Orff Echo, 51*(2), 18–21.

Cole, J. (2009, Summer). Milestones in the history of Orff Schulwerk in the United States. *The Orff Echo, 41*(4), 27–30.

Cole, J. (n.d.). *Before there was AOSA*. Retrieved May 19, 2021, from https://aosa.org/experts-blog/before-there-was-aosa/

Frazee, J. (2010, Fall). From the old world to the new. The genesis of the American edition of Music for Children. *The Orff Echo, 43*(1), 30–33.

Give A Note Foundation. (2017). *The status of music education in United States public schools – 2017*. Reston, VA. https://www.giveanote.org/media/2017/09/The-Status-of-Music-Education-in-US-Public-Schools-2017_reduced.pdf

Maschat, V. (2011). Music for Children – American Edition or: Why the American edition of Orff Schulwerk was born in Salzburg. *Orff-Schulwerk Informationen 85,* 290. https://www.orff-schulwerk-forum-salzburg.org/magazine-osh

McGraw Hill. (n.d.). *Spotlight on music*. Retrieved May 25, 2021, from https://www.mheducation.com/prek-12/explore/music-studio/spotlight-on-music.html

National Association for Music Education. (2014, June). *Music standards*. https://nafme.org/my-classroom/standards/core-music-standards/

Orff, C., & Keetman, G. (1957–1966). *Orff-Schulwerk. Music for children* (Vols. 1–5) (English adaptation by M. Murray). London: Schott.

Regner, H. (Coordinator). (1977, 1980, 1982). *Music for children, Orff-Schulwerk American edition: Vol. 2. Primary; Vol. 3. Upper elementary; Vol. 1. Pre-school*. New York: Schott.

Regner, H. (2011). "Musik für Kinder – music for children – musique pour enfants." Comments on the adoption and adaptation of Orff-Schulwerk in other countries. In B. Haselbach (Ed.), *Texts on theory and practice of Orff-Schulwerk: Basic texts from the years 1932–2010* (pp. 220-244). Mainz: Schott. (Original work published 1984)

Savvas. (n.d.). *Interactive music*. Retrieved May 25, 2021, from https://www.savvas.com/index.cfm?locator=PSZu-Wi&PMDbSiteid=2781&PMDbSolutionid=6724&PMDbSubSolutionid=&PMDbCategoryID=818&Filter_423=

Statista. (n.d.). *Wealth distribution in the United States in 2016*. Retrieved May 22, 2021, from https://www.statista.com/statistics/203961/wealth-distribution-for-the-us/

Stewart, C. (1998, Summer). Orff Schulwerk in the United States of America. *Orff-Schulwerk Informationen, 60,* 41–48. https://www.orff-schulwerk-forum-salzburg.org/magazine-osh

U.S. Census. (n.d.). *Quick facts*. Retrieved May 22, 2021, from https://www.census.gov/quickfacts/fact/table/US/PST045219

Periodicals

The Orff Echo. Quarterly journal of the American Orff-Schulwerk Association.

Reverberations: Teachers Teaching Teachers. Weekly, online publication for AOSA members.

ASIA

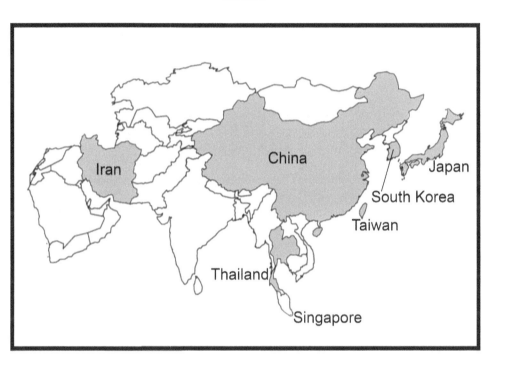

Orff Schulwerk in China: An Ongoing Development

Compiled and edited by Xu Mai and Sarah Brooke [1]

History of music education in China

China has developed a rich and complex musical legacy with a tradition of music education going back to the Zhou Dynasty (1075–256 BC). Each of the subsequent dynasties supported a strong music education which added to the rich cultural heritage of China.

The twentieth century saw the development of music education follow the political, social and psychological changes that occurred in China. During the first decade, some Chinese musicians studied abroad and brought their experiences back to China, leading to an attentiveness to Western classical music. Following the last of the dynasties and the establishment of the Republic of China in 1911, music education curricula included an appreciation of this music plus traditional Chinese music and contained repertoire that would be learnt in schools and used for civic and national gatherings. The texts of composed school songs called for patriotism and portrayed the national identity of China at that time.

When the People's Republic of China was formed in 1949, the government emphasized regional folk music to encourage an embracing of the people's music. School music textbooks began to include folk songs from minority groups in China, each with its own unique style, but often reconstructed with new lyrics written in praise of China's leaders, or with a patriotic theme.

The Cultural Revolution launched in 1966 saw a change in education as the youth were called to revolution by Chairman Mao Zedong. The population was urged to rid itself of the "Four Olds": Old customs, old culture, old habits, and old ideas. Traditional Chinese music and Western music were both banned at this time and school music repertoire focused on creating revolutionary spirits and national cohesion. Compositions were created for school music textbooks with little regard for any pedagogical aspects.

A broader music education was implemented from the late 1970s coinciding with the "open-door policy" towards Western culture, allowing an exchange of ideas between China and the West. This was reflected in school music programs where the elements of music were studied through Chinese repertoire and also from a variety of cultures across the globe.

A national curriculum was created at this time that focused on students developing knowledge about music and improving their technique in singing/making music. This curriculum was presented as textbooks for students and compulsory for all schools across China. In 2001, a new way of thinking about music education resulted in activities to encourage creativity being included in curriculum standards for the first time. Teachers and schools could be more flexible in how they approached music education, and a variety of textbooks were made available, some provinces focusing on the music of their region or ethnic group.

---

1 With grateful thanks to the following for their valuable contributions: Liao Naixiong, Li Danna, Xu Peiran, Werner Beidinger, Susie Davies-Splitter, Wolfgang Hartmann, Catherine West, Manuela Widmer

Over the past decades, China has been more open to a diversity of pedagogical styles and now holds a more holistic view of music education. In 2011, updated textbooks reflected an acceptance of research identifying how children learn, and how best to teach. Aesthetics was placed at the core of music and arts education.

Today, music education in schools has various objectives. This education is not specifically to develop expert musicians, but to imbue culture, attitudes, and social ideals. Song repertoire includes traditional patriotic songs, Western folk material, songs of the many ethnic minorities, and composed songs and rhymes. Alongside the song material, students from a very young age engage in listening activities in order to appreciate various musics. This ranges from Western classical music to Chinese classical, traditional, and contemporary music in different genres.

The Chinese music curriculum's foremost aim is to highlight the characteristics of music, and for students to recognize the emotive aspects of music. The current Chinese music curriculum standards lists imitation, exploration, experiencing, co-operating, and comprehending as the steps students cycle through in order to understand these characteristics.

History of Orff Schulwerk in China

In 1980, Liao Naixiong, a professor from the Shanghai Conservatory of Music, visited Carl Orff at his home in Bavaria where Orff gave Liao some of his Schulwerk publications and sound recordings and explained his system of elemental music education. Following this visit, Liao introduced Orff Schulwerk to the Chinese music education community. At this time, education reform was occurring in China, and the value and impact of music education for all was being rediscovered. It was an ideal time to introduce a new way of thinking about music education, and this brought about a wave of interest and excitement about Orff Schulwerk. Liao published articles and translated textbooks so that teachers could extend their understanding. He stressed that the Schulwerk promoted a way of music education that developed the human, the playful, the elemental, and he highlighted the unity of music, language, and movement. Liao felt this way of thinking linked to the traditional music of China and was the way for moving forward.

From 1981, Liao travelled to various cities and provinces in China to give lectures. Those teachers attending were interested in the philosophy of the Schulwerk and were keen to expand their understandings.

The introduction of Orff Schulwerk to China was a major impetus to actually reform school music education. It set in motion the first venture of school music educators to do something completely new, experimental, and ground-breaking in the classroom. Although this was welcomed, it appeared rather superficial in the first phase.

In 1984, after his second study tour of Germany and Austria, Liao organized an Orff Schulwerk introduction course, presented by Margot Schneider from Berlin. Following this, in 1988, the first Orff Schulwerk training course was held in Beijing with instructors Peter Cubasch, Wolfgang Hartmann, and Manuela Widmer from the Orff Institute in Salzburg.

Following the success of this, a group of Chinese teachers regularly met and discussed Orff Schulwerk at the Shanghai Conservatory. This led in 1989 to Li Danna taking a delegation of music educators to Germany and Salzburg to learn more about Orff Schulwerk.

In the same year, Li began the preparatory work for the forming of the China Orff Schulwerk Association (COSA) which was then registered in 1991. The influence of Liao and Li is testament to the ongoing interest in Orff Schulwerk. Many international guests and local presenters have been invited by COSA and other educational groups to teach workshops and courses to continue developing understandings of Orff Schulwerk. Some of those Chinese educators who have been interested in continuing their studies have completed various training both in China and overseas, several graduating from the Orff Institute in Salzburg.

From the mid 1990s, the cooperation of Liao and Hermann Regner (representative of the Carl Orff Foundation and former director of the Orff Institute) focused on the Orff Schulwerk finding its way into the music pedagogy of the conservatories. In 1998, Wolfgang Hartmann was entrusted with the task of presenting a five-year plan in which the conservatory music pedagogy students had an annual work phase "Orff Schulwerk" included in their studies. This was concluded together with Andrea Ostertag and Manuela Widmer from the Orff Institute, first with the Shanghai Conservatory, then also with the Central Conservatory in Beijing.

In addition to these studies, the Carl Orff Foundation collaborated between 2002 and 2004 with the Conservatory in Shanghai, the Central Conservatory in Beijing, and the Chinese Orff Schulwerk Association to offer a "Training Course for Future Orff Schulwerk Instructors," hosted at the Central Conservatory in Beijing. This was also conducted by Wolfgang Hartmann, Manuela Widmer, and Andrea Ostertag.

Even after the completion of the five-year plan further invitations from the conservatories were extended to Wolfgang Hartmann. In cooperation with the heads of the music education departments, the focus on forms of sequencing teaching (not just exemplary individual lessons) and the application of the Schulwerk in teaching elementary and middle school students was considered of primary importance. Therefore, extensive teaching practice periods were included in each visit.

In 2004, Liao created a Chinese adaptation of the Musik für Kinder volumes published by the Shanghai Educational Publishing House and Schott Verlag. He elected to include various model pieces taken from the five volumes and added pedagogical notes and explanations into one book. This one volume differs from other adaptations around the world in that there are no exercises or stand-alone ostinato examples, nor are there any pieces related to the Chinese culture.

International Orff Schulwerk in China

The Orff Schulwerk has now been part of the official curriculum of the conservatories in Shanghai and Beijing for many years. The Central Conservatory in Beijing is of particular interest as far as the country's music pedagogical line is concerned, due to the fact that it is directly subordinate to the Ministry of Culture. Both Wang Yang (Beijing) and Chen Rong (Shanghai) have been instrumental in presenting Orff Schulwerk at the conservatories.

The growing interest in Orff Schulwerk across China has led to more and more invitations from institutions and private organizations to internationally known Orff Schulwerk pedagogues. It is not possible to mention the countless private courses, but a few co-operations with international Orff Schulwerk institutions and organizations are briefly mentioned here.

Activities of the Orff-Schulwerk Gesellschaft Deutschland in China
(Excerpts from a report by Werner Beidinger, President of OSG Germany)

The director of Sino IMEX GmbH first contacted the board of OSG Germany in 2010 in order to sound out the possibilities of cooperation in the spread of Orff Schulwerk in China. Barbara Schönewolf and Mica Grüner were the first representatives of our team of lecturers who taught a 2-3 day "Orff Schulwerk course" (later referred to as "introductory" course) in various cities and regions of China. The German Orff-Schulwerk Gesellschaft deliberately does not use the term "level course" and emphasizes that it does not issue any kind of teaching qualification.

We were aware of the internationally discussed problem of "cultural colonization" by foreigners from the very beginning and that is why we insisted on translators who have completed either the special course at the Orff Institute or diploma studies in elemental music education in Germany.

With more than ten years of cooperation, 149 courses have occurred to date, 7 of which were held in Germany and 142 were spread across China.

"Music and Dance for Children"
(Excerpt from a paper by Manuela Widmer, Lecturer and former director of the Orff Institute Salzburg and Co-Editor of *Musik und Tanz für Kinder.*)

This teaching concept for early childhood as a starting point for versatile further education in the sense of the Orff Schulwerk in China has been developed from the cooperation of teachers and graduates of the Orff Institute in Salzburg and the promotion company Eurovista (Beijing).

Authorized by the publisher Schott Verlag, Eurovista began in 2017 exclusively with the large-scale music education project around the early childhood education publication *Musik und Tanz für Kinder* (Music and Dance for Children). In a process lasting several years, the editors (Micaela Grüner and Manuela Widmer, based at the Orff Institute) were committed to a careful translation through constant discussion with Chinese colleagues who had specialist training in the fields of elementary music education and rhythmics. The wish to include Chinese cultural material (nursery rhymes, songs, dances) in the textbook was met only to a limited extent. With reference to the number of Chinese regional languages and ethnic groups (more than 60), which could not be taken into account in a balanced way, it was decided to use a standard translation in Mandarin, so that regional supplements could be considered later. In addition, the Chinese experts pointed out the need of Chinese users (teachers as well as parents) for orientation and participation in Western culture. Once the teachers' commentaries and the children's booklets were translated into Chinese, the first introductory events for it were held in several cities in China and the subsidiary "MUT[1] International Education" was founded. With the translation of the material for early childhood education *Music and Tanz für Kinder*, which is widely used in German-speaking countries, Schott Verlag is setting new impulses with a modern presentation of Orff Schulwerk pedagogy for the preschool sector in China. Under the leadership of the two editors with the constant and competent support of the managing director of Eurovista a team of experts from China and abroad conducted the training activities twice a year between 2017 and 2019.

In the later training courses attention was repeatedly drawn to the basic principles of the Orff Schulwerk and its transcultural idea, and the participants were encouraged to transfer the presented teaching models to their regional culture and to actively introduce their own cultural material.

The cooperation with the Beijing New Talent Academy (BJNTA), which offers a designated artistic focus for its students, proved to be particularly fruitful. By the end of 2019, six further training courses on "Music and Dance for Children" had taken place, which, in addition to teaching the diverse content areas, were primarily aimed at providing a didactic foundation based on the Orff Schulwerk.

---

1 Musik und Tanz

International Centre for Excellence in Music Education (ICEME)
(Excerpts from a report by Catherine West, Director of Orff Teacher Education, Royal Conservatory of Music, Toronto, Canada)

From 2016 to 2019, Catherine West was invited by a Chinese private music education company (Xunmeng Education) to present Orff Schulwerk levels training courses based on the Canadian model under the newly founded ICEME. Fellow Canadians Marcelline Moody, Hong Hanbing, Joy Reeve, and Brenda Harvey also taught in these courses. Orff Schulwerk strategies became a way to unlock content that was already familiar to the participants, allowing for the co-creation of new approaches. Of necessity, the instructors needed to be responsive to how the particular content was received, abandoning some traditional songs and games quickly or embracing different versions. As respectful outsiders, the instructors stressed that the ideas for creative exploration could be adapted for many different materials, perhaps ones more appropriate than those being modelled.

Australian National Council of Orff Schulwerk (ANCOS) levels courses in China
(Excerpts from a report by Susie Davies-Splitter, Course instructor for ANCOS)

Following many years of Australians presenting workshops in China for a local private music education company (Topsky Education) in Shenzhen, the ANCOS levels training courses began in that city in 2010. This was borne out of the requests for a more sequential and in-depth study that was not possible through workshops alone. Susie Davies-Splitter and Sarah Brooke initially taught the courses while mentoring Xu Mai from China. She was able to be included in the teaching team in 2013. From 2014–2018, the levels courses were endorsed by the China Music Education National Journal. At this time, Carol Richards (the Chair of ANCOS levels courses) was invited to teach courses for private music education companies in Shanghai and Hong Kong which continued for approximately four years.

The courses conducted by ANCOS needed to follow the guidelines set by this association, and Australian certificates were provided to those who successfully completed the course. Presenters constantly considered the needs, language, environment, and culture of the Chinese participants, and Xu Mai and previous Chinese levels courses participants acted as consultants bridging the gaps between the two. They were able to provide repertoire and context that would not otherwise have been available to the Australian presenters.

It was always the understanding that the courses would in time be made available under a Chinese authority, and specifically created to meet the specific needs of Chinese educators. The contribution made by ANCOS has resulted in many educators considering a more creative and inclusive music education, and we are very pleased that participants from the levels courses in Shenzhen have worked together to form a local organization to continue the work of training in Orff Schulwerk.

Orff Schulwerk in Chinese education today

With nearly 40 years since Orff Schulwerk was introduced in China, the biggest question for schools remains the same. How can teachers integrate this approach into their teaching of a music curriculum set by the government?

Chinese music is primarily melodic rather than harmonic. Songs can lack repetition of rhythmic and melodic motifs so are not always easy to learn, and phrases can vary in length and in number within a piece of music. Although Chinese songs are often pentatonic, the tonal center may move several times within a single piece of music. Songs are not always conducive to accompaniments with Orff instruments, or appropriate for improvisation or modification. The distinctive tone colors of some of the traditional Chinese melodic instruments are not often integrated with the Orff instruments, the latter often considered an "educational" tool particularly for early childhood, and not for use at a performance level.

These aspects of some of the repertoire in the curriculum for Chinese students have a direct effect on how Orff Schulwerk is adapted and adopted by teachers. Although the tuned percussion instruments are popular and enjoyed in schools, teachers may lack the skills to use them for improvisation or to encourage creativity. Untuned percussion instruments, including traditional Chinese drums and gongs, are far more adaptable and accessible media with this repertoire.

Chinese schools have a tradition of music performance, and teachers are accountable for the quality of these performances. Many cities hold competitions for students, and for the teachers this can create a results-driven ethos. Teachers enter competitions where they demonstrate their ability to teach their students, and choirs and ensemble groups are assessed based only on the quality of the performance. The success of the teacher at these competitions can lead to a higher position, more resources for their music education program, and being held in high regard by their peers. These events put pressure on teachers and can reduce interest in considering alternatives to the traditional style of teaching.

Those teachers who have been exposed to an understanding of Orff Schulwerk often feel it gives them a window to include all children in music learning and build their confidence. However, it is still very commonplace that students are selected for choirs or ensembles based solely on their abilities. Some schools offer Orff ensembles for those who wish to play music, with no barriers to their participation. Yet it can also happen that schools with such groups may then be selective about who can participate in a performance. The quality of performance is still seen in Chinese culture as the overriding goal.

The traditional pedagogy in Chinese music classes is one of the teachers providing instruction, done through rote learning, PowerPoint, or demonstration. Techniques such as call and response, or question and answer, are generally only used by those who have experienced these techniques through various training courses. Traditionally teachers would teach a song by singing it themselves while the students view the song and notation in their textbooks. If a teacher lacks confidence in his/her ability, audio recordings and videos are provided by the government to use as the demonstration models. Many children sing in schools to recorded accompaniment tracks.

There are significant logistical and spatial aspects to be considered by teachers in Chinese schools including the size of classes (up to 50 children in primary and 60 in middle school classes). The physical space in many schools does not allow for any kind of movement, and if so, teachers are often reticent about so many students moving in the space. Teachers face the reality of testing their students through government set examinations and can feel the weight of this affect their teaching. Taking time for students to create, or improvise, or learn through movement, is often seen as taking time away from learning the specific material required for the examination.

Adapting Orff Schulwerk into the mainstream Chinese school education is not easy and it takes time. It is not just the teachers who need to reflect on how best they can support their students. Parents of today's students went through an education system in China vastly different to the one that an Orff approach presents. The school community, curriculum writers, and government officials require evidence that children can have a music education through the Schulwerk that matches their requirements.

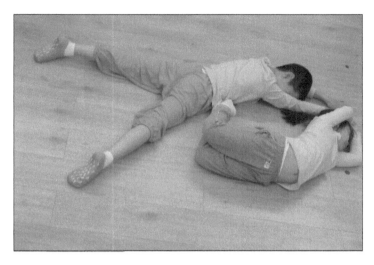

Playing instruments and moving
Photos: Private collection

Orff Schulwerk in different settings in China

Orff Schulwerk has a strong presence in preschools in China where children have an education that encourages an active engagement in music. Although the Schulwerk was traditionally seen as most appropriate for early childhood education, primary school teachers are attending workshops and training courses and incorporating the philosophy in their teaching. Some music educators in middle schools who have found difficulties in engaging their students have found Orff Schulwerk a rewarding and motivating way to approach their teaching.

China has many providers of after-school music education programs, and these have benefitted greatly from the influence of Orff Schulwerk. Without the need to satisfy government requirements regarding specific learning outcomes, they are more able to cater to students' needs and interests. Parents can be enthralled with the notion of a different way of learning and providers are able to capitalize on this.

Universities and teachers' colleges are seeing the benefit of the Orff instrumentarium. However, it can be that the pre-service teachers learn only specific repertoire on these instruments, and the training is focused more on how to ensure that their future students meet the curriculum standards. The joy, collaboration, creativity, and independence embedded in Orff Schulwerk is not always evident.

Moving forward

Since the registration of COSA in 1991 this association has been instrumental in continuing to provide training courses and workshops to music educators around the country, under the continuous leadership of Li Danna.

Other organizations and individuals offer courses and workshops throughout China, some targeted at specific groups (such as early childhood education), and others offering broader creative experiences. There is no regulatory body that monitors the providers of training, and as such China has had difficulties with some of the quality of the training, and with the qualifications of the educator providing the training.

The Institute for Music and Movement Education Advancement (IMMEA China) is a not-for-profit association based in Shenzhen. A group of educators supportive of Orff Schulwerk saw a need to offer training courses in line with the guidelines set by the International Orff-Schulwerk Forum Salzburg (IOSFS), in order to ensure that the quality of the training is in line with best practice. This group came directly from teachers who had attended the ANCOS levels courses in China, and in 2020, IMMEA China was formally accepted as one of the Associated Schools and Institutions by the IOSFS.

China is a big country with a large population. There are many differences between it and the country where Orff Schulwerk began. For some countries, the adapting of the Schulwerk has been an organic and easy process. For others, adaptation is fraught with difficulties and is a constantly evolving process. China has made great headway into considering more engaging and humanistic ways of educating students. Teachers invest in students through their schooling so that they can contribute positively to their society. The music traditions in China are strong and valued, and the community wants music and music education to be important in the lives of its members. It is an ongoing process to consider how best to provide for this. Chinese educators committed to the philosophy of Orff Schulwerk will continue to promote and exchange ideas in order to encourage others to adopt this holistic and inclusive approach.

Bibliography

Gersdorf, L. (2006). *Carl Orff* (Wang Tianruo, Trans.). People's Music Publishing House.

Grüner, M. (2018). *Orff instruments and how to play them* (Tong Xin & Gao Bo, Chinese Trans.). Beijing: Schott and Central Conservatory of Music. (Original work published 2011)

Haselbach, B. (Ed.). (2014). *Texts on theory and practice of Orff-Schulwerk: Basic texts from the years 1932–2010* (Liu Pei, Chinese Trans.). Beijing: Central Conservatory of Music Press. (Original work published 2011)

He, L. (2014, November). Curriculum review and expectations of Chinese Orff committee. *China Music Education*.

Hua, Y. (2012). *Living history—20 years music education in China for Hartmann*. [Unpublished master's thesis]. Shanghai Conservatory of Music.

Keetman, G. (1987). *Elementaria* (Liao Naixiong, Trans.). Anhui Literature and Art Publishing House.

Keller, W. (2003). *Introduction to "Music for Children"* (Jin Jinyan, Chinese Trans.). Mainz: Schott and Shanghai Education Publishing House. (Original work published 1963)

Li, D. (1995). Orff Schulwerk in China, the new voice of Yue-Fu. *Journal*. Shenyang Conservatory of Music.

Li, D., Xiu, H, & Yin, A. (2002). *Orff Schulwerk music education philosophy and practice.* Shanghai Education Publishing House.

Liao, N. (2018). An introduction of music pedagogy (Volumes 1 and 2). Central Conservatory of Music Press.

Orff, C., & Keetman, G. (2004). *Music for children* (Liao Naixiong, Chinese adaptation). Schott and Shanghai Education Publishing House. (Original work published 1950)

Roscher, W. (2020, September). The explanation of "Elementar" from Carl Orff: For music educators in China (Yu Danyong, Chinese Trans.). *Art of Music Journal.*

Wang, L. (2012). *Research on localization of Orff Schulwerk teaching method* [Unpublished doctoral dissertation]. Northeast Normal University.

Wu, B. (2014, November). Orff Schulwerk [Speech transcript, Orff Music and Arts Education Forum]. *China Music Education.*

Wu, M. (2016, December). Interview with Sarah Brooke and Xu Mai transcript. *China Music Education.*

Xu, P. (2015, November). Localization of Orff in practice and exploration. *China Music Education.*

Xu, W. (2015, November). The practice of the Orff approach in school music education. *China Music Education.*

Orff Schulwerk in Iran: A New Beginning
Adamak and elemental music education in contemporary Iran

Kamran Ghabrai, Nastaran Kimiavi, Mastaneh Hakimi,
Farzan Farnia, Shahrzad Beheshtian

The history of Schulwerk in Iran

The history of Orff Schulwerk in Iran can be traced back to the 1960s, when a workshop for "Art and Literature" was set up in the Iranian National Broadcasting Company to educate a selected group of children. A set of Orff instruments was imported to Iran for this occasion. Never before had there been any sign of usage of such instruments in Iran. However, these instruments did not come to Iran along with accompanying theories or educated commentators. Thus, they were inevitably used in the very same way Carl Orff had warned about: "Mistaken interpretations and the nonsensical misuse of the instruments threatened in many places to turn the whole meaning of Schulwerk into the very opposite of what had been intended." (Orff, 2011, 150). Therefore, though most instructional tools and even the well-known *Musik für Kinder* volumes had entered Iran, there was still a long way to go in order to learn how to use these tools and resources in the same context as Carl Orff, Gunild Keetman, and their colleagues had in mind.

In the first decade of the 21st century, a small number of Iranian music teachers had the opportunity to study at the Carl Orff Institute and become directly acquainted with the theory and approach of Orff Schulwerk. In 2011, at the eighth Orff Schulwerk Symposium, board members of the Orff-Schulwerk Forum proposed to the Iranian graduates to establish a base for Orff Schulwerk in their own country.

Returning to Iran, these alumni organized a group of enthusiastic teachers, chose the name of "Adamak" and pursued formal goals such as raising consciousness about Orff Schulwerk, adapting this approach, paving the way for developing the knowledge of music teachers, and providing a space for the exchange of these ideas in Iran. The scope and depth of Adamak's activities have increased since that time. Moreover, the establishment of the Iranian Orff Schulwerk Association was on its agenda as well. This was done with the assistance of Barbara Haselbach, the then director of the Forum. Thus, the Iranian Orff Schulwerk Association was formally established with the approval of the Orff-Schulwerk Forum.

Some details of Schulwerk's story in Iran have been described in various writings, including "Adamak–The New Orff Schulwerk Association of Iran" (Kimiavi, 2015). What is important here is the evolution of Schulwerk in Iran. That is the narrative that started from the day of the arrival of Orff instruments in Iran and has continued to the day of the establishment of the Iranian Orff Schulwerk Association in the first decade of the twenty-first century.

To begin the story of how Schulwerk has been integrated into Iranian culture, we will give a description of Iranian music and a short account of the features and possibilities of this culture and the challenges that Schulwerk teachers face.

But before that, it has to be mentioned that music and movement education in modern day Iran is not public, and in the absence of a public music education, each institution adopts a different method according to its arbitrary requirements.

In the present paper, after an introduction to Iranian music, we will focus on movement/dance in Iranian educational systems. Then, we will discuss the speech and features of the Persian language and the challenges related to the rhythm in this regard, and finally we will give a brief account of how Adamak faced these challenges in the past decade.

Iranian music and the Orff Schulwerk approach

Iranian music can be divided into two general categories: "folklore" and *"Dastgāhi."* However, this categorization is independent of the common types such as pop, jazz, & etc. Due to the diversity of Iranian ethnicities, folklore music, whether instrumental or vocal, is very diverse in Iran.

Much of Iranian musical heritage has been partly or completely lost. Yet, the remaining part has been compiled in a collection called *Dastgāh*. *Dastgāhi* music refers to a set of melodies and rhythmic patterns that can be called Iranian classical music. Nowadays, *Dastgāhi* music is taught in various educational institutions. These melodies are remnants of the musical heritage of Iran, which was collected in the present form during the 19th century.

It is crucial to note that when the term "local music" of Iran is used in this text, it refers to the collection of *Dastgāhi* and folklore music of Iran.

The local music of Iran is modal, and it uses intervals that are not necessarily semitones. That is, quarter tone and three-quarter tone intervals are also used in this music. The various tetrachords made up of these intervals are categorized into twelve *Mâyehs*.[1] The structure of these *Mâyehs* arises from various combinations of a major second, semitone, quarter, and three-quarter tone intervals.

Since the late 19th century, due to the import of instruments, works, and theories of Western music into Iran and as a result of incompatibility of modal structure with tonal harmony, a number of musicians, inevitably, sought to adjust the intervals of Iranian music. Prior to this integration with Western theories and instruments, Iranian music ensembles consisted of a set of Dastgāhi instruments, that all played monophonically and in unison. Yet, after this integration with Western polyphonic music, it was no longer possible to preserve the identity of the Iranian modal structure, therefore, this modal structure was tied to the tonal structure through various procedures.

The Orff instruments are not compatible with the quarter tones and three-quarter tones of Iranian music, and the instructors who use these instruments for playing melodies, are unable to play various Iranian pieces.

It is obvious that Orff Schulwerk teachers do not have enough historical material to introduce Iranian music in their classes, particularly in ensembles. Therefore, they are compelled to make new compositions without changing the structure of the *Mâyehs* and to find a new way to adapt the modal system of Iranian music to the basic principles of Schulwerk.

The local music of Iran is based on tetrachords. It is usually the middle tones of each tetrachord that undergo changes in quarter tones or three-quarter tones. Thus, the fourth and fifth intervals of each *Mâyeh* can be used to make drones and ostinati without having problems with quarter tones. It is obvious that we have to either play the melodies—due to their untempered

---

1   Mâyeh is synonymous with Mode. In Iranian local music, each Mâyeh is made up of two tetrachords, but due to the quarter/three-quarter tones, no Mâyeh could be compared to Gregorian modes.

intervals—with the appropriate instrument or sing them and use Orff instruments to create the accompanying context. However, we must pay attention to the fact that all 12 Iranian *Mâyehs* are not capable of such design.

Teacher training course
Photo: Kaveh Seyedahmadian

Adamak teachers and students with traditional instruments
Photo: Shirin Kheiri

Adamak performance ensemble
Photo: Kaveh Seyedahmadian

The place of movement and Schulwerk in Iran

Dance is divided into three categories in Iran: folklore, ritual, and artistic. However, there are no official institutions and centers for teaching and promoting artistic dance. That is—except for a few cases that are in the form of theater—there is no official phenomenon called "stage dance" in contemporary Iran. Nevertheless, different ritual and folklore dances can still be seen in various regions and cities of Iran.

Folklore dances usually have specific forms and movements, each of which is known by a specific name within each region, and usually each dance has its own melody and rhythm. Obviously, if we collect and categorize these movements, we will have a huge resource for working in music classes.

A manifestation of movement in contemporary Iran can be traced in the ceremony of *Muharram*,[1] a religious ceremony in which mostly men perform mourning, self-flagellation, and marching, accompanied by the rhythmic sounds of various kinds of drums and cymbals, with predetermined movements. This ceremony is one of the cases in which one can find the connection between movement and music in public and collective rituals. Muharram ceremonies have found their own movements, rhythms, songs, and rituals in different parts of Iran and there are local varieties in each region. Another instance of movement events can be found in places called *Zurkhāneh*, where special movements are taught with percussion instruments, such as bells and a kind of bass drum. Yet, this activity has always been for men, and has been kept alive only by the efforts of a few centers.

However, like music education, there is no sign of dance or movement training in the official education system of Iran and in the absence of such formal education, music teachers generally turn a blind eye to the relationship between music and movement. This makes it difficult to use movement in the classroom and to show the relationship between music and movement. It can be inferred that generally—but not necessarily—Schulwerk teachers encounter a population that is alien to dance or even expressive gestures and movements or is ashamed to move in the presence of others. This is one of the obstacles an Orff Schulwerk teacher or any other teacher who intends to enter this field may face. However, we can assume that we need long-term planning and effort to show the relationship between music and movement.

Perhaps here we can use Orff's definition of the place of movement and dance in music classes. Orff considers elemental movement to consist of the most natural movements that human beings, particularly children, have an innate tendency to perform. The most important step in moving a community that refuses to dance is to encourage them to do natural locomotion. Walking, running, jumping, moving, etc., are manifestations of the fundamental movements that Orff expected to be used in any culture, with the least reluctance, due to their naturalness. Movement games are an effective tool for all age groups, from young to old, and of course they are elements of Orff Schulwerk, which were somehow neglected from the time instruments arrived in Iran until about a decade ago.

Using movement games, students can get acquainted with their bodies, so that they can use this means for expression. Using rituals and local dances is also a helpful activity. For example, it is possible to introduce movement training into the classroom and reveal the relationship between movement and music by using movement materials and movement games of different ethnic groups. It should be noted that music and dance are fundamentally created by the most natural and primitive elements and gradually expand until artistic maturity is finally achieved.

---

1   The first month of the Islamic calendar

Finally, it is noteworthy that what is more important than anything else is the connection between music and movement, and in this respect, Iranian local and ritual dances and games, or materials from other nations and ethnic groups can be used equally in movement topics.

Students with balloons
Photo: Sepand Saedi

Speech and the capacities of Persian language

The issue of speech usage in Schulwerk is slightly different from the other issues. To clarify this, we must talk about poetry and the meter of words in Persian.

Prior to the modern era, literacy was practiced by the use of classical poetry and word-based methods and designated meters called *Arūd* (prosody). Thus, it can be inferred that music and literature instruction have long been intertwined in Iran—for example, exactly like troubadours and minnesingers, Iranian minstrels and storytellers were poet-musicians who narrated their stories in the form of musical narratives to the people. These narrators usually kept a rhythm consistent with the rhythm of speech.

In the contemporary era and with the introduction of modern methods of music education to the big cities of Iran, those who wanted to instruct music in these new ways, have largely sacrificed the meter of Persian words to Western melodies. Persian words have a mixed rhythm and therefore, they take a variety of rhythmic patterns. This causes the rhythm of Persian words not to be compatible with the meter of the imported melodies.

In practice, many of those who used Orff instruments, actually receded from the principles of Schulwerk. Because when they used imported melodies, they translated the poems of the pieces and, instead of sticking to the rhythm of words, kept the rhythm of the melodies.

In such an atmosphere, it is obvious that pieces made for Iranian children will emerge with exactly the same translational, not interpretational approach, in which the music and words are not integrated.

Although there have always been teachers who have tried to teach rhythm to children using the possibilities and variety of Persian word meters, one of the main elements of Schulwerk, i.e., speech, has not played an independent role in most children's music classes in Iran. Undoubtedly, it is possible to draw the teacher's attention to the meter of speech and the need for its natural expression, by use of Orff Schulwerk theory. That is, more than anything else, it should be noted that the words deserve to be used as an independent and rich source of rhythm.

Iran is the land of poets and has a rich treasure trove of poems, proverbs, verbal games, and poetic stories. Creating melodies that are compatible with these words will, more or less, solve the problem of the incompatibility between the meter of words and the rhythm of the music. Thus, by re-reading and interpreting Schulwerk in the local music of Iran, the Iranian cultural heritage can be added to music classes. Moreover, the Persian poems and words can be used in classes independently and without the need for any melody and musical rhythm.

Adamak and the future of elemental music education in Iran

Iranian society is a growing society, and this growth has been accompanied by an increase in the need and demand for education. If we look at the growth of Schulwerk from this perspective, we inevitably should have long-term plans for the future. The development of Schulwerk in Iran requires the dissemination of this approach through various seminars, the publication of theoretical and practical content, and the holding of workshops and training courses for educators. Instead of being content with educating children, it is necessary to educate parents and music teachers as well.

There are not many existing musical materials consistent with the criteria mentioned in the earlier sections. In fact, the production of a kind of audio-visual resource complying with native identity is necessary. In this regard, an effort that has been made in the last decade is the production of collections such as *Namak*,[1] in which Iranian folklore songs are arranged for Orff instruments while preserving the identity of each song. The *Namak* collection is the result of Adamak's attempt to bring Indigenous and Iranian roots to the current audio culture, in which Orff Schulwerk elements are used alongside familiar melodies so that cultural and educational goals are met. The songs contained in this collection sound different to Iranian ears because there are very few examples of Iranian melodies that are accompanied by modal parts in modern settings. Of course, this would cause quarrels among advocates of traditionalism, but the positive aspect is that Iranian children can hear and work with their national heritage and use these native songs to create their own modern compositions and works of art.

There will be some challenges when using Iranian folklore songs during instruction. For example, in some folklore pieces, the length of the phrases changes dramatically. Also, sometimes the structure of rhythmic patterns is broken, and a free rhythm phrase is performed. This is a characteristic of local music of Iran and should be savored. Therefore, in arranging the songs of the *Namak* collection, a simple and easy-to-understand structure is created, in order to establish a clear relationship between music and movement in instruction. Solutions such as creating an introduction and a middle section for each song, a tangible compositional arrangement of phrases and middle sections, as well as choosing parts with specific and clear lengths, make it easy for the students to understand the form of each song.

On the issue of movement and dance education, it can be noted that the introduction of movement arts into the formal education system faces a problem that arises as a result of a cultural situation. Here, we are not simply dealing with an educational and musical issue, so it is not enough to theorize and produce content. The issue at hand is rather a sociological and historical phenomenon. Also, there is a long way ahead to bring movement into the field of public education and the importance of movement and music is yet to be revealed.

For this reason, Adamak has presented the importance of movement and the need to bring it to education. That is, from the very first teacher training workshop in 2011 until today, more than 70% of the instruction hours and activities are dedicated to movement and the demonstration of the relationship between music and movement. Nowadays, many of the participants who once sat in their places during movement activities and had no desire to play movement

---

1   Folklore songs for children (Namak is the abbreviation of folklore songs for children in Persian), 2015.

games now come to the fore with ease and, clearly, grasp the relationship between music and movement through various actions.

On the subject of literature, it should be noted that from the very beginning of instructing children's music in Iran, poetry and music have been together in the classrooms, but this association was not necessarily consistent with the idea of the correlation of music and speech. Thus, the main issue is the production of content in which this relationship is presented. Therefore, in the workshops of the past decade, Adamak has used Persian poetry to clarify the importance of this for music teachers.

Should all these conditions be met, we would be able to achieve our goal in cultivating a culture of learning-oriented music education, and to make way for a generation that learns to be creative through the means of Orff Schulwerk, a generation that makes contemporary art using materials extracted from Iranian culture. After all, that is what we all pursue.

Adamak has come a long way in bringing this cultural treasure to music classes and connecting music, literature, and movement, but it still has a long way to go. First, we had children in our planning and started to work in children's classes, but gradually we broadened our perspective and now we are trying to work out a more inclusive approach and reach various target groups like seniors and special needs learners. Although this path is very challenging, the prospect is clear: Iran is a land of fruitfulness, a land rich in cultural resources, and home to more than twenty different ethnic groups, whose culture is diverse. So, in hope for a brighter future, we keep paving the road to Orff Schulwerk's growth in Iran.

Translation: Kamran Ghabrai

Adamak's Bibliography:

• *Namak* Collection (Iranian folk songs for children)

– *Namak I*, Adamak Pub, (2015)

– *Namak II*, Adamak Pub, (2018)

• *Where?* Collection

– *At the Farm*, Adamak Pub, (2017)

– *In the Forest*, Adamak Pub, (2019)

– *In the sea*, Adamak Pub, (2021)

• *Namak* Music Score (Teacher's Book)

– *Namak I* Music Score, Adamak Pub, (2016)

– *Namak II* Music Score, Adamak Pub, (2021)

• *Texts on Theory and Practice of Orff-Schulwerk, Vol. I* (Translation into Farsi)

Ghabrai, K. Hamaavaz Pub, Adamak Pub, (2016)

• Publishing articles (writings or translations) in different local and international music magazines

References

Kimiavi, N. (2015, Winter). Adamak–The new Orff-Schulwerk association of Iran. *Orff-Schulwerk Heute*, 93, 92–93.

Orff, C., & Keetman, G. (1950–1954). *Orff-Schulwerk. Musik für Kinder.* Mainz: Schott.

Orff, C. (2011). Orff-Schulwerk: Past and future. In B. Haselbach (Ed.) *Texts on theory and practice of Orff-Schulwerk: Basic texts from the years 1932–2010* (pp. 134–156). Mainz: Schott. (Original work published 1964)

Adaptation of Orff Schulwerk in Japan

Masayuki Nakaji, Tohru Iguchi, Junko Hosoda,
Junko Kawaguchi, Wakako Nagaoka

1. Historical development

In 1953, Naohiro Fukui traveled from Japan to attend an ISME congress in Brussels, Belgium. It is reported that before going to Brussels, he attended a meeting in Salzburg at which Carl Orff was also present. He brought *Musik für Kinder*, volumes 1–5, back to Japan and instructed his student Hisao Kawamoto to study it. This is considered to be the beginning of Orff Schulwerk in Japan.

In 1962, Carl Orff and Gunild Keetman's visit to Japan exerted a decisive influence on the acceptance of Orff Schulwerk in Japan. At the invitation of NHK (Japan Broadcasting Corporation), they gave lectures and concerts with Japanese children in seven major Japanese cities. These were also broadcast on radio and television. Soon thereafter, Orff Schulwerk received a great response from music educators.

From the latter half of the 1960s, Japanese interest in traditional and folk music from around the world has increased, along with a growing awareness of the question of whether music education in the home country should be devoted to Western music. In addition, improving likability of music in schools has come to be discussed. Orff Schulwerk has suggested new possibilities for such situations.

Even before Orff's visit to Japan, Musashino Academia Musicae—the elementary school attached to the University of Tsukuba—along with Takehaya Elementary School—attached to Tokyo Gakugei University—had begun researching Orff Schulwerk and practicing it with elementary school students as well as university students. This work continues to this day. In addition, after Orff's visit to Japan, some Japanese music educators who were impressed by the educational philosophy began studying abroad and training at the Orff-Institute in Salzburg. After returning, they contributed to the spread of Orff Schulwerk in Japan.

In Musashino Academia Musicae, and their attached kindergarten and music school, courses related to Orff Schulwerk were set up for students and children. In some general elementary schools, Orff Schulwerk was used for teaching instrumental ensembles such as recorders (it was not always based on Orff's philosophy, however). Orff instruments started to be manufactured and sold by Japanese musical instrument companies, and this continues today.[1]

In 1973, Yoshio Hoshino and Tohru Iguchi started research activities on Orff Schulwerk at Takehaya Elementary School. Through this activity, it was pointed out that the Orff Schulwerk-related studies up to that point were almost all concerned with introducing the practice but neglected the philosophy behind Orff Schulwerk. This research activity became the basis of the current Orff Schulwerk Association in Japan.

---

1 These companies include Nikkan, Korogi, and Suzuki, among others.

From the 1970s to the present, Japanese Orff Institute graduates have further developed the Orff Schulwerk philosophy at various teacher training institutions, miscellaneous schools and facilities, adapting it to suit the actual situation of Japanese education.

2. Relationship between Orff Schulwerk and Japanese culture

Following Orff and Keetman's visit to Japan, the German version of the Schulwerk was translated into Japanese and published (Orff & Keetman, 1963). In the Japanese translation, most of the melodies of the German version were retained with an unnatural Japanese translation of the lyrics applied. In general, this translated version did not follow the Schulwerk's philosophy of starting education from one's own culture. Overall, the translated version did not reflect the language and musical culture of Japan, leading to some misunderstandings and thus, the transient "Orff Boom" of the 1960s in Japan came to an end. For Japanese music educators at that time, it was difficult to understand and practice music activities with children that centered around improvisation and did not use printed music.

Reflecting on that failure, some music teachers during the 1970s attempted to practice the concept of Schulwerk based on Japan's own culture. They used Japanese rhymes, riddles, choral speaking, traditional children's games (movements), traditional Japanese pentatonic scales, ostinati of Japanese traditional music, traditional musical instruments, traditional dance, and many other traditional elements.

Japanese folk musicologist Fumio Koizumi's studies of *Warabeuta* (Japanese traditional play songs for children) exerted a great influence on adaptations of Orff Schulwerk in Japan.

For example, the rhythm and high-low accents of the Japanese language, scale theory of children's songs, and traditional music provided the basis for Orff Schulwerk practice. The characteristics of Japanese music culture related to the Orff Schulwerk philosophy can be summarized as follows.

Language: The musical elements of the Japanese language have different characteristics from German and other European languages. Japanese has high and low accents rather than strong and weak accents, and the musical rhythm and melody are influenced by this.

Rhythm: Ostinato accompaniment is often used in folk music. In addition, traditional music is characterized by free rhythms (parlando-rubato) and rhythms in which beats expand and contract, a feature specific to Japanese children's game-songs.

Musical Scales: The traditional Japanese pentatonic was the focus of Koizumi's attention (1958/2009).[1] He organized the basic scales used in traditional Japanese music into four types. These also include the scales of Okinawa (southern island of Japan), which has a cultural history distinct from that of the main islands of Japan.

Four types of musical scales in Japanese traditional music
(Whole notes mean the "Finalis")

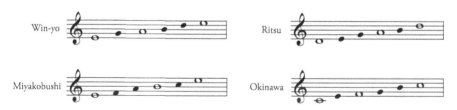

Min'yō is often found in nursery rhymes and folk songs. *Miyakobushi* is used for some folk songs and traditional Japanese music of the Edo period (1603–1868). *Ritsu* is used for *gagaku* (Japanese imperial court music). *Okinawa* can be seen in the music of the southern islands Okinawa and Amami and shares similarities to other Southeast Asian music.

Texture: Japanese traditional music is dominated by heterophony, well suited to bordun accompaniment. Harmonic music has been influenced by Western music since the Meiji era (1868–1912), and children's songs of this type predominate.

Musical Instruments: Japanese drums and other percussion instruments have also come to be used in the practice of Orff Schulwerk. The koto (13-stringed zither) is suitable for ostinato and pentatonic improvisation because its tuning can easily be changed by moving the bridges to match the tuning of an Orff xylophone or metallophone. Recorders are often used in schools because many traditional Japanese wind instruments are difficult for children to play.

Movement: Movement in Japanese Orff Schulwerk focuses mainly on traditional play and folk dance. Dances in traditional Japanese performing arts (Japanese Noh dance) have different styles from those in Europe and the United States in terms of foot movements and hand gestures, but their practice in children's education is limited.

Impact on Education: After Orff's visit to Japan, the 1968 *Course of Study for School: Music* (Monbukagakusho[1]) includes activities found in Orff Schulwerk, such as improvisation with rhythm and "Question and Answer" (Iguchi, 2006). In the current Course of Study for School: Music promulgated by the Ministry of Education (Monbukagakusho, 2017), reference to a specific music education approach such as Orff Schulwerk is avoided. Orff Schulwerk has also come to be practiced in music education situations outside of the school classroom.

A Japanese version of Orff Schulwerk and books on Japanese adaptive practices are being published based on research of Japanese traditional music and educational situations.

Koto class at Hiyoshidaihikari Kindergarten
Photo: Kunihiko Iwamoto

---

1   Monbukagakusho is the Japanese Ministry of Education, Culture, Sports, Science, and Technology.

Wadaiko drumming
Photo: Wakako Nagaoko

3. Implementation of Orff Schulwerk in Japan

The establishment of the Orff Schulwerk Association Japan (OSAJ)

As mentioned in the first section, in the early stages of adaptation in Japan, Orff Schulwerk was incorporated into music education classes of several educational institutions. Beyond those educational institutions, the Orff Schulwerk Association of Japan (OSAJ) was established in 1988.[1] Following this, people who were interested in Orff Schulwerk continued to gather for study-groups and workshops throughout the country, culminating with a small group from all over the country coming together in Tokyo in 1988, where they decided to hold study-group meetings on a regular basis. Since then, this study-group has been making steady progress for more than 30 years, with more than 1,000 participants thus far and a current regular membership of about 150. The two main areas of activity that grew out the study-group are holding seminars and workshops and publishing research journals.

Seminars and workshops

Seminars are held for two days each summer, and workshops are held for either a full or half-day each in autumn, winter, and spring. Participants include teachers from kindergartens, elementary, junior, and senior high schools, nursery school and teacher training university researchers, and individuals who work with people of differing abilities. There are many types of courses for each subject: comprehensive learning courses, and workshops that focus on sound, language, and movement/dance. Activities that focus on any of these three areas are mutually integrated, with an emphasis on improvisation and creativity. The idea of integrating basic movement/dance into music education has been accepted by the members of this study-group. The basic movement/dance is an extension of everyday movement such as walking, running, and jumping, and movement/dance is a medium of expression and communication. In addition, the content of the workshops also includes integration with the fine arts (pictures, photographs, picture books, calligraphy, etc.) and contemporary music techniques (Hoshino, 1993).

The instructors are graduates of the Orff Institute, and various educators and artists who sympathize with the Orff Schulwerk philosophy. Their areas of expertise are diverse and include

---

1   The Orff Schulwerk Association of Japan homepage is https://www.orff-schulwerk-japan.com

recorder, percussion, early music, musical instrument making, grass whistle, drum circles, samba, poetry, language, baroque and contemporary dance, pantomime, and more.

At the seminars and workshops special guest experts on Japanese drums, *Koto* (Japanese zither), *Noh*-theater (using Japanese traditional masks), *Ohayashi* (Japanese festival music and dance), Japanese folk songs, *shakuhachi* (bamboo notched end-blown flute), Okinawa nursery rhymes, etc. are invited to discuss the possibilities for Orff Schulwerk in Japan.

Our subjects expand further outward from Japan to include other East Asian music, for example Korean *samulnori* and Indonesian *gamelan* music and dance. The Association conducts numerous workshops and symposia for students and teachers, but carries out no levels courses, because we regard Orff Schulwerk as an idea and not as a method.

In addition, symposia and practical reports on the possibilities of further Orff Schulwerk development in Japan are held by members and educators as the need arises. Seminars also offer the opportunity for discussion and provide a place for information exchange between participants. These discussions are divided into target groups, such as early childhood education, school education, special needs education, childcare worker training, teacher training, music school, etc. We are learning from the practice and seminars by members while integrating various school levels and types. We are also exchanging opinions on the possibility of putting Orff Schulwerk to practical use. In addition to the reports and research published in *Studies in sound and movement* (OSAJ, 2013–2020), members of OSAJ can learn about the application of Orff Schulwerk educational practices from fellow participants.

Research journals

Initially, the research journal was published twice a year (OSAJ, 1988–2013), but since issue no. 41 in 2013, a new issue has been published once yearly (OSAJ, 2013–2020). In recent years, the number of voluntary research submissions has increased, and they are peer-reviewed before publication. In addition, Japanese translations of Orff Schulwerk-related German articles have been included. Contributing to the further development of Orff Schulwerk in Japan, OSAJ published a comprehensive compilation of research on Orff Schulwerk music education in 2015: *The Theory and Practice of Orff Schulwerk* (Iguchi). The book, which was sold at bookstores nationwide, was written by 15 key members of OSAJ[1] and has detailed and contemporary content.

4. Adaptation to Japanese teaching practice

Today Orff Schulwerk is practiced in various schools throughout Japan, including kindergartens, nursery schools, primary schools, junior and senior high schools, schools for special needs, childcare worker training, teacher training (university), and music schools. Teachers who sympathize with Orff Schulwerk base their practice on the concept of Orff Schulwerk in the context of their own particular educational situations. This includes practice with social and therapeutic pedagogy and music therapy approaches. In addition, there are private organizations[2] that invite officials from the International Orff-Schulwerk Forum Salzburg (IOSFS) to serve as lecturers who speak about various topics such as inclusion education and training.

Although the term Orff Schulwerk is not used in the *Course of Study for School: Music* by the Ministry of Education (Monbukagakusho, 2017), this document has been influenced by

---

1   Tohru Iguchi (ed.), Masayuki Nakaji, Junko Hosoda, Mamiko Kumaki, Wakako Nagaoka, Junko Kawaguchi, Mieko Iguchi, Taku Kosokabe, Noriko Ishigami, Reiko Shibata, Tomoko Nasukawa, Akiko Iizuka, Noriko Matsushima, Noriyuki Suzuki, and Sayaka Arimura.

2   See, for example, MUSE Company: http://www.musekk.co.jp/

activities related to the Schulwerk, such as language, movements and sounds, rhythmic activities using body percussion, question-answer, speech pieces, improvisation and composition using the pentatonic scale. In early childhood education, interest in Orff Schulwerk emphasizes integrated expression through improvisation and composing.

In the Heisei period (1989–2019), the educational direction of Japanese schools changed significantly. In music education, improvised expression was advocated along with the creative music making of John Paynter and others. Orff Schulwerk was favorably re-evaluated along these lines. Activities using body percussion and verbal rhythms have become widespread in schools, along with an emphasis on traditional Japanese music. Pentatonic scales, ostinato, and bordun were to be used in new educational contexts. In addition, the content common to Orff Schulwerk is included in cross-curricular and comprehensive learning.

During this period, the content area "Music Rhythm" was changed to "Expression" in the Ministry's *Course of Study for Kindergarten* (COSK) (Monbukagakusho, 1989). Thus, the relationship between music and other modes of expression became more important. Here again, Orff Schulwerk was re-evaluated. In particular, the concept described in the current COSK (Monbukagakusho, 2017) and the Orff Schulwerk philosophy have much in common. The "Basics of Kindergarten Education" in the COSK states as follows:

a. Encouraging children to undertake voluntary activities and allowing them to lead a life appropriate to early childhood, based on the idea that young children utilize experiences essential to their development through fully demonstrating their abilities in an emotionally stable manner.
b. Ensuring that the aims outlined in Chapter 2 are comprehensively achieved through play-centered instruction by taking into account the idea that play—a spontaneous activity of children—is an important aspect of learning which cultivates a foundation for the balanced development of both physical and mental aspects.
c. Ensuring that instruction in line with developmental issues is carried out based on the individual characteristics of each child by taking into consideration that early childhood development is achieved through diverse processes and interactions between various aspects of both physical and mental elements, and that the life experiences of each child are diverse. (Monbukagakusho, 2017, p. 3)

These pedagogical ideas are similar to those of Orff Schulwerk. They are also keys to aesthetic education that are in common with Orff Schulwerk, which regards expression as an essential part of human life. This is shared with the modern way of thinking about music and movement education. Furthermore, in the COSK, the role of the teacher includes co-working, acting as role model, supporting play, etc. This is the same role as any teacher of Orff Schulwerk.

In Japanese institutions of higher education (junior colleges, universities, graduate schools) one cannot major or specialize in Orff Schulwerk. However, Orff Schulwerk, along with Dalcroze Eurhythmics and the Kodály Method, is recognized as one of the main pillars of music education in the 20th century that influenced music education in Japan. Almost all teacher training and music education books contain a description of Orff Schulwerk as an important component of 20th and 21st century music education. In addition, due to the aspects of Orff Schulwerk that are shared with the COSK and *Course of Study for School: Music*, the principles and practices of Orff Schulwerk are taken up by members of OSAJ in various classes during general teacher training in Japan.

The main issues for OSAJ in the future are the study of cross-disciplinary learning, inclusive education, traditional Japanese music, and Asian music. It is also essential to consider the possibility of activities using digital tools and the Internet since the outbreak of the corona pandemic.

Translation: Masayuki Nakaji and Christoph Mau

References

Hoshino, Y. (1979). *Orff Schulwerk – Theory and its practice.* Tokyo: Zen-On Music Company Ltd.

Hoshino, Y., & Iguchi, T. (1984-1985). *Orff-Schulwerk. Music for children* (Vols. 1–3) (Japanese adaptation). Tokyo: Schott Music.

Hoshino, Y. (1993). *Music learning to create and express. From the perspective of environmental education of sound.* Tokyo: Ongaku no Tomo Sha.

Hosoda, J. (2006). *Exciting sound play easy presentation, from hand clap game to instrumental ensemble.* Tokyo: Suzuki Publishing.

Iguchi, T. (1987). Carl Orff's music for children. In N. Kimura & T. Iguchi (Eds.), *Children and music: Vol. 9. Characteristic music education* (pp. 33–66). Tokyo: Dohosha.

Iguchi, T. (2006). Historical research on the introduction and deployment of Orff Schulwerk in Japan. In M. Kawaguchi (Ed.), *60 years of postwar music education in Japan* (pp. 163–175). Tokyo: Kaisei Publishing.

Iguchi, T. (Ed.). (2015). *The theory and practice of Orff Schulwerk.* Tokyo: Asahi Press Inc.

Kawaguchi, J. (2009). Learn from Orff's music education. In R. Ishii (Ed.), *Learn while practicing – Children's musical expression* (pp. 106–117). Osaka: Hoiku Publishing.

Koizumi, F. (1958/2009). *Study of traditional Japanese music.* Tokyo: Ongaku no Tomo Sha.

Miyazaki, K. (2013). *Carl Orff's musical education.* Tokyo: Styletone.

Monbukagakusho. (1968 & 2017). *Course of study for school: Music.* https://www.mext.go.jp/component/a_menu/education/micro_detail/__icsFiles/afieldfile/2009/04/21/1261037_7.pdf

Monbukagakusho. (1989 & 2017). *Course of study for school: Kindergarten.* https://www.mext.go.jp/content/20201022-mxt_youji-000004376_1.pdf

Musashino Academia Musicae. (1990). *Together with Orff, theory and praxis in 25 years.* Tokyo: Musashino Academia Musicae.

Nagaoka, W. (2016). Today's development of Orff's music and movement education. Reconsideration on the revised edition of "Musik und Tanz für Kinder." *Journal of Music Education Practice,* 14, 125–136.

Nakaji, M. (2000). Problems and potential of the Orff approach in Japan: A comparative study between Japan and German speaking areas. In Japan Music Education Society (Ed.), *Music education studies 1, theoretical study of music education* (pp. 307-321). Tokyo: Ongaku no Tomo Sha.

Nakaji, M., & Tanikawa, S. (1994). *Music for children, words, plays and songs.* Tokyo: Schott Music.

Orff, C., & Keetman, G. (1963). *Orff Schulwerk music for children: Vol. I. Pentatonic* (Japanese translation by Naohiro Fukui, Kan Ishii, et al). Tokyo: Ongaku no Tomo Sha.

Orff Schulwerk Association Japan (Ed.). (1988–2013). *Orff - Music for children reports, 1-40.*

Orff Schulwerk Association Japan (Ed.). (2013–2020). *Studies in sound and movement, 41–48.*

Shibata, R. (2009). *Fun Sound Play for Children.* Tokyo: Ongaku no Tomo Sha.

Orff Schulwerk in Singapore

Paul Grosse

Orff Schulwerk had quiet beginnings in Singapore. During the early 1980s, Singapore's Ministry of Education sent a few teachers to the Philippines to attend introductory Orff Schulwerk workshops. This was in tandem with the proposed new music syllabus that Singapore was then finalizing, which introduced active music making/learning as opposed to passive reception of perceived knowledge in a music class.

However, there was no mention of the Orff Schulwerk philosophy or pedagogy for decades after the initial foray. It was not until 1996 when Yvonne Yong came back from her studies in both the University of St. Thomas, USA, and the Orff Institute, Austria, that once again saw Carl Orff's multi-faceted and holistic music education trying to take root in Singapore.

Orff Schulwerk taking root in Singapore (1995–2005)

After initial conversations with different stakeholders in Singapore, it was decided that Orff Schulwerk would be used within the social work context as Yong was invited to start a program with a "before and after school-care" center in the east of the island. This dealt primarily with challenging children and other children-at-risk, and an integrated arts education program was set up with developmental and intervention goals in mind. It was noted that children who had experienced failure and difficulties in school found success in the arts to be a very positive and motivating experience. Children from the 1995 group are now in their adult years. They have found skills and values appropriate for their work, family, and study as they cope with the developmental challenges in life. A few years later, 1998, the Orff-Schulwerk Society of Singapore was founded by Yvonne Yong.

Foundation of Orff-Schulwerk Society Singapore

The early aims of the Orff-Schulwerk Society Singapore were stated as:

1. to promote the knowledge and understanding of Carl Orff's pedagogical concept.
2. to support the personal and professional development of teachers, therapists, and artists.
3. to work in collaboration with various other arts organizations to research and develop meaningful ways of teaching.

Orff Singapore focused particularly on working with the following groups:

1. day care centers, where children are cared for before and after school
2. wards for children with cancer
3. retirement homes that are open to intergenerational programs
4. centers for early education

During this period, several Orff Schulwerk courses took place in Singapore, led by Mei-Lien Lemye and Yvonne Yong. These workshops were targeted to early childhood educators.

A collaboration with the Lambaga School in Medan, Indonesia, of which Mei-Lien was the director, was planned.

Due to the success of the above Orff Schulwerk courses in Singapore, further introductory workshops were organized for those working within the social work sector to share the ideas and philosophy of the Schulwerk with a larger audience. However, as many of those who attended the workshops are non-music trained, it was felt that a modicum of basic music literacy and music skills would be a beneficial pre-requisite for future participants.

Spreading roots and branches: Orff Schulwerk in Singapore, 2003-2021

The Orff Schulwerk was further utilized by another Voluntary Welfare Group (VWO) from 2003 to 2013. The purpose of the music program was to provide children under this organization's care with the opportunity to learn music. During the initial years, lessons were like any other Orff Schulwerk class, featuring chants, songs, simple arrangements with home-made instruments, and with many performing opportunities. In 2005, a performing group called *Sounds of Providence* was formed. This group consisted of beneficiaries of the VWO charity.

In this program, one could witness the children's growth in confidence and self-esteem as they grew in the mastery of the instruments in the different performances that they participated in. In that short decade, movement, folk-dancing, and percussion instruments were progressively incorporated into the program. The children have benefited from the above through increased use of body coordination and sense of spatial movement. Through improvisation in a highly structured setting, the children have also discovered their innate ability to create something that they can call their own. All this time the children were using local songs and dances of the major ethnic groups found in Singapore: the Chinese, the Malay, and the Indians. Any English songs that were taught were the childhood songs of the author, remnants of the former British colonists.

However, to give them a larger sense of the actual world, many folksongs from different parts of the world were introduced to the children. Through intense work on their voices, the group has managed to sing simple part songs as well as to improve their singing abilities. The children participated in caroling at old-folks' homes and hospitals. This is how they could give back to the community through their artistic performances: they performed for patients in a locked ward in a mental hospital, to mothers nursing their new-born babies.

In the early days, the children had no access to Orff instruments, or had only very few non-pitched percussion instruments. Hence, body percussion, self-made instruments, every-day objects were used to underpin the lessons. It was only after prospective donors saw the success of the program that Orff instruments were made available to the respective centers.

An important development of this decade was in 2006 when the Singaporean government started a program in a school for youths who had failed a national exam twice. In order for these students to stay within the system, an integrated arts program was developed. This program used drama, visual arts, dance, and music in addition to other vocational skills like culinary and basic accountancy skills. The government officials saw the possibility of how the Schulwerk encourages music and movement lessons in a more holistic manner.

Kem Kawan Kawan

A unique program of this period was Kem Kawan Kawan (Friendship Camp). This camp was based on an American music program called Sounds of Hope, which is located in St. Paul, Minnesota, USA. Friendship Camp was envisaged to preserve our own folk songs and dances, as Asia itself has a rich ethnic cultural heritage. Children and their adult companions from Myanmar, Thailand, Malaysia, Indonesia, Nepal, Japan, Philippines, and Singapore came together for ten days to learn each other's songs and dances as well as those from other countries. Through the Orff Schulwerk process, performances were workshopped every two years so that these children as well as adults were given the opportunity to give performances to the wider community.

Most days were spent in rehearsals, working, laughing, and sharing as they learned songs in each other's language and dances from each other's culture. The performances were designed to be cooperative in nature so as to allow the group to learn and present songs and dances from every participating culture.

In rehearsals, the children learned discipline and patience. They discovered a sense of community and feelings of pride and satisfaction. From their artistic experiences, they shared the thrill of creating something special and beautiful together. By staying together as a community, the children also learned to overcome barriers of language and culture.

The adult companions shared in every aspect of the program and had some special activities of their own. They acted as interpreters for the children and provided support and encouragement throughout the days of the program.

Through the opportunity to perform together for the public the children became a living message of international cooperation and friendship, how people of different races can live and work together in harmony and peace.

All those that were involved, the participants, the adult companions, the junior team, the volunteers as well as the organizing committee came away deepened by this experience.

Orff around Southeast Asia

Important growth during this period occurred through connections with people around Southeast Asia. Outreach programs, which in turn became teacher-training programs, were established in Myanmar. Other countries that were visited included Northern Thailand, Laos, Indonesia, and Malaysia. It is important to note that the training or sharing was done in a non-commercial manner, i.e., these trips were on the basis of "teaching locals to fish rather than giving them the fish." Lately there were sessions with boys in a remand school that saw youths and children participating in sessions that were cathartic for a few, including the local teachers.

Workshops and levels training

Other Orff Schulwerk pedagogues travelled to Singapore to give workshops both to the locals as well as to the international schools within Singapore. Esteemed colleagues such as Robyn Staveley, Suzie Davies-Splitter, and Sarah Brooke were invited by private music schools and early childhood experts to train educators here. Both Davies-Splitter and Brooke started levels training under the umbrella of the Australian National Council of Orff Schulwerk. The last training was held in 2017 helmed by Nikki Cox and Bethany Rowe. Through this early training, many early childhood educators in the private sectors started to use the Schulwerk within their schools and lessons.

Other prominent Orff Schulwerk practitioners like Doug Goodkin, Richard Gill, and Kofi J. S. Gbolonyo were invited by international schools to give workshops for their staffs. Local teachers were unable to attend due to many bureaucratic reasons.

Establishment of Orff-Schulwerk Association of Singapore (SingOrff)

SingOrff, the newly resurrected Orff-Schulwerk Association of Singapore, was re-established in 2017 as it was felt that there should be a critical base to sustain its efforts nationally. It is presently run by volunteers.

SingOrff presented their inaugural levels training in 2018. That year saw 46 participants split into two classes. The participants were both local and international, with many coming from international schools around the region. In 2019, both levels 1 and 2 were conducted concurrently. Singapore levels are helmed by Peta Harper, Andrea Ostertag, and Wolfgang Hartmann, who constituted our foreign trainers, whilst the local trainers were Abdul Hakim, Rebecca Lau, and Paul Grosse.[1] In the same year, Barbara Haselbach was invited to give talks and to teach the participants.

Orff Schulwerk within the Singaporean education system

In 2010, the Singapore government established the Academy of Singapore Teachers (AST), primarily to spearhead the professional development of the Ministry of Education staff, strengthening local teachers' knowledge as well as pedagogical training. The Singaporean Education Ministry is currently looking into strengthening both primary and secondary teachers' musicianship, pedagogical skills, and musical knowledge. Experts from Kodály, Dalcroze, and Orff Schulwerk were invited to hold five whole-day workshops, deemed "Milestone workshops," for government music teachers, both primary and secondary. Andrea Ostertag, Mary Walton, Sarah Brooke, and Paul Grosse were trainers in this program over the years. Teachers who had attended these workshops were then allowed to attend "Orff Plus" workshops, again conducted by different Schulwerk experts like Andrea Ostertag, Mary Walton, and Paul Grosse. Orff Schulwerk practitioners like Doug Goodkin were invited to conduct shorter whole-day courses on jazz and blues.[2]

From 2011 onwards, returning teachers enrolled in a professional development course in a local teacher-training university have been exposed to the Orff Schulwerk philosophy. Through this course, many primary school teachers have been inspired to learn more and even volunteer their time in the rejuvenated Orff-Schulwerk Association of Singapore, SingOrff, since 2017. Six teachers are now presently attending the satellite European Mentorship Program. Sharing sessions with local trainee teachers as well as other people keen to know more about Orff Schulwerk have been conducted in the past and there are definitely more to come. Workshops, both face-to-face and online, have been organized to whet the appetite of those wanting to learn more about the Schulwerk.

Other avenues

Since 2014, Paul Grosse has been going into both secondary and primary schools to mentor teachers in the finer details about the philosophy of Carl Orff in a program sponsored by the National Arts Council of Singapore, in partnership with the Ministry of Education. Initially, many teachers were only interested in the activities but lately, it has been possible to marry the philosophy, i.e., the 'why' together with the 'how'—the process/activities. It has to be said

---

1 Individual chapters in Orff Schulwerk books are given to SingOrff's levels participants as reading assignments. See bibliography.
2 The books by Orff practitioners are found within the library and widely read by those interested in the Orff Schulwerk. See bibliography.

that primary schools have been more receptive to the Schulwerk, though secondary schools are slowly warming up to process rather than product-driven pedagogy.

In various universities, one can see Orff Schulwerk inspired lessons being offered to undergraduates taking an education degree. In these universities, local folk tunes were adapted to the Orff Schulwerk approach, which has been customized successfully in Singapore's context. As there is no "one size fits all" model, whenever there is a new cohort, the activities and lessons are adapted and tweaked to the students' needs and capabilities.[1]

The assessments at the end of the course are context driven, where students are expected to identify the constraints of conducting an exclusively Orff Schulwerk class in Singapore schools.[2] They are expected to propose solutions on how they might adapt the Orff Schulwerk approach and overcome the issues they identified. For example, both improvisation and movement are foreign to teachers as well as pupils. Through the mentorship program as described earlier, the Artist in School Scheme (AISS), opportunities were presented to empower both teachers and students to become more adept in using their bodies for moving, as well as being improvisers.

Through the process, students are taught to be independent creative problem solvers too. They are also expected to support their analysis based on theories they have learnt in class. Assessment is applied driven and needs to be evidenced based.

The direction Orff Schulwerk has taken in Singapore

Within the last decade, much research has been utilized and papers were written, and much practical work was initiated in the following areas:

1. How can Cantonese opera and other forms of Chinese opera be adapted into the Schulwerk?
2. The applicability of Orff Schulwerk within the Singaporean classrooms with relevance to social and emotional learning (SEL)
3. The use of improvisation/exploration to facilitate the child's critical and inventive thinking
4. The impact of group work within the Orff Schulwerk class on communication and collaboration skills of the students within the primary school
5. The training of the Orff Schulwerk teacher—artistic facilitator or well-rounded pedagogue—the differences in training within the Orff Schulwerk movement

Orff Schulwerk and SPED (special education) schools in Singapore—how the open-endedness of Orff's philosophy enables students to find success in their lessons

The above were research papers completed in the government primary schools with the research platform called "research in action."[3] It is hoped that more research will be done in the future in the Singaporean context.

In 2016, Orff Schulwerk was introduced into the special needs school where much success was encountered. The students ranged from the deaf, to cerebral palsy clients, and students with autism.

---

1 In local public schools, the masterplan is to have an eclectic music education syllabus, rather than just relying on any one pedagogy.
2 Paul Grosse has been teaching to the trainee teachers in a local teacher training undergraduate program since 2008, giving them insights into the Orff Schulwerk. However, it has to be said that these pedagogy units are not purely about the Schulwerk.
3 The research papers were published under the government and meant to encourage local teachers to be active researchers as well. They are unfortunately not for the general public. The fruits of the research on Chinese operas can be seen in levels training and international conferences. The others are still ongoing.

In present day Singapore, Orff Schulwerk is used both commercially as well as within the public school system.[1] In the latter, there are many teachers who identified with the Orff Schulwerk philosophy. Though these teachers have to subscribe to an eclectic syllabus/style, they are passionate to attend workshops and training outside of their designated professional development hours in order to have greater insights into the Schulwerk. One, too, can see it being used in many child-care centers, early childhood education establishments, and in special needs schools. In the latter, many teachers have found the elemental technique suitable for working with their students.

Bibliography

Estrella, E. (2019, January 24). *The Orff approach to music education for children.* Liveabout dotcom. https://www.liveabout.com/the-orff-approach-2456422

Frazee, J., & Kreuter, K. (1997). *Discovering Orff.* New York: Schott.

Frazee, J. (2007). *Orff Schulwerk today: Nurturing musical expression and understanding.* London: Schott.

Frazee, J. (2012). *Artful, playful, mindful: An essential guide for Orff music teachers.* London: Schott.

Goodkin, D. (2002). *Play, sing & dance: An introduction to Orff Schulwerk.* New York: Schott.

Goodkin, D. (2008). *Intery mintery: Nursery rhymes for body, voice and Orff ensemble.* San Francisco: Pentatonic Press.

Haselbach, B., (Ed.). (2011). *Texts on theory and practice of Orff-Schulwerk: Basic texts from the years 1932–2010.* Mainz: Schott.

Hogan, D. (2014, February 11). *Why is Singapore's school system so successful, and is it a model for the West?* The Conversation. http://theconversation.com/why-is-singapores-school-system-so-successful-and-is-it-a-model-for-the-west-22917

Jorgenson, L. B. (2010). *An analysis of the music education philosophy of Carl Orff* [Master's Seminar Project Report, University of Wisconsin - LaCrosse]. UW-L Seminar Papers. https://minds.wisconsin.edu/bitstream/handle/1793/49113/JorgensonLisa2011.pdf?sequence=1&isAllowed=y

Orff, C., & Keetman, G. (1957-1966). *Orff-Schulwerk. Music for children* (Vols. 1–5) (English adaptation by M. Murray). London: Schott.

Shamrock, M. (1997). Orff Schulwerk an integrated foundation, *Music Educators Journal, 83* (6), 41–44.

Steen, A. (1992). *Exploring Orff: A teacher's guide.* New York: Schott.

Thomas, J. (1980). Orff-based improvisation. *Music Educators Journal, 66* (5), 58–61.

---

1   In public schools, the lessons are Schulwerk-inspired as the whole music curriculum uses Informal Learning, Kodály, Dalcroze, and Orff Schulwerk. It is up to the individual teachers to decide how they want to deliver their lessons. A few definitely lean more toward Orff Schulwerk.

Orff Schulwerk in South Korea

Hye-Young Kim, Sung-Sil An, Hyeon-Kyeong Kweon
(Sr. Johannita), Young-Bae Yun, Oh-Sun Kwon, Yeni Kim,
In-Hye Rosensteiner

Introduction

Geographically positioned as a peninsula between Asia and its island chains, Korea's culture relates closely to the cultures of its neighbors, a convergence of diverse traditions. Thus, Korean traditional music has long incorporated Chinese and—starting in the last century—also Western influences, which after the 1900s developed the musical culture and traditional music style on the peninsula. Although music education since modern times has emphasized Western styles as its most important foundation, traditional Korean music must also be included, thus highlighting our efforts to provide national and international learning platforms. Carl Orff himself postulated that the original idea of the Schulwerk should be integrated into the traditional culture of each country.

1. The culture of Korea

1.1. Traditional Korean music

Traditional Korean music can be classified as **Court Music** (*Jeongak*) and **Folk Music** (*Minsokak*)

Court Music (*Jeongak*) was played during feasts or ceremonies held in palaces, royal processions, military parades, and was enjoyed by aristocrats outside the palace grounds. Today it is mainly performed in concerts and also for tourists.

Types of Jeongak:

- *Jeryeak* - Music for Ancestral Ceremonies
- *Jongmyo Jeryeak* (Royal Ancestral Ritual Music) - https://youtu.be/GmT4WiU2QTQ
- *Munmyo Jeryeak* (Confucian Shrine Music) - https://youtu.be/adcGeuTMmBA
- *Yeonryeak* (Court Inquiries, Banquet Music) - https://youtu.be/OJ_XKkUjHq8
- *Gunryeak* (Military Parade Music) - https://youtu.be/vlWM6WhpiFY
- *Jeongga* (Korean vocal music such as songs, lyrics, and traditional three-verse Korean poems) - https://youtu.be/XQuVvhp5PLg

Folk music (*Minsokak*) was and is an expression of joy of life or sadness of the local people but was also often connected with the physical labor of the rural population, including work songs to enhance the efficiency of their collective hard work. Also, most children's games involve singing and movements and are part of the tradition of our folk music.

Types of Minsokak:

- *Pansori* (A long epic chant with a single singer accompanied by a drummer) - https://youtu.be/QkwEaU6RgLA
- *Byongchang* (Any part in a pansori accompanied by the stringed instrument gayageum) - https://youtu.be/mcBrdW9-u5Y
- *Sanjo* (A form of instrumental solo under Korean folk music) - https://youtu.be/ldU-9jZQtYbs

1.2. The characteristics of Korean traditional music

Melody and scale: The concept of Western harmony in music does not apply because the music was made using the characteristics of the melody itself. It is based on playing a melody even when various instruments are performing. Korea's five-note system is separated into two parts: *pyong*-scale and *kyemyun*-scale.

- *Pyong*-scale—A scale arranged in Sol, La, Do, Re, Mi and is similar to the Western G pentatonic scale.
- *Kyemyun*-scale—A scale arranged in La, Do, Re, Mi, Sol and is similar to the Western minor pentatonic.

Rhythm: *Jangdan* is a general name for rhythm, meaning the speed, pulse, and time structure of a song or movement.

Various types of singing

- Call and response. A singer improvises a song (Give - *megigi* 메기기 in Korean), several people sing the refrain together (Receive - *batgi* 받기 in Korean).
- Alternation: A singing form in which two people or two groups sing alternately with each other.
- Singing storytelling: The lyrics are more important than the melody, the soloist decides when it is more of a recitative or a certain repeated melody.

Notation (the *Gibo* method):

King Sejong created in the 15th century a notation called *jeongganbo*. It is written from top to bottom and from right to left. The notation of rhythm in *jeongganbo* form can easily be used with children. Today Western notation is also used.

King Sejong's legacy: Korean notation (jeongganbo)
https://www.youtube.com/watch?v=wz4wvLwr8aY&feature=youtu.be

1.3 Characteristics of the Korean language

Korea has its own original alphabet, known as *hangeul*, with 14 regular consonants and 10 vowels. Hangeul was invented by King Sejong, the 4th King of the Joseon Dynasty (1392-1910).

Before *hangeul* was invented, people in Korea learned *hanja* (Chinese characters), which was very difficult to learn. Therefore, there were many illiterate people. *Hangeul* is a phonetic writing system that allows us to represent the individual sounds of consonants and vowels in writing. Korean sentences have the form "subject + object + predicate." Korean has a rich vocabulary for describing emotions as well as expressing subtle differences, and it also uses a great deal of onomatopoeia.

The language is characterized by very complex phonological composition, which produces various sounds depending on the combination and sequence of words. The meaning of words in terms of accentuation and intonation generally does not change, except by raising the pitch at the end of an interrogative sentence. Across the country, regions are distinguished by slight dialectal colorations, and sometimes even different words and intonations are used for the same terms.

There are many forms of traditional folk literature (proverbs, riddles, fairy tales, fables, children's rhymes, etc.) that are still alive in families and in the everyday life of children and are used in Orff Schulwerk classes as well.

1.4 Instruments

Most educational institutions have traditional percussion instruments (for example, *kkwaeng-gwari* and *jing*—metal instruments similar to smaller or larger gongs—and *janggu* and *buk*—two types of double skin drums) that are used for the traditional Korean percussion quartet, *samulnori*. These instruments are also played by dancers to accompany their own group dances. In addition to percussion instruments, there are various traditional Korean stringed instruments such as *gayageum* (twelve-stringed arched board zither), *geomungo* (six-stringed zither), and *haegeum* (two-stringed tubular spike violin). Some examples of wind instruments are *piri* (cylindrical double-reed instrument made of bamboo), *daegeum* (bamboo transverse flute), and *taepyeongso* (the metal shawm). Class teachers learn to teach instruments during training, but external specialist teachers are usually invited to play traditional Korean instruments.

The four types of percussion instruments in the samulnori: kkwaenggwari, jing, janggu, buk
Photo: Hyo-Jung Lee
See also: https://www.youtube.com/watch?v=W-xYoK3fQrk

1.5. Current types of music in South Korea

In modern South Korea, the genre K-pop (South Korean popular music) is gaining more and more popularity. Famous examples of current idol groups are BTS and Blackpink. In addition, original well-known musicals from the West, as well as South Korea's own creative musicals of different genres are popular. In the field of "classical" serious music, too, one can find numerous soloists, ensembles, and orchestras in South Korea.

As singers, dancers, and rappers, the K-pop musicians are role models for many children and young people. As in the Orff Schulwerk, music, dance, and language are always connected in the K-pop world. There are more and more Orff Schulwerk teachers who use K-pop in their lessons as an improvisational impulse.

Traditional Korean music is still cultivated in various forms. *Samulnori* (traditional percussion quartet), one of these popular musical activities that has been preserved to this day, used to be played in the context of agricultural work. Due to the vitalizing character of the music, *samulnori* gained international recognition and has an inspiring effect on many areas of music. Collaborations with jazz musicians, classical orchestras, and dance performances have been established.

2. A brief description of the South Korean state music education

Music lessons are offered in South Korean schools for all age groups. In kindergarten and primary school, the class teacher teaches music along with all other subjects. In private schools or, in special cases, in public schools, a trained music educator teaches the subject of music. In the middle and upper school classes, a separate teacher is usually responsible for each subject. From middle school onwards, there is little instruction in the area of the integration of the arts because the educational focus is on the main subjects (math, Korean, English).

Since the early childhood education guidelines were revised in 2019, there are once again more opportunities in education to awaken children's interests in creative arts and aesthetics. Formerly, musical activities consisted of music and dance as separate activities in schools. In kindergarten, however, these components were now integrated. With the recent introduction of the Orff Schulwerk concept into the curriculum, interest in elementary music and dance education has also increased among many teachers, who offer some form of integrated aesthetic education themselves. This is still done through individual efforts and is mostly still limited to kindergartens and primary schools. In 2020, "improvisation," "creativity," and "music and dance" were integrated into the basic plan for revitalizing arts education in schools. The learning process in the areas of "artistic expression" and "creative thinking skills" can thus be promoted.

3. The development and adaptation of Orff Schulwerk in South Korea

3.1 The foundation of the Korean Orff Schulwerk Association (KOSA)

During the 1970s, Orff Schulwerk was introduced to South Korea by Professor Jeong-Sik Jeong and Sister Myung-Ja Hwang (Sr. M. Michaelis), who had studied at the Orff-Institute, but it was not yet widely spread. Since then, people who operated a music education research institute gathered together to found KOSA. At the same time, educational institutions for Orff Schulwerk were assembled and organized as affiliated organizations of KOSA and began to educate teachers and issue certificates.

History of (KOSA) chairpersons:

1st & 2nd 2004–2008:	Myung-Ja Hwang (Sr. M. Michaelis)
3rd & 4th 2009–2012:	Young-Jeon Kim
5th & 6th 2013–2016:	Hee-Sook Lee
7th 2017–2018:	Kyu-Sik Kim
8th 2019–Current:	Hye-Young Kim

3.2 Orff Schulwerk certificate course

A certificate course is open and operated by five affiliated institutions:

- Orff Schulwerk Music Center Institute: Hye-Young Kim
- Notre Dame Orff Schulwerk Education Institute: Hyeon-Kyeong Kweon (Sr. Johannita)
- Korean Orff Schulwerk Music Education Institute: Kyu-Sik Kim
- Elemental Music Pedagogy Institute: Hee-Sook Lee
- Korean Orff Schulwerk Institute: Young-Jeon Kim

In 2019, we reorganized our certification course into three levels, implemented in September 2020.

3.3 International Orff Schulwerk seminar

Since founding the association, KOSA has invited international Orff Schulwerk teachers from the Orff-Institute and elsewhere every year from 2005 to 2015. (Werner Beidinger, Christa Coogan, Ari Glage, Doug Goodkin, Micaela Grüner, James Harding, Barbara Haselbach, Insuk Lee, Sofía López-Ibor, Andrea Ostertag, In-Hye Rosensteiner, Shirley Salmon, Karin Schumacher, Doris Valtiner, Manuela Widmer, Michel Widmer, Christiane Wieblitz, Angelika Wolf).

Every second year since 2016 the seminars are held with national instructors in order to strengthen and develop South Korean Orff Schulwerk teachers' capabilities and to discover new domestic instructors.

3.4 Publication of a magazine

All issues published from 2007 to the 20th issue in December 2020 provide information on Orff Schulwerk news at national and international levels, with the arts and education as primary topics of discussion. For more information, please refer to the website of the Korean Orff Schulwerk Association http://www.eng.korff.or.kr/

3.5 The situation at present

Recently at the national level, the educational approach has changed to student-centered education and encouraged play-oriented, creative education. For this reason, music areas that have been separated are now integrated into the arts education policy.

In addition, the number of ethnic minorities and immigrants has been increasing in South Korea recently, and many are becoming students. Thus, multicultural elements are widely used in music education as they share their own culture, art, and lifestyle as part of the school curriculum. Traditional folk songs, dances, and songs from various cultures, including Africa, the Americas, Europe, and Asia are used as class materials.

In South Korea, most students stop their artistic activities at the age of nine and begin to focus on their main studies. Sometimes training in musical instruments is offered at a private school. Therefore, in order for music education to develop robustly, it is necessary for the state to focus on arts education, hire new arts teachers, and distribute musical instruments and materials to provide arts teachers with diverse and broad opportunities.

Currently, there are not many teachers who can teach integrated arts in public education institutions, so professional instructors are invited to provide students with an opportunity to experience the arts even for a short period of time. However, instructors often complain of difficulties because they have to concentrate on product-oriented evaluations.

3.6 The connection between traditional Korean arts and Orff Schulwerk

South Korean Orff Schulwerk teachers creatively use the diverse traditional materials of music, dance, and language in the classroom. The traditional choreography of the dances can be varied in a modern way in class, e.g., the *buchaechum* (fan dance) or the famous *talchum* (mask dance), which used to caricature and criticize the rulers. In this way, various stories can be told in music-theatrical form. Painting, which has always been an important genre in Korean art, along with calligraphy, which shows lines and shapes in artistic form, serve as impulses for music and movement improvisation.

4. At present Orff Schulwerk is taught in the following target groups:

1. Private kindergartens and daycare centers: Most of them are group classes with 10 to 25 students. (Proceeds as a regular course)
2. Although there are a small number of private elementary schools or foreign schools that have designated Orff Schulwerk courses as regular subjects and qualified teachers, they generally conduct classes in the form of special lectures, not regular courses.
3. Arts education has been largely overlooked due to Korea's still great emphasis on entrance exams, but the number of arts education courses has been increasing in recent years. These courses consist of either a large group for all classes or as a small group in the form of a club, also inviting arts instructors separately.
4. University: The Western music education methods, including Orff Schulwerk, are being taught alongside *gugak* (traditional Korean music) education in universities that focus on early childhood and primary education.
5. Training of Orff Schulwerk teachers: The five institutions that belong to the aforementioned collaboration have trained teachers who specialize in Orff Schulwerk pedagogy and certified those who have completed education under the KOSA name.)
6. Music Therapy: Several music therapists with certificates from KOSA apply experiences to their own treatment sessions. In addition, there is a place where an Orff Schulwerk ensemble is formed around the developmentally disabled (Hanwoolim Band - leader Bo-Hye Shin).
7. Facilities and Welfare Centers for seniors are interested in Orff Schulwerk classes. Currently, teachers (Hyeon-Kyeong Kweon /Sr. Johannita, Jin Kim, etc.) who have received Orff Schulwerk certificates work with group classes at a small number of facilities, and this is expected to expand gradually.
8. Commercial institutions: In addition to the five institutions recognized by the association, people who do not obtain Orff Schulwerk teacher certificates may offer courses under unofficial entities for business purposes, with or without sufficient knowledge of Orff Schulwerk. These places require observation.

Translated and adapted Publications

Lee H. S., & Rosensteiner, I. H. (2007). *Music and Dance for Children*. Samho Music.

Translation

Kim Y. J. (2006). *Carl Orff. The Schulwerk*. Music World.

Domestic publication

Kim J. S., et al. (2010) *Orff and EMP*. Dongmunsa.

Kim Y. J. (2008). *How to Compile Orff Instruments*. Music World.

Kim Y. J. (2009). *Children's Song Ensemble with Orff Instruments*. Music World.

Lee H. S. (2013). *Orff Music Trip by the Giant and Mouse*. Music World.

Orff Music Center Institute. (2011). *Fun fun Orff Classic & Fun fun Orff Christmas*.

Orff Music Center Institute. (2013). *Orff Program for Teachers*.

Exciting Mu & Mo Orff 1, 2, 3. (2018). *Mu&Mo* [Mu&Mo stands for Music & Movement].

Articles in the international magazine *Orff-Schulwerk Heute* (formerly *Orff-Schulwerk Informationen*)

South Korean as well as visiting international guest teachers have written several articles about the development of Orff Schulwerk in South Korea. (see Index in: www.orff-schulwerk-forum-salzburg.org/magazine-osh)

Closing remarks

South Korea places a very high value on education and most of the education is aimed at going to a good university. Therefore, many young people give up their artistic activities because they concentrate on learning the main subjects of math, Korean, and English. Exceptions are students who want to prepare for a professional career in the arts. Here, too, the competition in Korea is very high.

Although the Orff Schulwerk has not existed for very long in South Korea, it has grown rapidly since KOSA was founded. KOSA strives to integrate the spirit of Orff Schulwerk into the strongly performance-oriented South Korean educational reality in order to promote the development of the individual personality through creativity, Korean cultural assets, and the arts in education. With its work, KOSA wants to achieve that as many people as possible find carefree access to the arts through music and movement as well as integrated artistic activities.

References

Ministry of Health and Welfare. (2019). *Notice of Nuri program by age of 3–5 years old*, general revision. Ministry of Health and Welfare No. 2019-152.

National Folk Museum of Korea. (2021, January). *Encyclopedia of Korean folk culture*. https://folkency.nfm.go.kr/en/main

National Gugak Center. (2021, January). http://www.gugak.go.kr/site/main/index-001?menuid=001&lang=en

Wikipedia. (2021, January). *Music of Korea*. https://en.wikipedia.org/wiki/Music_of_Korea

Orff Schulwerk in Taiwan

Fang-Ling Kuo [1]

Some historical aspects

The beginnings of Orff Schulwerk in Taiwan fall into the period of social, economic, and political openings of the country. Taiwan entered a period of economic growth and industrialization during the 1960s. This was often referred to as the "Taiwan Miracle." The democratization phase in the 1970s went hand in hand with a process of "Taiwanization," which meant that local culture and history were promoted more. At the same time, independent and creative thinking began to blossom in Taiwanese society. New values, a different way of life, and new attitudes created an atmosphere of openness and curiosity. New ideas in the arts, music, dance, music education, and cultural development by and large were flourishing. Through seminars and courses, Orff Schulwerk activities began to influence and enrich music education in Taiwan from the late 1960s onwards. At the time of the creation of this article it has been 50 years since the first seeds of the Orff Schulwerk concept began to bear fruit in educational settings of Taiwan. It is worth taking a brief look at the beginnings of the Schulwerk in Taiwan.

An early development

In the late 1960s Reverend Alphonse Souren was one of the first teachers who worked with Orff Schulwerk in Taiwan in Guangren (Kuang Jen) Elementary School situated in the Wanhua district of central Taipei. Souren had studied Orff Schulwerk pedagogy in Belgium and established a small Orff Schulwerk professional development center in Guangren in 1969. The period between 1969 and 1980 was the foundation period of Orff Schulwerk in Taiwan. En-Se Su, Jong-Teh Lin, Tseng Liguang, and Hwei-Ling Chen, were some of the initial leading developers of this educational idea. Based on the German original, the first Chinese model examples were created and published. The first volume carried the subtitle *Five Tone Scales* (1972) and the second volume, Major (1979). During the following years a number of publications by the Sin Lau Children's Music Centre in Tainan and the Catholic Hua-Ming Publishers generated more children's songs, basic music books, and musical arrangements for Orff instrumentation. These efforts in conjunction with a proliferation of private music and movement studios contributed to the growing popularity of the Schulwerk in Taiwan. The idea began to spread further in different regions of Taiwan. Many international interchanges took place between European, American, and Taiwanese teachers. The following people and interchanges represent some of many occasions that contributed to the continuing and lasting growth of the Schulwerk in Taiwan over the next five decades:

---

1 The editor acknowledges Christoph Maubach with grateful thanks for his diligent editing of this article.

- Jos Wuytack, a lecturer from the University of Leuven in Belgium, held a three-day Orff Schulwerk workshop in 1977. Three hundred primary and secondary school teachers participated.
- As a result, quite a few teachers felt inspired to travel to Europe to study the applications of Orff Schulwerk as elemental music and movement education.
- Hwei-Ling Cheng (1954-2013) studied Orff Schulwerk with Wuytack in Belgium and began to write musical arrangements for Taiwanese folk songs based on the Schulwerk.
- Jong-Teh Lin established his own elemental music and movement studio in Tainan in 1971.
- In 1983 Barbara Haselbach undertook a two-week workshop/seminar for more than 150 participants in Taipei. This can be seen as a key event for growing a deeper understanding of elemental music and dance education and for the proliferation of Orff Schulwerk in Taiwan.
- Another outcome of Haselbach's visit in Taiwan was Chia-Shu Liu's enrolment in the Advanced Studies in Music and Dance Education at the Orff-Institute in Salzburg (the Special Course).
- Upon her return to Taiwan Chia-Shu Liu developed the Ren-Ren Children's Music Studios in Taipei, Taichung, and Kaohsiung. Over many years these studios were very successful and contributed significantly to the spread of Orff Schulwerk in Taiwan.
- Ching-Mei Lee was one of many Taiwanese teachers who attended the Orff Institute Special Course.
- The work of Hwe-Ling Cheng and other Taiwanese teachers who studied elemental music and movement education overseas shaped the Orff Schulwerk in Taiwan into the late 1990s and beyond.
- By the end of the 1990s, 20 Taiwanese teachers had participated in the Special Course in Salzburg. Many more undertook the Salzburg course in the decades that followed later.
- Teachers also attended Orff Schulwerk teacher education courses in the USA, Australia, and New Zealand, and others attended summer courses at the Orff Institute.

Adaptation

The beginning phases of the Schulwerk adaptation in Taiwan saw only minor modifications from its original German language concept. What followed next, if one were to follow Carl Orff's image of the wildflower development, could be termed a period of cultivation of Orff Schulwerk in Taiwan (1980-1995). During this phase, the actual application of Schulwerk in practice, i.e., elemental music and dance education, was stimulated largely by workshop experiences with international Orff Schulwerk exponents including many teachers from the Orff Institute as well as returning graduates.

More than in previous periods, however, Taiwanese Orff Schulwerk enthusiasts now began to develop the core principles of the idea for their own cultural and educational settings. Because a focus on energetic and persistent learning with repetition and diligence are part of the national psyche in Taiwan, the teachers took on the ideas of Orff Schulwerk with great enthusiasm. Elemental music experiences came into practice in group activities, often in large numbers. As a consequence, Orff Schulwerk children's classes grew steadily in popularity throughout Taiwan. Creative group activities, observing others in their creative endeavors and relating back to what was already part of their educational repertoire gave Taiwanese participants the confidence to slowly and carefully grow the seeds in their own flowering way.

The place of dance and movement in Taiwanese and other Asian communities is defined in particular cultural ways. To have movement and dance included in music and aesthetic education was sometimes new for Taiwanese kindergartens, schools, and community centers. Nevertheless, the idea of incorporating dance and movement in creative pathways for heightening sensibilities and for deeper artistic understandings was accepted in many different ways. Exploring and creating with stimuli such as poetry or stories, recorded music or visual imagery, body percussion, melodies or rhythms and then combining this with local materials such as Taiwanese instruments, melodies, dances, shadow plays, and instrumentations became eventually part of the Taiwanese oeuvre.

From the 1990s onwards music education in creative and playful ways fit with a changing *Zeitgeist* in Taiwan. When creative processes were guided in scaffolded pedagogical ways, Taiwanese educators and students were the most comfortable. Becoming conscious of the elements of dance and music in intentional ways, developing ideas creatively whereby the playful processes become as important as the musical or dance outcomes, these were, broadly speaking, the goals of elemental music and movement education in Taiwanese settings.

Period of development and cultivation

Classes in the first three decades of Orff Schulwerk in Taiwan took place in after-school sessions or Saturday morning schools, and more often than not in private music studios. This development dovetails a growing small business culture driven by the very curious and industrious Taiwanese people. Buddhism and Confucianism have contributed to a lifestyle that encompasses the belief that self-cultivation and self-creation are desirable, and citizens can be taught in many personal and communal accomplishments. People in Taiwan thrive for success in many areas of life, and music and other artistic expressions belong in these areas as well. Families send their children to extracurricular activities, sometimes for several hours after official primary school hours. In private music studios, creative music and movement as part of music learning became very popular. Teachers were able to set up large studios with parquetry floors, mirrors, and extensive sets of imported Orff Schulwerk instruments, melodic and non-melodic percussion instruments, as well as recorders. In these first decades the Taiwanese adaptation of elemental music and movement education came to the fore largely as an imported Western educational concept rather than one that is interwoven with local musical experiences and expressions.

The development of the next decades shows a transformation of Schulwerk with an outlook and focus on more holistic ways in education and with efforts to integrate local non-Western music and movement. This later development also includes the integration of music and movement for children as a pedagogy in tertiary education and formal teacher training. Elemental music pedagogy has spread and is now practiced and adapted for different settings and populations in Taiwan, including kindergartens, primary schools, and tertiary schools. If one were to summarize key teaching-learning processes they would contain the following:

- Guided creative activities are important features in children's lessons and workshop sessions.
- Various forms of imitation appear during the session.
- Guided exploration and free exploration foster creative processes.
- Brief models by small groups or individuals can serve as examples.
- Improvisation in movement and music follow.
- Music and dance improvisation build the foundation for composition.

- The desire to "fix" a composition leads to an engagement with literacy.
- Pictorial and non-traditional notation precede traditional notation of music and dance.
- Principles such as "simple to complex" and "begin with a small seed of an idea and let it sprout to a larger artistic whole" have become part of elemental music and movement in Taiwan.

A holistic approach

Ching-Mei Lee was one of the teachers who returned from Salzburg to establish her own music studio in Taipei, called the "Genesis Orff music private classroom." Her particular interests and activities included music and movement with disadvantaged learners and also the engagement with local Indigenous Taiwanese minority groups. Her initiatives, her awareness of the local customs, language, and needs opened new doors for Taiwan's music education. Other Orff Schulwerk enthusiasts followed the path that Ching-Mei Lee began. In the eastern inland mountains of Taichung and in the Pingtung region of the south, Orff Schulwerk teachers began conversations and activities with some of the 15 different cultural and language groups of Taiwan.

The Indigenous people of Taiwan, often referred to as Gāoshān people, make up about 3% of the entire population of Taiwan, which totals about 23.5 million. Of the different Indigenous language and cultural groups, the Ami people are the most well-known. Indigenous Taiwanese show that music, dance, and cultural expressions are still healthy and functioning, and meetings with Orff Schulwerk teachers can be fruitful for both parties: The Orff Schulwerk teacher learns about language, custom, dance, and essential cultural expressions while sensibly sharing the process of creative education in a tactful and unpretentious way. Music and movement with fringe and other community groups became part of the Taiwanese Schulwerk growth.

Since the mid-1980s there has been a development of a deeper understanding of movement and dance in elemental music education and aesthetic education in general. Enabling and enticing participants to find their own movement vocabulary and expressiveness—even when the well-developed traditional Taiwanese dance forms and mannerisms seem a closer option—has been like cutting the Gordian knot.

The role that the media can play in the proliferation of the Orff Schulwerk approach is demonstrated in the 1988 example of a Taiwanese television program produced by Orff Schulwerk exponent Ching-Mei Lee. The TV series showed 13 programs in which creative processes and outcomes of the Orff Schulwerk approach were shown. They were loosely based on a famous Taiwanese tale, *The World of the Winter Watermelon*. The popularity of the TV series and the proliferation and growth of other private music studios with their varied music and movement offerings helped popularize Orff Schulwerk amongst children and parents. The encouragement of children's creative abilities in emphasizing Chinese culture and folk music along with a spirit of collaboration and physical and emotional growth represent significant qualities of the Taiwanese Schulwerk development. From about 1988 the Orff Schulwerk was widely adopted. The spark was ignited, and it sprang over to many educational institutions.

Taiwanese Orff-Schulwerk Association—establishment and activities

Following these diverse and occasionally disparate developments, a volunteer group of teachers got together and in 1992 formed a support association, the Chinese Orff-Schulwerk Association of Taiwan. In 2009 the name was incorporated and changed to Taiwanese Orff-Schulwerk

Association (TOSA).[1] The majority of TOSA's members are teachers of music in kindergartens, preschools, and primary schools. The TOSA board is composed of 15 members. TOSA membership has, as it often happens with Orff Schulwerk associations, a fluctuating membership ranging between 30 and 150 members. The board, which aims to meet four times a year, is elected every 2 years. TOSA organizes workshops with local and international presenters and publishes a bimonthly bulletin. It also offers regular TOSA yearbooks, which are based on a particular theme related to the adaptation of Orff Schulwerk in Taiwan. TOSA board members often provide professional advice to potential members and newcomers of the organization.

Within the most recent decade there has been a strong increase in the dissemination of Orff Schulwerk in the university sector of Taiwan. Teacher education programs as well as professional music performance courses nowadays include units of work with a focus on elemental music and dance education. TOSA sees its purpose in fostering the art of music and movement teaching in all areas of education. It hopes to provide pathways for advanced Orff Schulwerk teacher education, and it aims to fulfill social responsibilities as well. This last aspect comes into focus through the engagement with disadvantaged and Indigenous populations.

TOSA has established and disseminated numerous Orff Schulwerk teacher education and professional development initiatives in Taipei, Taichung, and Kaohsiung. Increasingly it provides opportunities with in-service training for early childhood and primary school teachers. Often a number of students from university courses join these in-service sessions at reduced cost. This is one way that enables TOSA to maintain a younger membership and curate a careful succession in the future. Central beliefs, techniques, and processes of Orff Schulwerk are being re-echoed through the workshops, seminars, and now also online events that TOSA organizes. On TOSA's future agenda rest issues such as more integration of original local music and dance, maintaining good quality Orff Schulwerk development, and the perspectives of a unneighborly exchange possibly through an Asian Orff Schulwerk Alliance.

Practices and trends

Many deeper insights and experiences of Orff Schulwerk as an aesthetic and holistic education are fostered. Taiwanese Orff Schulwerk teachers embrace the basic principle that the Schulwerk includes the unity of music, dance, and speech and that this type of learning is creative, artistic, and experiential. Theoretical knowledge is gained through experiences with music, movement, and the arts, which develop in process and outcome correspondingly. In addition, we consider that music and movement are also for personal development. The period after 1995 and until 2020 can be described as a growing phase of TOSA. Orff Schulwerk has well and truly taken a foothold in Taiwan. The following key expressions affirm some of the current Taiwanese Schulwerk practices and trends:

---

1   http://www.orff.org.tw

- Movement brings the participants into creative spheres, inwardly and outwardly.
- Sensitization opens the mind.
- Listening is paramount.
- Imagining and comprehending sound and music are part of education.
- Creative movement experiences are essential.
- Intentional movement experiences nurture kinetic learning.
- Stories and poetry provide stimuli.
- Fine arts examples can offer different entries to artistry in music and movement.
- Local instruments and vocal expressions are integrated with traditional Western sound sources.
- Local cultural languages, customs, and expressions are integrated.

In summary, the characteristics of local traditions and mores, Taiwanese and Chinese languages, Chinese poetry, songs and artistic expressions as they are unique to Taiwan, including puppetry, traditional dances, and local instruments all have now become part of the Orff Schulwerk oeuvre in Taiwan. There has been a very considerable proliferation of Orff Schulwerk, and applications are found in school, community, and welfare education settings, private music studios, kindergartens, primary schools, some secondary schools, in undergraduate teacher education courses, in graduate diploma and master's in education degree programs, music performance courses, in some dance studios, and in situations with disadvantaged and minority groups.

Bibliography

Keetman, G., & Lin, J.-T. (Eds). (1986). *Taiwanese and Chinese children's songs for voices and Orff instruments. Texts in English, German, and Chinese.* Taipei, Taiwan: Lin Jong-Teh.

Lin, J.-T. (n.d.). *Class textbooks 1–3* (in Chinese). Tainan, Taiwan: Lin Jong-Teh Music Education Centre.

Su, E.-S. (Ed). (1972). *Orff Schulwerk. Music for children, Chinese edition, Vol. 1. Pentatonic.* Taipei: Catholic Hua-Ming Publications.

Tseng, L., & Chen, H.-L. (Eds). (1979). *Orff Schulwerk. Music for children, Chinese edition, Vol. 2. Major.* Taipei: Catholic Service Centre of Historical Relics.

Orff Schulwerk in Thailand

Krongtong Boonprakong, Wittaya Laithong,
Amanut Jantarawirote, Geeta Purmpul, Sakrapee Raktaprajit

Orff Schulwerk is one of the most well-known music teaching approaches used in music education with its essential characteristic of child's play. Thailand has been adopting Orff Schulwerk in its way of music teaching since 1971. Since then, Orff Schulwerk in Thailand has found its way to flourishing in its new home by integrating and adapting to Thai art, music, culture, and education. This article will depict the history and journey of Orff Schulwerk in Thailand. The authors hope that those interested could incorporate the following knowledge and experience in order to further the Orff Schulwerk with the essence of Thailand.

Introducing the knowledge and philosophical concept of Orff Schulwerk to Thai music education

Sowing seeds of Orff Schulwerk in Thailand

The founding of "Somprasong school" by MomDusdi Paribatra Na Ayudhya in 1955—the first nursery in Thailand for children from age 2-4 years and later extended to the elementary level—marked the beginning of Orff Schulwerk in Thailand. MomDusdi Paribatra Na Ayudhya strongly believed that learning started even from the time in the womb, and that early childhood is the foundation of one's development and life. She believed that the knowledge and philosophical concept of Orff Schulwerk is the most appropriate educational approach for early childhood (Paribatra Na Ayudhya, 1979).

In 1971, with collaboration from the Embassy of Germany in Bangkok, the Deutscher Akademischer Austauschdienst [German Academic Exchange Service] (DAAD), and the Goethe-Institut in Thailand, MomDusdi Paribatra Na Ayudhya invited Hermann Regner and Barbara Haselbach from the Orff Institute of the Mozarteum University Salzburg, Austria to provide training for preschool and elementary teachers in Thailand. The workshop received much attention. This success encouraged many educators who were interested in applying the Orff Schulwerk approach for the improvement of learning and teaching methods in Thai's education system to further their knowledge and education. Among those who went on to further their training in the Orff Schulwerk approach are Kamolvan Ungphakorn-Punjashthithi, the first Thai to attend the Orff Institute in Salzburg (1972–1973) and Krongtong Boonprakong (2000–2001), the founder of Jittamett Kindergarten, where the Orff Schulwerk approach has become an essential part of its curriculum.

Thai Orff-Schulwerk Association (THOSA)

After Jiitamett Kindergarten had been a significant part in the development of Orff Schulwerk in music education in Thailand for some time, Barbara Haselbach and Sofía López-Ibor suggested the founding of an Orff Schulwerk association in Thailand. Thus, in 2008, the Thai

Orff-Schulwerk Association (THOSA) was founded by MomDusdi Paribatra Na Ayudhya, who served as the first president of the association. To date, the Thai Orff-Schulwerk Association has become well-known both nationally and internationally through its work of educating in the Orff Schulwerk approach and encouraging and advising others in pursuing their education.

The connection of the Orff Schulwerk concept with Thai cultural background

The Orff Schulwerk and Thai cultural background in language, music, art, dance, poetry, folk play, cultural festivals or events, and even in Thai cuisine, share a similarity in their philosophies, concepts, and practices.

Language

Thai language is a tonal monosyllabic isolating language in which morphemes[1] can be strung into words or complement each other to create a new meaningful word. There are various ways and techniques of forming words, such as using duplicated words together and combining words with the same meaning, as well as rhyming and spoonerism techniques. These forms and structures of Thai language are practiced in colloquial conversation or even a playful conversation. These implementations in Thai language are similar to the concept of improvisation in the Orff Schulwerk approach, which aims to promote enjoyment and creativity through music activities.

Dance and visual art

The implementation of methods for the formation of words and new words in Thai can be seen in the process of creating Thai classical and folk dance. The dancers create a new dance by stringing the basic dance movements into a pattern. The dance movement in Thai classical and folk dance is meaningful because a story can be told solely by the dance itself. The pace, tempo, position, or even articulation in movement imply the dancers' situation, status, relationship, gender, and emotion. The same concept is presented in Thai classical visual arts, such as the *Kranok* pattern, representing the beautiful Thai traditional movement in art.

Music

Percussion instruments and drums are the main instruments in Thai classical music. Some of them are melodic instruments (e.g., *ranat* and gongs) and others are un-pitched (e.g., *klong yao, ching, krap*, and *mong*). Thai percussion instruments and drums produce sound that is consistent with the sound characteristics of Orff instruments. Thus, the natural role of Thai percussion instruments, drums, and ballad recitation or improvisation can be used in Orff ensembles and arrangements. This results in innovation and diversity in musical style that is consistent with the cultural context.

An important and worth mentioning case for the application of Orff Schulwerk in promoting language with traditional dance, visual art, and music in Thailand is the Phleng Khorat (Khorat Song): An intergenerational project of THOSA (Boonprakong & Utamaphethai, 2018). Its unique content is that the lyrics are in Khorat dialect. It is a Jataka tales dance (Bureau of Culture Nakhon Ratchasima Province, 2015; Jataka tales, 2021). The Orff Schulwerk approach was incorporated into this project by first introducing children and youths to the folk dance, encouraging them to express or tell the story they heard through painting, and finally

---

1 A morpheme is the smallest meaningful unit in a language (root or base, prefix, suffix, etc.).

collaborating with the locals in adapting the performance. This promoted the development of self-confidence by participating in performance and creativity through movement. By the end of this project, the Orff Schulwerk in Thailand attained its new roles in cultivating networking and bonding, promoting mutual awareness and appreciation of self-worth in generational diversity, and creating bonds and admiration in the new generation toward traditional folk arts.

Cuisine

Thai cooking and its corresponding eating customs reflect the Thai culture that is compatible with Orff Schulwerk. Doug Goodkin stated and explained this notion during his lecture at the Orff Schulwerk seminar in Thailand in 2007. He made reference to the eating custom that corresponds to Thai cuisine called *Miang kham*. In this custom, one's choices from an assortment of foods are wrapped and then topped with sweet sauce. This reflects the notion that Orff Schulwerk's way of offering choices from an assortment of options is already a part of the Thai way of life (Goodkin & López-Ibor, 2007).

Orff Schulwerk and the music education system in Thailand

The principle of education for early childhood in Thailand focuses on holistic development and the importance of self-development and executive function skills (Ministry of Education, 2020). Thus, the Ministry of Education only provides a framework and learning standards for teaching and learning in early childhood. The curriculum for early childhood is varied among early childhood education institutions because they can develop their curricula as they see appropriate.

Likewise, there are guidelines and framework for music education. However, music as a subject in early childhood institutions is not required. Most kindergartens and early childhood development facilities could not provide an opportunity for music activities. Music education and lessons are considered afterschool hobbies or weekend lessons at various music academies. Only a small number of schools offer music and movement lessons, such as Changphueak Kindergarten and Jittamett Kindergarten (López-Ibor & Boonprakong, 2010).

Children of Jittamett Kindergarten (Bangkok)
Photos: Ann Warangkana Siripachote and private collection

For the elementary and secondary levels (Grades 1-12), the Ministry of Education announced the *Basic Education Core Curriculum B.E. 2551 (A.D. 2008)*, which provides a framework and guidelines for all basic educational institutions and facilities in planning the pertinent curriculum in accordance with their priorities and readiness. Arts, with the main aspects of visual arts, music, and dramatic arts, are prescribed as one of the learning standards and indicators areas (Ministry of Education, 2008a). Ultimately, the standards in the arts learning area help to develop learners in various aspects that will lead to creative works for the benefit of life, society, and the environment. Furthermore, arts learning helps to strengthen self-confidence in learners, thus providing a foundation for future education or professional lives (Ministry of Education, 2008b).

Chuppunnarat, Laovanich, and Laovanich (2018) found that there are three types of music teaching approaches proven to be a success in music education for elementary and secondary students. They are:

1. Approaches and methods that develop from foreign music education philosophies and principles (e.g., Dalcroze, Kodály, and Orff Schulwerk)
2. Developing a way of learning that is suitable with environment and context
3. Instrument teaching through oral tradition (prominent in learning a Thai classical instrument)

The Orff Schulwerk approach and the oral tradition of teaching both apply observation and imitation, in which the learner is continuously watching and listening, and an active chain of perceiving, memorizing, and performing is essential. The difference is that Thai classical instrument students are not allowed to have an opportunity to improvise or freely create sound or music until the students have attained a certain level of skill and knowledge. In contrast, the Orff Schulwerk approach encourages students to improvise at the early stage of learning.

There are 48 higher education institutions in Thailand that offer degrees in music and music coursework such as Western music, Thai music, music business, music technology, folk music, and music education. The music education program is designed to educate students in various teaching philosophies and methodologies such as Dalcroze, Kodály, and Orff Schulwerk at the introductory level. Only a few institutions offer Dalcroze, Kodály, and Orff Schulwerk as their own separate subjects. Chulalongkorn University, Mahidol University, and Kasetsart University are some of the few higher education institutions that offer Orff Schulwerk as its own course. However, while Orff Schulwerk is currently a part of the curriculum in music degrees, it is not found as a major area of study in any university in Thailand.

Academic books and documents on Orff Schulwerk concept

The academic books and documents published by Thai scholars are not widely distributed at the international level due to the language barrier. Such a barrier limits the ability to translate and interpret Orff Schulwerk's academic books into Thai. Thus, Orff Schulwerk documents and books that exist in the Thai language are those that have been translated and rewritten by university professors and scholars who have been trained and have knowledge in Orff Schulwerk. These transcribed documents are widely used as learning material for students in music education programs and by others interested in Orff Schulwerk.

Examples of various academic books and documents that are widely used for reference in Thailand are the following:

MomDusdi Paribatra Na Ayudhya: *Basic Music and Dance*

MomDusdi Paribatra Na Ayudhya: *Basic Teaching Methods for Traditional Music and Dance*

Thawatchai Nakwong: *Teaching music for children Based on The Concept of Carl Orff* (Orff- Schulwerk)

Thawatchai Nakwong: *Orff Songs*

Jane Frazee and Kent Kreuter: *Discovering Orff: A Curriculum for Music Teachers*

Doug Goodkin: *Play, Sing, and Dance: An Introduction to Orff Schulwerk*

James Harding: *From Wibbleton to Wobbleton - Adventures with the Elements of Music and Movement*

Barbara Haselbach: *Dance Education—Basic Principles and Models for Nursery and Primary School*

Barbara Haselbach (Ed.): *Texts on Theory and Practice of Orff-Schulwerk: Basic Texts from the Years 1932–2010*

Gunild Keetman: *Elementaria - First Acquaintance with Orff-Schulwerk; Rhythmische Übung; Pieces for Xylophone*

Sofía López-Ibor: *Blue is the Sea - Teaching the Whole Child Through Music and Visual Arts*

Carl Orff and Gunild Keetman: *Orff-Schulwerk - Music for Children Vols. 1–5* (English version adapted by Margaret Murray)

Hermann Regner: *Music for children (American Edition) Vol. 1, Pre-School; Vol. 2, Primary School*

Brigitte Warner: *Orff-Schulwerk, Applications for the Classroom*

Summary

Five decades have passed since the seeds of Orff Schulwerk were sown in Thailand. Orff Schulwerk sprouted and has been growing through the climate and weather of Thai arts and culture, the education system, and Thai ways of life. To date, Orff Schulwerk is flourishing and prospering while improving education that aims to foster children as a whole, to promote their capacity to understand and respect the natural environment and the interdependence between people and other beings, and to empower them to live quality lives in the ever-changing society.

Translation: Nuttha Udhayanang

Bibliography In Thai

Bureau of Culture Nakhon Ratchasima Province. (2015). *Phleng Khorat* (press release). Retrieved from https://www.m-culture.go.th/nakhonratchasima/ewt_news.php?nid=25&filename=in dex

Chuppunnarat, Y., Laovanich, V., & Laovanich, M. (2018). *The status and approach of music education resource management in Thailand's institutions: Ministry of Culture's policy formulation and implementation.* Ministry of Culture.

Jataka tales (2021, 14 January). In Wikipedia, the free encyclopedia. Retrieved from https://th.wikipedia.org/wiki/%E0%B8%8A%E0%B8%B2%E0%B8%94%E0%B8%81

Ministry of Education. (2008a). *Basic education core curriculum B.E. 2551 (A.D. 2008).* Bangkok: Agricultural Co-operative Federation of Thailand Ltd.

Ministry of Education. (2008b). *Learning standards and indicators, learning area of arts of basic education core curriculum B.E. 2551 (A.D. 2008).* Bangkok: Agricultural Co-operative Federation of Thailand Ltd.

Ministry of Education. (2020, August 7). *Announcement of the ministry of education on policies and practices for educational management and learning for early childhood* (press release). Retrieved from http://academic.obec.go.th/images/official/1600765436_d_1.pdf

Paribatra Na Ayudhya, Dusdi. (1979). *Basic teaching methods for music and dance* (1st edition). Bangkok: Department of Academic Affairs, Ministry of Education.

Thai Orff-Schulwerk Association (n.d.). About Thai Orff-Schulwerk Association. Retrieved from http://www. thaiorff.org/thaiorff.org/rucak_rea.html

Bibliography In English

Boonprakong, K., & Utamaphethai, N. (2018, Winter). Orff and community project: Pleng Korat. How Orff-Schulwerk brings a local community together in a folk art learning project. *Orff-Schulwerk Informationen*, 99, 68–70.

Goodkin, D., & López-Ibor, S. (2007, Summer). Orff-Schulwerk seminar in Bangkok April 2-7, 2007. *Orff-Schulwerk Informationen*, 77, 55–57.

Zach, A. (2007, Summer). Orff-Schulwerk Kurs an der Mahidol Universität in Bangkok. *Orff-Schulwerk Informationen*, 77, 57–58.

López-Ibor, S., & Boonprakong, K. (2010, Winter). Jittamett Kindergarten, Bangkok. *Orff-Schulwerk Informationen*, 84, 70–73.

EUROPE

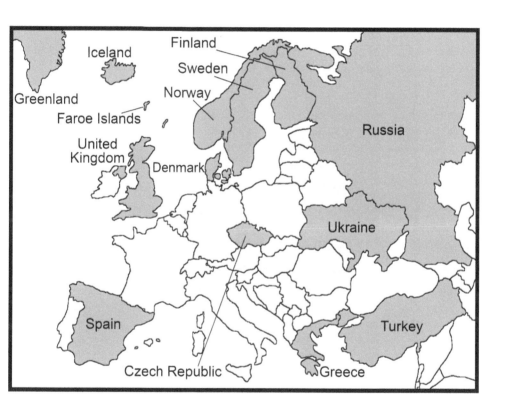

The Czech Orff Schulwerk

Jiřina Jiřičková

The country, its language, music, and dance

The Czech Republic (Czechia), part of Czechoslovakia until 1992, is a country that is bordered by Germany and Austria, Poland and Slovakia. Actually, all residents of the Czech Republic speak Czech. Czech is characterized by an accent on the first syllable, long and short vowels, unusual consonant clustering (*zmrzlina*) and a unique consonant, "ř" (as in Dvořák). In terms of musical folklore, for most of the territory of the Czech Republic (historically called Bohemia) and for the western part of Moravia, typical major periodic songs are in 2/4 and 3/4 meters. Many songs have a dance character and tell about the lives of people and events of everyday life.

The most famous national dance is *polka*. One of the most typical dances is called *furiant*. It represents both the cheerful nature of the Bohemian folk and a parody of the rich farmer with his wife. The Czech variant of the waltz is called *sousedská*. Mazurka was also popularly danced and coincides with the Polish model in 3/4 meter and a slightly fast tempo. There are dances called mateník too, whose meter is variable. The most common dances are spinning dances consisting of three parts, namely the pre-singing of a dance song, a common whirl, and a separate dance performance of a boy and a girl. Another group of folk dances are figural dances. They imitate activities where the first half of the dance is, for example, polka or sousedská, and the second half depicts a selected work activity (e.g., shoemaker's dance), or the dances are based on the typical movements of animals (e.g., pheasant dance). Among the folk dances, prankish Moravian male dances that involve improvised leaping (dances called *odzemek, verbuňk*) are abundant. The typical instruments were dulcimer, bagpipe, clarinet, violin and double bass, supplemented by typical Czech folk instruments *vozembouch* or *fanfrnoch*. The more recent type of music is the music of brass instruments (*dechovka*), which prevailed, thanks to the military service that the musicians had to complete in the past. The eastern region of the country, especially eastern Moravia, and in the past the whole of Slovakia are characterized by music of a purely vocal character in which the minor tonality predominates, and also modal tonality often occurs. For the western part of the country, regular rhythmic values are most often applied, while the rhythm of the eastern part of the country is much more varied. Generally, there is considerable affinity between the western type of folk songs and those of Germany and Austria, whereas the vocal expression of eastern folk songs tends toward that of the Carpathian region.

Contemporary musical influences in the Czech Republic can be characterized as a mix of diverse musical styles and genres, where the worlds of Czech musicians, dancers and performers intersect with the influence of globalized personalities from the world of classical, popular, and world music.

Orff Schulwerk in the Czech Republic

Improvisation and creativity as integral components and the basic principle of music education were officially anchored in school documents at Czechoslovak primary schools in 1976. The ideas of Orff Schulwerk significantly contributed to and were applied in this new concept of music education. However, they were not practically implemented, as Jaroslava Kotůlková claimed in a personal interview in October 2020.

The publication that "codified" Orff's principles in Czechoslovakia and was inspired by Orff's *Musik für Kinder*, is called *Česká Orffova škola*. It is translated as Czech Orff Schulwerk.[1] Looking back, in the history of Czech music pedagogy one can find personalities who in many ways anticipated Orff's principles many years before. One of them was Jan Amos Komenský (1592–1670, in English, Comenius). This "teacher of nations," as he is called, wrote more than 300 years ago: "Music is most natural to us" (Comenius, 1952, p. 34). In his book *Informatorium maternum*, he calls for children to be given "a whistle, a drum, a children's violin, etc., so that they may whistle, squeak, strum and thus bend their hearing to various glares and get used to something" (Comenius, 1952, p. 34).[2]

The actual expansion of Orff's ideas in Czechoslovakia took place during the 1960s. Approximately forty teachers from Czechoslovakia participated in the 1965 conference of the International Society for Music Education (ISME) in Budapest (Poš, 1969, p. 137).[3] It was the first immediate Czechoslovak encounter with Orff Schulwerk. Independent of this event, the first attempts to mass-produce children's musical instruments occurred that same year. (Salvet, 2008, p. 44).[4] Shortly after the conference in Budapest, Wilhelm Keller visited Prague. Vladimír Poš introduced him to the composers Ilja Hurník and Petr Eben. They soon went to visit the Orff Institute and agreed to work on the Czech adaptation of Musik für Kinder.

Between 1965 and 1968, research was carried out at the Department of Music Education, Faculty of Education, Charles University, to prove that music pedagogy based on the principles of Orff Schulwerk can ensure effective music education. In 1967, a gramophone record called *Music for Youth—Schulwerk* was published for the general public. It contained 45 compositions by Carl Orff, Ilja Hurník, and Petr Eben. Finally, in 1969, the first volume of the Czech Orff Schulwerk was published.

In 1968, new curricula for music education in schools were proposed. They literally stated: "We place the greatest emphasis on children's own creativity" (Budík et al., 1968, p. 16). In the same year, Soviet troops invaded Czechoslovakia and the political conditions and social situation changed drastically. The "Western" Schulwerk could not be talked about too loudly. Nevertheless, Schulwerk ideas were incorporated into the curriculum during the 1970s, thanks

---

1 It was released between 1969 and 1996.

2 Elements of Orff's Schulwerk were anticipated by the patriotic cantors Jan Jakub Ryba (1765–1815) and Jan Nepomuk Filcík (1785–1837), who literally surrounded their students with music during the day. Already at the beginning of the 20th century, the follower of pedocentrism, František Čáda, recommended "to use children's musical inventions and desires for naive composition and to make them together with the rhythmic basis of music education" (Sedlák, 1977, p. 53). According to Sieber (2005), other significant Czech music teachers Ferdinand Krch and Josef Křička were inspired by Dalcroze and other progressive ideas.

3 As early as 1960, experimental curricula were developed that expressed an effort to change the content of school music education. So far, the question of creativity and instrumental activities has not been raised in Czechoslovakia. A significant shift in this issue was recorded after the ISME conference and the reflection on the state of music pedagogy in Czechoslovakia in comparison with world developments

4 These experiments were initiated by Ladislav Daniel, 1961-1970, a head of the Pedagogical Institute in Olomouc. He implemented various teaching aids in music, promoted playing the recorder, and significantly contributed to the establishment of schools with extended music education in Czechoslovakia.

to a group of enlightened experts, and were included in the new music school textbooks published from 1975 to 1983. Despite the fact that Orff instruments (Czech produced, as mentioned) were placed in schools and the progressive ideas were set down in school documents, most of the music teachers—themselves not guided to creativity—were not able to follow the written rules.

The first volume of the four-part series entitled *Czech Orff Schulwerk—Beginnings* was published in 1969. In addition to progressively arranged themes for elementary improvisation, folk songs and word games, the authors present detailed methodological instructions. They clarify how the aesthetic perception and creativity of children can be developed through work with rhymes, activities developing children's singing and intonation skills, and using Orff instruments. Methodical instructions are supplemented by photographs of teaching situations. The authors also mention methodological instructions concerning the possible construction of a lesson, the location of the lesson, the placement of children in the space, and their clothing. The publication is further enriched with elementary instrumental compositions and a collection of movement exercises and games, which, according to the authors, are intended for children aged five to seven.

The second volume of the Czech Orff Schulwerk, called *Pentatonika*, contains monophonic vocal and instrumental compositions, two- and three-part songs, canons, songs with variable meters and free meter. The tonal range of these songs varies from two-tone mode to five-tone mode, and the authors orchestrated well-known Czech, Moravian, and Slovak folk songs, or used folk literature as their starting point (Hurník & Eben, 1969b).

In 1970, the Czech version of Orff Schulwerk was handed over to Carl Orff. He declared: *"Something completely different, but very good"* (Regner, 1984/2011, p. 235). Orff relinquished his copyright and the Czech Orff Schulwerk can thus be described as an original author's work, which significantly exceeds the concept of adaptation of Orff's *Musik für Kinder*.

In 1972, the third volume of the Czech Orff Schulwerk, called Major-Minor was released. This volume contains a large number of widely known folk songs that the authors deliberately selected from the songbooks for children in the first through fourth grades of primary school, and which the authors orchestrated for Orff instruments.

The last and fourth volume of Modal Tones (Hurník & Eben, 1996) was published after a 20-year pause in 1996. Thanks to the support of Liselotte Orff and the Carl Orff Foundation, the fourth volume was published with a slight delay in commemoration of the 1995 centenary of Carl Orff's birthday. The volume contains songs and instrumental compositions in modal tonalities.

The fifth volume of the Czech Orff Schulwerk, intended by these authors, was to contain a selection of original compositions from the five volumes of Orff's *Musik für Kinder*. It was never published due to the revolutionary political and social changes of the 1990s when Czechoslovakia split into two separate countries.

Czech Orff Schulwerk is a collection of texts for rhythmic and melodic exercises, rhythmic texts, melodies, songs, small instrumental compositions, and medieval compositions for Orff instruments, all based on the texts, rhythms, and melodies of Czech, Moravian, and Slovak songs. At the same time, Czech Orff Schulwerk respects the main Orff Schulwerk principles, and "has its specific features that distinguish it from Orff's original" (Hurník & Eben, 1969,

p. 7). [1] These features are mainly seen in the style of accompaniment, the use of special instruments, and the development of the tonal range during singing. Compared with Orff's *Musik für Kinder*, the Czech Orff Schulwerk pays more attention to the methodological and pedagogical side. The music material inside the individual volumes follows a logical sequence. Compared with the German original, the publication includes fewer supplementary exercises, topics for improvisations, and rhythmic exercises. On the other hand, it brings new exercises for the creative development of singing and the preparation for the singing of canons. It is devoted to improvisation in an *aba* form, rondo form, and variations. According to Poš, the Czech Orff Schulwerk consists of "much easier accompaniments" (Hurník & Eben, 1969, p. 8).

The progressive ideas of Orff Schulwerk motivated music educators to look for new ways of teaching music at a time when the state of music education in general education schools was mostly perceived as unsatisfactory. It encouraged a reassessment of the current concept of just singing and listening to music.

Clapping game in a Czech kindergarten
Photo: Václav Jiřička

Children's musical
Photo: Václav Jiřička

---

1   The traditional rhymes, songs, and fairy tales are captured in the significant publication *The Czech Year in Fairy Tales, Songs, Games and Dances, Rhymes and Riddles*, collected by Plicka, Volf, Svolinský in the first half of the 20th century. Back In the time of the national revival in the 19th century, many Moravian folk songs (collected by e.g., Bartoš, Sušil) and Czech songs and rhymes (collected by Erben) were gathered. These collections became an important source for creative music teachers many years later.

Teacher training

Educational seminars have been held since 1965 and regular multi-day courses since 1966. Every year, educators met, were instructed, and some of them taught during these seminars and courses. They shared a common interest in the concept of Orff Schulwerk, and further spread Orff's ideas mainly through their direct pedagogical work.[1]

In 1995, Pavel Jurkovič, pedagogue, musician, and an author of a large number of songbooks, instrumental accompaniments of songs, and compositions, founded the Czech Orff Society and became its chairman.[2] Following Pavel Jurkovič, Jarmila Kotůlková was the head of the society during the years 2000–2014. The current chairwoman of the society is Lenka Pospíšilová, who in her pedagogical, creative, and teaching work follows Pavel Jurkovič. During its 25 years of activity, the society has organized dozens of conferences, courses, and summer activities for teachers of all types of schools, social and educational workers, therapists, and parents.

The Czech Orff Society maintains contacts with the International Orff-Schulwerk Forum (IOSFS) in Salzburg. The courses of the Czech society are not structured according to different levels, and its own instructors in general have not studied in specialized long-term Schulwerk courses. However, the society's committee carefully selects its teaching team, whose members are mostly music educators who themselves have attended numerous Orff Schulwerk conferences, significantly demonstrated their professional and human qualities, and further spread Orff's principles through their active pedagogical work.

Instructors of the Czech Orff Society educate children of various ages, students, people with disabilities, and seniors, both irregularly and regularly. The humanistic conception of education through Orff Schulwerk and the emphasis on the dignity and uniqueness of humans at various stages of their lives, regardless of the degree of their talent, fully correspond to the concept of education in the 21st century. In Czechia, teachers proudly refer to Comenius' legacy. Elementary creativity and so-called "experiential pedagogy" are successfully included in the work of many teachers, social workers, and educators at all levels of schools in the framework of school curricula of individual schools. Based on many years of experience, it has been proven to be a great benefit to combine movement, music, speech, and work with simple musical instruments in creative extracurricular activities with seniors and families. This helps to break down barriers between generations and nationalities and unites families from different social groups within a locality. The inclusion of these elements and their connection to the requirements of conscious development of creativity, self-reflection, relaxation, and release of imagination are highly topical and timeless and bring joy to both teachers and students.

Since 2006, the instructors of the Czech Orff Society have been co-creating cycles of musically creative workshops for the children of the Fík club[3] of the Prague Symphony Orchestra (Kotůlková, 2008). In addition, they actively cooperate with the Czech Philharmony, Prague Philharmony Orchestra, and Janáček Philharmony Orchestra. The instructors of the Czech Orff Society work at primary schools with extended music education, at the departments of

---

1 To the leading personalities of the courses belong Pavel Jurkovič and Jaroslav Herden. There were publications released that represented Orff principles in work with local music material. Jurkovič never published the methodology. He was followed by Jana Žižková and Ludmila Battěková, and mostly by Lenka Pospíšilová and her practical examples of teaching Orff Schulwerk that inspired and motivated creative music teachers.

2 E.g., Songbooks *Na orffovských cestách I–III* (translated as On Orff's Road), *Hudební nástroj ve škole* (transl. Music instrument in school)

3 Prior to a concert by the Prague Symphony Orchestra, children in the Fík Club meet with Orff Schulwerk teachers and play with the music they will then hear the orchestra perform. Following the workshop, children actively participate in the concert. The project is called "Music to Touch."

music education of the pedagogical faculties of the Czech Republic (Charles University in Prague, Masaryk University in Brno), at the Prague Conservatory and basic music schools, as well as at general schools. Ramona Schulz is the leading personality of the Elementary School of German-Czech Understanding in Prague, which in 2019 became the Czech Republic's first Associated School member of the IOSFS.

Throughout the Czech Republic, the principles of Orff Schulwerk are naturally incorporated into the content of basic music education and are also applied in the education of preschool children. However, there is no institution in the Czech Republic that would be officially integrated into the education system and that would allow teachers to obtain a special certificate of completion of Orff Schulwerk. Related to this is the fact there are no specific curricula created for this type of study in Orff Schulwerk. Methodological instruction remains anchored in the original Czechoslovak publication Czech Orff Schulwerk. In the Czech Republic, there are a number of qualifying diploma publications that deal with the ideas of Orff Schulwerk and that describe the specific significance of the Czech Orff Schulwerk at the time of its establishment. However, a comprehensive systematic research study has not yet been conducted that would cover the entire subject of the Czech Orff Schulwerk from the 1960s to the present.

Despite the facts mentioned above, awareness of Orff Schulwerk among Czech music educators, thanks to the work of the Czech Orff Society, a number of its regular Orff conferences, and the pedagogical work of their lecturers at various pedagogical institutions and in various areas of social and cultural life, is relatively widespread. It is a joy that Czech educators, unlike before 1989, are now free to draw on a wide range of Schulwerk inspirations from around the world and meet prominent personalities who share our interest in Orff Schulwerk.

The motto of the Czech Orff Society is a summary of the efforts of Czech music educators, which subscribes to the still current legacy of Orff Schulwerk:

1. humanistic approach - faith in every child
2. working in an atmosphere of trust, joy, and also the desire to know and know more
3. combining singing, speech, instrumental expression, and movement into one whole
4. inspiring the desire and the need to express oneself in one's own way, to be creative in developing a harmonious personality that finds a relationship with one's neighbor and responsibility for working together
5. showing children the possible path they can walk on their own in the future.

Children performing with teacher Lenka Pospíšilová
Photo: Zbyněk Hraba

Concert in Czech Music Museum, Prague
Photo: Jan Zákravský

References

Bartoš, F. (1982). Nové národní písně moravské [New Moravian national songs]. Brno: K. Winiker.

Budík, J., et al. (1968). Návrh učebních osnov XIV: Problémy modernisace základního vzdělávání. Část D [Design of curriculum XIV: Problems of modernization of basic education. Part D]. Praha: VÚP, 16.

Erben, K. J. (1984-1988). Prostonárodní české písně a říkadla. Část 1-5 [Nationwide Czech songs and rhymes. Vols. 1-5]. Praha: Panteon.

Hurník, I., & Eben, P. (1969). Česká Orffova škola I. Začátky [Czech Orff Schulwerk I. Beginnings]. Praha: Editio Supraphon, 5-8.

Hurník, I., & Eben, P. (1969b). Česká Orffova škola II. Pentatonika [Czech Orff Schulwerk II. Pentatonic]. Praha: Editio Supraphon.

Hurník, I., & Eben, P. (1972). Česká Orffova škola III. Dur – moll [Czech Orff Schulwerk III. Major - minor]. Praha: Editio Supraphon, 4.

Hurník, I., & Eben, P. (1996). Česká Orffova škola IV. Modální tóniny [Czech Orff Schulwerk IV. Modal modes]. Praha: Editio Supraphon, 2.

Jurkovič, P. (2007, 2009, 2012). Na orffovských cestách I – III. [On Orff's roads I – III.]. Netolice: Jv-Audio.

Jurkovič, P. (1997). Hudební nástroj ve škole [Musical instruments at school]. Praha: Muzikservis.

Komenský, J. A. (Comenius). (1952). Informatorium školy mateřské [Kindergarten]. Praha (SPN), 34.

Kotůlková, J. (2008). Sergej Prokofiev's Ballet Suite Romeo and Juliet. A project of the Prague Symphonic Orchestra and the Czech Orff Schulwerk Society. Orff-Schulwerk Informationen 80, 14–18.

Plicka, K., Volf, F., & Svolinský, K. (1948). Český rok v pohádkách písních, hrách a tancích, říkadlech a hádankách. Jaro [The Czech year in fairy tales of songs, games and dances, rhymes and riddles. Spring]. Praha: Vydavatelstvo Družstevní práce.

Plicka, K., Volf, F., & Svolinský, K. (1950). Český rok v pohádkách písních, hrách a tancích, říkadlech a hádankách. Léto [The Czech year in fairy tales of songs, games and dances, rhymes and riddles. Summer]. Praha: Vydavatelstvo Družstevní práce.

Plicka, K., Volf, F., & Svolinský, K. (1980). Český rok v pohádkách písních, hrách a tancích, říkadlech a hádankách. Podzim [The Czech year in fairy tales of songs, games and dances, rhymes and riddles. Autumn]. Praha: Odeon.

Plicka, K., Volf, F., & Svolinský, K. (1969). Český rok v pohádkách písních, hrách a tancích, říkadlech a hádankách. Zima [The Czech year in fairy tales of songs, games and dances, rhymes and riddles. Winter]. Praha: Státní nakladatelství krásné literatury, hudby a umění.

Poš, V. (1969). Malá historie Orffovy školy v ČSSR [A small history of Orff Schulwerk in the Czechoslovak Socialist Republic]. Praha: Supraphon, 136–137.

Regner, H. (2011). "Musik für Kinder—Music for Children—Musique pour Enfants." Comments on the adoption and adaptation of Orff-Schulwerk in other Countries. In B. Haselbach, B. (Ed.), *Texts on theory and practice of Orff-Schulwerk: Basic texts from the years 1932–2010,* (pp. 220–244). Mainz: Schott. (Original work published 1984)

Salvet, V. (2008). Orffův Schulwerk v české hudební výchově [Orff Schulwerk in Czech music education]. Praha: Charles University, PedF, 44. Habilitation.

Sedlák, F. (1977). Nové cesty hudební výchovy [New ways of music education]. Praha: SPN, 53, 55.

Siebr, R. (2005). Novátor hudební výchovy Josef Křička: učitel, skladatel, člověk [Innovator of music education Josef Křička: teacher, composer, man]. Praha: Sobotáles, 24.

Sušil, F. (1951). Moravské národní písně [Moravian national songs]. Praha: Vyšehrad.

Orff Schulwerk in Greece: Past and Present

Maria Filianou

The Symposium of the International Orff-Schulwerk Forum Salzburg (IOSFS) that took place at the Carl Orff Institute Salzburg in 1995 had the title: *The Inherent—The Foreign—In Common*. "The inherent" means the acquaintance of each country with its traditions, whereas "the foreign" refers to different aspects of teaching and learning suggested by the Orff Schulwerk approach as well as understandings gained through communication with people of different cultures. This acquaintance with "the foreign" proves one of the basic functions in Orff Schulwerk, which is related to the adaptation and development of the Orff Schulwerk approach in our country.

Brief historical review of the Greek 'Inherent'

"The inherent" that Greeks share includes Greek traditions, customs, dances, musical instruments, songs, and rhythms. A characteristic example of a Greek custom that is still alive after hundreds of years takes place on New Year's Eve in Sourva, Thrace. On that day young men gather in church and sing Christmas carols. They light a fire in the center of the church square in order to drive away bad spirits, and they invite people to come by ringing the church bells. They take a long dogwood branch, tap a fellow villager with it, and sing: "Sourva, Sourva strong body like silver, like a dogwood, and next year may everyone be healthy and kind-hearted."

Dancing can also be thought of as part of "the inherent." Traditional dancing is a communal aspect in community activities. Local feasts, weddings, carnivals, as well as festivities of any kind, offer great chances for dancing. The existence of these dances reinforces the belief of an uninterrupted sequence that characterizes Greek tradition. As is the case today, many types of songs already existed in Homer's time (late 8th or early 7th century BC), such as patriotic songs, laments, work and play songs, amusing narrative songs that are sung and danced by choirs of children and adults (West, 1999, p. 439).

During the period from the 8th to the 4th century BC, the Greek world experienced great intellectual growth (Mossé & Schnapp-Gourbeillon, 2005, p. 388), and music was considered a major means of education. Musical scales such as the tetrachord, pentatonic scales, and archaic scales were known as *harmoniai*, and in the 5th century BC they were thought of as contributing to children's education and development. Every *harmonia* had its own inherent aesthetic and emotional qualities. Many philosophers, such as Plato, Aristotle, and Aristoxenos, ascertained that music influences the morality of the individual (West, 1999, pp. 224, 229, 249–257).

During the Hellenistic period (4th–1st century BC), music was developed as a universal art that all people could share. It is proven that the Greek music of the Roman period (end of 1st century BC to end of 3rd century AD) is connected with Byzantine music (West, 1999, pp. 501, 517). From this inheritance of the Byzantine period (3rd–15th century AD) the Greek language developed in two ways: a scholarly tradition (*katharevousa*) and a popular tradition (*dimotiki*)

(Tomadakis, 1993, pp. 26–31, 77). Through the texts of popular literature, the Modern Greek language has been formulated.

After the fall of Constantinople to the Ottomans (1453 AD), a large number of Byzantine intellectuals established themselves in the West, while those unable to follow consoled their sorrow with traditional songs. The Greek-speaking population under Ottoman rule gradually adopted the ideas of the European Enlightenment by creating the Modern Greek Enlightenment, born in the 18th century and expressed by the erudite literary tradition and by the popular tradition of the *klephtic*[1] songs. Through these songs, the Greeks narrated their suffering and gained strength for their struggle for freedom (Politis, 2004, pp. 112–113). In the beginning of the 19th century, the declaration of the Greek Revolution (1821) took place, and liberation from the Ottoman yoke was achieved. The formation of the Greek State in 1832 was based on democratic ideals.

Personalities in the discipline of ethnology, such as Nikolaos Politis, Stilpon Kyriakides, and George Megas, devoted themselves to highlighting the continuity of the Greek language (Tomadakis, 1993, 114–115), declaring that "the ancient Greeks would feel at home, if they found themselves in a modern feast" (Megas, 2001, p. 29).

Meeting the "foreign" (other civilizations) and seeking the "common" (through Orff Schulwerk).

George Chatzinikos (1996) confirmed that educated musicians were considered for a long time the only ones who were trained according to Western classical music. As he mentions, this music education and writing "neutralized" the rhythms that traditional music has offered us (Chatzinikos, 1996, pp. 9, 17). Thrasybulos Georgiades addressed this matter in 1936 with regard to the intake of Orff Schulwerk in Greece. He asked, "Can one educate Greek children in music through using a German Schulwerk?" The idea that makes such an approach exceptional is that it "can be used with the same success in countries with the most different musical cultures… In this case it would be most appropriate to incorporate the musical inheritance of the relevant culture as working material" (Georgiades, 2013, pp. 200–201). Later, Polyxeni Mathey, the teacher who imparted the principles of Orff Schulwerk in Greece, proposed that music and movement education should include not only the heritage of Western European culture but mainly melodies, rhythms, and dance forms of our country (Mathey, 1986, p. 18).

Fortunately, the unilateral perceptions about Western classical music were not adopted by enlightened Greeks such as the 20th century composers Nikos Skalkotas and Manolis Kalomoiris, who included in their work pure Greek aspects, like Greek rhythms. Dance teachers also, such as Koula Pratsika, Zouzou Nikoloudi, Agapi Evangelidi, Maria Hors, and many others who had apprenticed with Christine Baer-Frissell,[2] Mary Wigman,[3] and Rosalia Chladek,[4] paved the way for a new artistic expression that combined music, dance, and speech. In this generation of the 1930s, which led to a new stream of art and education, Mathey is considered to belong as well.

---

1 Klephtic songs belong to heroic folk songs.

2 Christine Baer-Frissell (1887–1932), rhythm teacher, collaborator with Jacques-Dalcroze, founder of the school Hellerau-Laxenburg.

3 Mary Wigman (1888–1976), German dancer and choreographer, founder of German expressive dance (New German dance).

4 Rosalia Chladek (1905–1995), Austrian dancer and dance teacher, developed the Chladek°system, a contemporary dance technique.

The main aspiration of all Greek protagonists who were inspired by and supported Orff Schulwerk was the connection and common course of "the inherent" and "the foreign." The multicultural aspect gives experiences of togetherness, acceptance, and harmonious cohabitation. For example, *Karagiozis*, a kind of shadow play,[1] is a pedagogical device used in teaching preschool and primary school children that offers opportunities for music and movement activities. The Greek character, *Karagiozis*, sings on stage a Byzantine song about Alexander the Great, an eastern song about Chatziavati, α *klephtiko* (traditional song) about Barba-Giorgo, and a serenade about Nionio (Baud-Bovy, 2007, p. 17).

The "in common" ideas

The humanistic, artistic, as well as educational axis of the Orff Schulwerk approach is where the "in common" is met. As Regner (2011) points out, Orff Schulwerk educational ideas are organized into a "didactic concept" that "describes as areas of learning activity those attitudes of behavior that should be internalized in young people through music education" (p. 178). Motivation, exploration, sensitization, psycho-motoric techniques, and structuring are included and bounded together in Orff Schulwerk implementation. According to Orff, its most important invention was a fundamental music education. This kind of music, that he calls "elemental music," "should be a foundation for all subsequent music making and interpretation" (p. 182).

Elemental music forms a unity with movement, dance, and speech. Singing, moving, and dancing, which are activities common to children everywhere and are the natural way that children choose to express themselves, play an important role in Orff Schulwerk. Expressive movements have been used by all peoples and cultures throughout centuries. Even in Greek playful songs, rhythm unifies speech and body music. Through tongue-twisters, nonsense-word songs, proverbs, and brain teasers that exist in our country, the game of discovering the musical elements of our language begins.

Orff Schulwerk as the unity of music, movement and speech features the "inherent" of Greek culture, and through these activities, children experience the value of their culture. For instance, the spring song "Chelithonismata," is one of many ancient customs still alive in our times. Athenaeos (6th century BC) wrote about it. In the 12th century, the French priest Benoit heard Greek students singing it in Rome. Nowadays children sing this song all over Greece to welcome spring (Baud-Bovy, 2007, p. 11). This custom is a favorite curtain-raiser in Greek Orff Schulwerk.

The concepts related to the group role and the development of individuals—through interaction, cooperation, and social acceptance—are "in common" for those who adopt the principles of the Schulwerk in their teaching. The exchange of ideas and the common experiences among group members during the experiential contact with music and dance formulate the frame of human communication and the feeling of belonging in a community that excludes no one. Therefore, this is not only a music and movement education but also a humanistic, artistic, and pedagogic approach.

Short history of the development of Orff Schulwerk in Greece

Polyxeni Mathey studied at the Günther-Schule in Munich (1935) and met Carl Orff there (Tsoutsia Loulaki, 2010,[2] p. 14). Shortly after her return to Greece in 1936, Orff Schulwerk

---

1 *Karagöz* in Turkish means black-eyed. It is a folk theatre found in Asia, the Middle East, North Africa, and the Balkans. Greeks met *Karagöz* of the Turkish shadow theatre in the Ottoman Era (1453-1821).

2 The entire 2010 issue of Rhythmoi is dedicated to Mathey.

began to spread in the country. Mathey's vision was that the Orff Schulwerk, as a wildflower that flourishes, could contribute to our cultural development. Mathey's two Greek Orff Schulwerk volumes (1963, 1968)[1] were the first attempt to adapt Greek traditional songs and dances for Orff instruments.

In May 1985, Fotini Protopsalti (a Greek graduate of the Orff Institute) with the support of Panos Milios and Mathey organized the first Orff Schulwerk seminar in the Moraitis School. The following year a one-year seminar incorporating Dalcroze and Orff Schulwerk was organized. Angelika Slawik, Nefeli Atesoglou, and Lily Arzimanoglou were responsible for this music and dance education. The program had great success, and it was the reason that Chrysanthi Moraitis-Kartalis and Katerina Moraitis-Kassimatis, the two directors of the Moraitis School, invited Hermann Regner in 1986 to organize the founding of a professional Orff Schulwerk course in Greece (Sarropoulou, 2013, pp. 84–85).

A postgraduate course was founded then, with the help of Mathey, as a two-year curriculum with daily attendance. For many years Regner was the mentor and supervisor of the program and Angelika Slawik was the first director of studies. Katerina Sarropoulou and Cornelia Flitner were the next directors. The two-year professional Orff Schulwerk course in the Moraitis School was upgraded in 2011 to a new structure of studies in three levels under the direction of Katerina Sarropoulou. Today the three-year post-graduate Orff Schulwerk course focuses on a broader education that encompasses the cultivation of the music-dance-movement relationship, integration of the arts, and adoption of pedagogical concepts and philosophy of Orff's approach. This reform in 2011 was systematically supervised by the International Orff-Schulwerk Forum Salzburg's (IOSFS) president Barbara Haselbach (Sarropoulou, 2013, p. 89).

A very important step in the history of Orff Schulwerk in Greece is the foundation of the Hellenic Orff Schulwerk Association (HOSA) in 1990, which includes all graduates of the course at the Moraitis School. HOSA aims to disseminate the pedagogical principles of Orff Schulwerk and organizes seminars and lectures, operates a library, and participates in conferences in Greece and abroad.

In 2002, the Hellenic Orff Schulwerk Association and President Maria Filianou organized a three-day event entitled "1st Panhellenic Festival Carl Orff." Many international Orff Schulwerk educators (Barbara Haselbach, Ulrike Jungmair, Doug Goodkin, Sofia Lopez-Ibor, Werner Beidinger) were invited to teach (Sarropoulou, 2013, p. 88) and many artistic groups presented their work inspiring Greek people.

Of major importance for the HOSA is its quarterly journal *Rhythmoi* (*Ρυθμοί*), which had published 42 issues before discontinuing in 2010.

During recent years, HOSA representatives have participated in IOSFS meetings and symposia. Many Greek artists and educators studied and were graduated from the Orff-Institute. The Moraitis School is an Associated School of the IOSFS.

---

1 The songs and dances from the Greek tradition were orchestrated for Orff instruments. Mathey's aim was to arrange them for children and make Orff's educational work known.

Students of the Musiki Kinetiki Agogi Orff building drums
Photo: Archive of the Further Educational Course in Orff Schulwerk Studies, Moraiti School

Orff Schulwerk and Greece's educational system

Orff Schulwerk has obtained an important position in education in our country. The musical pedagogic work of Carl Orff has left its footprint both in nursery and primary education. In 1988, the first music secondary school in Greece included in its curriculum some teaching hours of Orff's elemental music and movement education. In 2000, the Ministry of Education included a pilot program of Orff's approach for primary schools, which may have not gone any further but has boosted the dissemination of Orff's music education ideas. At the same time, the Moraitis School has been including Orff Schulwerk in its primary education schedule.

More specifically, in 1994, in primary music education the first book written for the music teacher *Musical Education I* (Hellenic Pedagogical Institute, 1994, p. 12) contains clear reference to Orff Schulwerk and emphasis is given to games with sounds, rhythm, and speech as well as construction of improvised musical instruments. In the Cross-Thematic Curriculum Framework (Hellenic Pedagogical Institute, 2003)[1] concerning music, the development of musical education to include experiential learning and active participation and agency from the students' side gained an active role.

Accordingly, in 1995, in the physical education curriculum, music and dance were introduced, especially in the early years. In 2003, in the same curriculum, music and movement games as well as traditional dances were included. There was also an effort in both teachers' and students' music and movement education books to include "contact with more expressive forms of movement." In this way, many educators were trained in music and movement education in the two-year professional Orff Schulwerk course at the Moraitis School (Agalianou, 2008, p. 55–56, 58).

Orff's approach is taught in the Department of Music Studies in the National and Kapodistrian University of Athens in the module called "Music Pedagogical Systems" (Chrisostomou, 2008, p. 59). The Department of Early Childhood Education and the Department of Primary Education mentioned the "Orff system" in their curricular programs in 1969 and later in 1984. Since 2018, Olympia Agalianou has been teaching in the Department of Early Childhood Education at the National and Kapodistrian University in Athens within the module called "Introduction to Orff Schulwerk Music and Movement Education" (Department of Early Childhood Education, 2020).

---

1   Cross -Thematic Curriculum Framework (2003) is the Curriculum that teachers of Early Childhood Education and those of Primary Education follow in their teaching wherever in Greece in public as well as in private education.

Today the music pedagogical work of Carl Orff not only contributes to musical and movement education in Greece. It also promotes the principles and means that enhance the Greek tradition to preserve its roots firmly and reveal every phase of its history as well as to recognize exchanges taking place with other people of its culture. The description made by Baud-Bovy is suitable: "like two different plants cultivated in the same pot and although they feel strange, their roots are mixed up underground and their branches over the ground and if you try to uproot them one follows the other" (2007, p. 41).

Bibliography

Agalianou, O. (2008). Musical and movement education in the curriculum of physical education. Music in the first grade. 5–6 *Association of Music Teachers in Primary Education* pp. 53–58.

Baud-Bovy, S. (2007). *An essay on Greek folk songs.* Peloponnesian Folklore Institution 5th Edition.

Chatzinikos, G. (1998). Music learning and education in Greece. *Rhythmoi,* 25, 3–19. Hellenic Orff Schulwerk Association.

Chrisostomou, S. (2008). *Music pedagogical systems.* Department of Music Studies, University of Athens.

Hellenic Pedagogical Institute. (2003). Cross thematic curriculum framework for compulsory education Diathematikon Programma. Hellenic Ministry of Education and Religious Affairs. Retrieved April 23, 2021 from http://www.pi-schools.gr/download/programs/depps/english/13th.pdf

Hellenic Pedagogical Institute. (1994). *Musical education I—Games with sounds, rhythms, melodies.* Teacher's book. Hellenic Ministry of Education and Religion.

Department of Early Childhood Education. (2020). *Directory of studies.* Retrieved February 14, 2021 from http://www.ecd.uoa.gr/wp-content/uploads/2013/05/%CE%9F%CE%A3-2020-F.pdf

Georgiades, T. G. (2013). The Orff-Schulwerk in Greece (1936) (M. Murray, Trans.). In M. Kugler (Ed.), *Elemental dance-elemental music: The Munich Günther School 1924–1944* (pp. 200–201). Mainz: Schott. (Original work published 1936)

Mathey, P. (1963, 1968). *Songs and dances for children* (Vols. 1–2). Mainz: Schott.

Mathey, P. (1986). *Rythmic (Rythmiki).* Nakas. Second edition.

Megas, G. A. (2001). *Greek feasts and customs of Greek devotion.* Estia.

Mossé, C., & Schnapp-Gourbeillon, A. (2005). *Precis d'histoire Greque* (2–31 B.C.). (L. Stefanou, Trans., 6th ed.). Papadimas.

Politis, L. (2004). *History of modern Greek literature* (14th Reedition). Cultural Association of National Bank of Greece.

Regner, H. (2011). Carl Orff's educational ideas – Utopia and reality (M. Murray, Trans). In B. Haselbach (Ed.), *Texts on theory and practice of Orff-Schulwerk: Basic texts from the years 1932–2010* (pp. 168–192). Mainz: Schott. (Original work published 1975)

Sarropoulou, K. (2013, Winter). The Moraitis School, Athens. *Orff-Schulwerk Informationen,* 89, 84–92.

Tomadakis, N. V. (1993). *Key for Byzantine philology. Introduction to Byzantine philology.* P. Pournara.

Tsoutsia Loulaki, E. (2010). Polyxeni Mathey, "Nice as a Greek." *Rhythmoi,* 42, 13–17. Hellenic Orff Schulwerk Association.

West, M. L. (1999). *Ancient Greek music.* Papadimas.

Periodical

Rhythmoi (Ρυθμοί). Quarterly journal of the Helenic Orff Schulwerk Association, published until 2010.

Orff Schulwerk in the Nordic Countries

Kristín Valsdóttir

The Nordic nations are a family of peoples that inhabit a relatively small part of the planet. They have various origins, and through the centuries they have either chosen or been led down different paths. For some periods, these paths have been conflicting. Still, for the last fifty years or so, the Nordic nations have increasingly sought similar solutions to the persistent challenges of human coexistence (Nordic Sounds, n.d.).

For such a small population of people in the Nordic countries, Nordic cultural diversity is noteworthy and reflected in our music and dance heritage. Each country's origin, geological position, and respective natural features have promoted a variety of traditions that reflect each nation's unique culture, customs, and lifestyle (Eriksen, 2019). The music tradition of each culture is influenced by particular places and times in which it is created and performed. Therefore, it can provide insight into what is familiar and where customs and cultures differ, but also what we share (Nettl, 1995; Jorgensen, 2003).

Cultural heritage

Different places and long distances have created diverse local customs and culture between areas. The often-harsh landscape and inhospitable wilderness are sources that shape the content and strange creatures of the Nordic fables (Nordic Sounds, n.d.). While in Sweden and Norway the pine forests and ancient fir trees with hanging ragged beard moss conjured images of trolls and fairies, for Icelanders it was the sea, wind, and the gloomy hills of the highlands' volcanic black sands and lava. Such creatures as the hidden people in Iceland and stories connected to them, the Kalevala in Finland and the Viking Age Archology have also served as a material for building a national identity among the Nordic countries (FROG, 2020)

Educational value of cultural heritage

According to some research, many of the cultural activities in the Nordic countries have educational as well as broader societal values (Karlsen et al., 2013). The educational role of music and folktales is even greater in the more remote and isolated areas and countries. An example is seen clearly in the Faroe Island tradition were parents and grandparents sang and danced with the children so that the Faroese legacy would survive (Nordic Sounds, n.d.). Another example is from Finland, where a well-known folktale tells of a little rabbit who wins a battle against the big Mr. Frost (representing the ice-cold and frosty winter). For a small country, it is essential to teach children that small ones can be strong (Nordic Sounds).

Considering that Greenlandic people did not have a written language, the music was the primary way of preserving historical stories that represent life in this extraordinary country. The Greenlanders used their songs and ballads for entertainment as well as for various other purposes. These include contacting the spirit world through music and work songs. Songs and stories were also used for educating and raising children.

The Icelanders have that in common with the Greenlanders because some stories and songs include messages about how to behave. One of these Icelandic songs tells the story of a child who fell through a hole in the ground and beneath the hole lived a monster that would beat them. Singing the horrible story for the children had the effect that they took more care when they were playing outside and were in less danger of falling into lava holes that are numerous in Iceland.

Musical elements and traditions

Despite these differences within the Nordic countries, there is a common theme when it comes to traditional folk music—at least familiar to most of the countries—and that is singing, storytelling, and ballads.

Songs and stories

The Nordic countries all have a rich tradition of ballads and epic songs from the Middle Ages. These songs seem to have a strong link to music and dance traditions of the Faroe Islands (Koudal, 1993). These familiarities between the cultures connected to the importance of singing and ballads in the traditional music culture are now, or for the longest time, most relevant in the west Nordic countries. The Faroese music tradition lies in ballads, circle dances, rhymes, and Kingo "hymns." Being without instruments until the mid-18th century the music lived in the voice and movements of the inhabitants (Visit the Faroe Islands, n.d.). Similar to the Faroese ballads, the traditional Icelandic music is mostly vocal and very closely related to the traditional form of Icelandic epic tales or *rímur* (Icelandic ballad) (Þorsteinson, 1906–1909). What differentiates Faroese from Icelandic tradition is dance. The circle dance accompanied by ballads survived only in the Faroe Islands, as the church banned it elsewhere because of its pagan origin. The Icelanders may have obeyed and stopped dancing, but they still sang in parallel fifths and the *Tritonus*, the "Diabolus in musica," which was also officially banned from church music (Ingólfsson, 2003).

Similar to the Icelandic epic poems and the ballads from the Faroe Islands, is the *Kalevala*, the national epic storybook of Finland. Even today, *Kalevala* is an inspiration for all art forms. A storyteller would often tell the old stories by singing a phrase that the listeners repeated, and this allowed everyone involved to remember the information. The hero of the story is Väinämöinen, and through singing, he won battles and enchanted animals. Maybe it can be concluded that this is the basis for the Finnish belief in the power of music and rhyme (Nordic Sounds, n.d.).

In the Norwegian solo folksong tradition is a form called *stev*, short four-line verses. These *stev* were sometimes used in an entertaining competition where singers improvised stories based on text fragments. The connection to the Scottish Islands is clear in the younger version of *stev* (Ling, 1997).

Both Norway and Sweden have a rich collection of herding songs and calls that arose from the extinct pasture culture between high mountains and in Norway's deep narrow fjords. Traditional calls, *kulning*, singing in the falsetto style, were used to call livestock from the mountains where they had been grazing during the day (Thun, n.d.).

Instruments

Traditional instruments in the Nordic countries can be classified by whether they have forests or not. Norway, Sweden, and Finland have immense forests that provided the material for making instruments. The old Norwegian instruments include the Jew's harp, willow flute, *lur*,[1] and *langeleik*.[2] Norway is known for the famous Hardanger fiddle, developed in the 15th century. All the instruments influence the characteristics of a song. For example, if the songs come from areas with the Hardanger fiddle, they have richer ornamentations (Nordic Sounds, n.d.). Similar instruments like fiddle, *lur*, and accordion were used in traditional music in Sweden, Finland, and Denmark. Then there are variations of the instruments within each country or between districts. In Sweden, there is, for example, the fiddle and *nyckelharpa*[3] and in Finland, among other instruments, the *Kantele*[4] that has deep roots in Finnish history. Although the *Kantele* is a historical instrument, it is still used today, flourishing among various musical styles (Virta, 2020).

Iceland, Faroe Islands, and Greenland did not have great resources to make instruments from wood. Nearly the only wood instrument known in Iceland is the *langspil*, which is believed to have come to Iceland around the 18th century. Whether it comes from Norway or elsewhere in Europe is not known, but the *langspil* belongs to the zither instrument family as does the Norwegian *langelek* (E. Eyjólfsson, personal communication, October 22, 2019). In Greenland, the Arctic drum, is the national instrument. It has a bone or wooden frame on which a membrane—usually made from intestines or skin from animals such as seals or polar bears—is suspended. The Arctic drum is an ancient instrument that has been traced back nearly 4500 years (Grønnow, 2012).

Project with a 5th grade class in Iceland building langspils
Teacher and photographer: Eyjólfur Eyjólfsson

Dances

The Greenlandic dance, drumming, and song are inseparable. The Greenlandic tradition of the drum-song is performed by a soloist, man or women, wherein the performance of the song, drumming, and dance are interwoven (Hauser, 1993). In that sense, it relates to the idea of the Orff Schulwerk that music, word, and movement form a whole and should be approached like that in education (Orff, 1964/2011, p. 144).

Apart from the traditional Greenlandic dances, all the Northern countries share a heritage of folk music and dance traditions up to a point, even if there are significant local variations.

---

1   A long natural blowing horn without finger holes that is played by embouchure. Lurs can be straight or curved in various shapes.
2   A droned zither that has only one melody string and up to 8 drone strings.
3   A "keyed fiddle" or literally "key harp" – a traditional Swedish instrument.
4   A plucked stringed instrument.

The songs for ballads are generally danced in circles, as in the Faroe Islands. In contrast, Norway, Sweden, and Finland share dances like polka or *polska*, danced in couples. These dances are typical in Europe, and the reason that they are common in the most southern part of the Nordic countries is their close contact to central Europe (Nordic Sounds, n.d.). Norway also has old dance styles like *gangar* (in English, walker) and *springer* (in English, runner) and *halling*. *Gangar* and *springer* are danced in pairs and have local variations, while *halling* is a traditional spectacular and powerful solo for a male dancer.

From what has been drawn from each culture above, there are some similarities but also significant differences in the traditional music and dance cultures in the north. What sets them apart is partly rooted in the dispersed settlement.

The Orff Schulwerk approach in the Nordic countries

Educational applications

The term "Nordic model of education" is relatively known and refers to the reform of the education system in the late twentieth century in the Nordic countries. The Nordic model was developed to enhance social justice and equality, aiming at every child getting an education independent of background and origin (Antikainen, 2006: Telhaug et al., 2006). It has however been pointed out, that over the past 20-30 years, the school model in the Nordic countries has changed to some degree. Nevertheless, we can argue that the ideology of the "Nordic model" is still prevailing and education in the Nordic countries is by core, built on equity and the holistic welfare of the individual child (Lundahl, 2016).

There might be a consensus in thinking about education and music, but there are not many direct links between Orff Schulwerk and the Nordic countries. While the Orff Schulwerk was developed in Germany, similar methods and approaches were developed in the Nordic countries. In Denmark, it was, for example, Astrid Gøssel. A pianist and a music educator who worked for many years teaching movement, she developed her ideas based on her education and practice as music- and movement educator (PædagogenDK, n.d.). The essential elements of her work relate to a great degree on the core ideas of the Orff Schulwerk approach. At a similar time, Minna Ronnefeld was working as a music teacher with strong connections to the Orff Schulwerk, both as a student of Gunild Keetman and later as a teacher at the Orff Institute (Bruland, n.d.). In Sweden, Daniel Helldén (b. 1917), a composer and music pedagogue studied with Carl Orff. Helldén developed Orff's pedagogical methods in his teaching in Sweden and introduced them in large parts of the Nordic region (Vem är det, 1993). Joar Rørmark (b. 1935), a Norwegian conductor and music educator, had a close working relationship with Helldén and was drawn to the ideas of the Orff Schulwerk. Rørmark's emphasis in his work is on all children and young people being allowed to develop their abilities to experience and express themselves through music (Ruth Wilhelmine Mayer, oral source, 2020, December 6).

Training courses and teacher education

According to the answers from a questionnaire sent out to selected music teachers in each of the seven Nordic countries included in the Nordic Sounds material, there are only two Orff associations in the Nordic countries at the moment—in Finland and Iceland. There was a Swedish association, FOSiTS, but that has not been active for some years. These associations are founded and, to a great deal, led by music teachers who studied at the Orff Institute.

The connection to teacher training institutions is not traceable in the Nordic countries except for Finland and Iceland—in both countries on an informal basis. There is no Orff Schulwerk-related degree offered through the institutions or universities that educate teachers. On the other hand, in both of these countries, members of the Orff associations are teaching music and movement in teacher training programs. It can be argued that, through this, developing teachers are to some degree influenced and trained according to the ideas of the Orff Schulwerk.

The only specific training courses that lead to an Orff Schulwerk teacher certificate are levels courses for teachers offered in Finland and organized by the Finnish Orff Schulwerk association, *JaSeSoi*. Although there are no levels courses in Iceland, SOTI, the Icelandic Orff Schulwerk Association, has provided courses for teachers—mostly general music teachers— taught by educated Orff Schulwerk teachers. In the other Nordic countries, there are no such courses offered. In Norway, Ruth Wilhelmine Meyer, a graduate of the Orff Institute, worked at the Grieg Academy in the department for music teachers using an Orff approach, 1992-1997. Pedagogues from the Grieg Academy in Bergen and the Oslo Metropolitan University have visited the summer courses at the Orff Institute and brought the creative music and dance approach to students at their institutes. The Orff Schulwerk is not explicitly written in the curriculum in the Nordic countries except for the levels courses offered in Finland.

Adaption of the Orff Schulwerk

Some adaptions of the Orff Schulwerk have been published in the Nordic countries. In Denmark Minna Ronnefeld's publication is the Orff-Schulwerk: Danske børne – og folkesange and Musik for Børn (1977). In Sweden, Musikmetodikk for barneskolen 1-6 by Hanna Asmussen, Klari Kredborg, and Daniel Helldén was published in 1962-1968, and a Norwegian edition came in 1982 by Joar Rørmark, Øystein Årva, and Torbjørn Dal. However, some material on music and dance education published both in Finland and Iceland are highly influenced by the Orff approach because the authors are educated at the Orff Institute. These are books such as Stafspil (barred instruments) by Nanna Hlíf Ingvadóttir and two other educational books on music and movement: Hring eftir hring (Round after the round) by Elfa Lilja Gísladóttir and Það var lagið (That's the spirit) also by Elfa Lilja, the author of this article. Soili Perkio, composer and music educator, also educated at the Orff Institute, has written more than seventy books and audio materials for general music education and early childhood music education (The University of the Arts Helsinki, n.d.). However, none of them is marked explicitly as an adaption of the Schulwerk, though they bear the mark of the holistic approach in music education that characterizes the Orff approach and the Finnish education policy. Perkio's publications are being used in teacher training for music-pedagogics in conservatories and universities. The latest of these publications is the web-material Nordic Sounds.

Nordic Sounds: Educational material in music and dance

The project Nordic Sounds is rooted in the Orff Schulwerk approach. The aim of this educational material is sharing our music and dance traditions and giving those outside the Nordic area insight into our musical heritage.

Through our studies in music and dance education at the Orff Institute, we (the editing team)[1] were reminded of and encouraged to learn about different cultures as well as maintaining and respecting our own. This emphasis deepened our understanding and skills as musicians and educators as well as Nordic citizens. We believe music and dance are vital elements of every culture and that each cultures' musical traditions shed light and give a distinct insight into what is common and where we differ.

---

1   Editing group: Elfa Lilja Gísladóttir (IS), Elisa Seppanen (FI), Kristín Valsdóttir (IS), Nanna Hlíf Ingvadóttir (IS), and Soili Perkio (FI)

In the material, traditional songs, games, musical elements, and pieces lay the foundation for developing new and creative ways to work with them. The process of meeting in different countries, sharing, and trying traditional material from each country with new ideas was both an incredible journey of learning about one's own music but also of others. Having learned a lot, we also wanted to give those outside the Nordic area an opportunity to celebrate Nordic music and dance heritage with us.

The principal result of the Nordic Sounds project is a website for educators. The website is open and available to everyone: https://www.nordicsounds.info/. The advantage of producing an online publication is the capacity to give examples of the pronunciation of each language, video examples of the work, along with links to performances and ideas to further extend the material.

The working team

The working group[1] along with the editing team came from different areas of music and cultures. The contribution of all participants in the project was based in their respective field of expertise within music, dance, traditional music-culture, and education. The cross-sectoral collaboration, testing, and implementation of ideas have merged to provide a high-quality educational resource with thoroughly grounded, professional instructions.

It is our hope not only that this publication strengthens and vitalizes the ideas and approach of the Orff Schulwerk in the Nordic countries, but also that our variable traditional music and dance cultures from the North can be an inspiration to music teachers and their students around the world.

References

Antikainen, A. (2006). In search of the Nordic model in education. *Scandinavian Journal of Educational Research,* 50(3), 229–243.

Bruland, I. (n.d.). Minna Ronnefeld (1931–). Dans kvindehistory. Retrieved from: https://www.kvinfo.dk/side/597/bio/1712/origin/170/.

Eriksen, T. H. (2019, April 1). The role of nature in the Nordic countries. Retrieved from: https://nordics.info/en/show/artikel/the-role-of-nature-in-the-nordic-countries/

FROG. (2020, March 23). Folklore in the Nordic countries. Retrieved from: https://nordics.info/show/artikel/folklore-in-the-nordic-countries/

Grønnow, B. (2012). The backbone of the Saqqaq culture: A study of the nonmaterial dimensions of the early Arctic small tool tradition. *Arctic Anthropology* 49(2), 58–71.

Haselbach, B., Grüner. M., & Salmon, S. (2007). In dialogue. Elemental music and dance education in interdisciplinary contexts. Hünfelden: Schott.

Hauser, M. (1993). Folk music research and folk music collecting in Greenland. *Yearbook for Traditional Music, 25,* 136–147. Doi:10.2307/768690

Ingólfsson, Á. H. (2003). *These are the things you never forget.* Ph.D. Essay in music, unpublished. Cambridge: Harvard University.

Jorgensen, E. R. (2003). Transforming music education. Bloomington: Indian University press.

---

1 Navarana Kristina Motzfeldt Berthelsen, music teacher (GL); Ruth Wilhelmine Meyer, singer and music educator (NO); Vuokko Rajala Nyvelius, music teacher and dancer (SE) along with Ann-Marie Ulfvarson, rhythmics teacher (SE); Ingrid Oberborbeck and Morten Mosgaard, music teachers (DK); and Katrin Jørgensen, trumpet player and educator (FO).

Karlsen, S., Westerlund, H., Partti, H., & Solbu, E. (2013). Community music in the Nordic countries: Politics, research, programs and educational significance. In Veblen, K. K., Messenger, S. J., Silverman, M., & Elliott, D. J. (Eds.), Community music today (p. 41-61). Plymouth: Rowman & Littlefield Education.

Koudal, J. (1993). Ethnomusicology and folk music research in Denmark. *Yearbook for Traditional Music, 25*, 100–125. Doi:10.2307/768688

Ling, J. (1997). *A history of European folk music by Jan Ling.* Toronto: Atticus Books.

Lundahl, L. (2016). Equality, inclusion and marketization of Nordic education: Introductory notes. *Research in Comparative and International Education, 11*(1), 3–12.

Nettl, B. (1995). *Heartland excursions: Ethnomusicological reflections on schools of music.* Urbana and Chicago: University of Illinois Press.

Nordic Sounds: Educational material for music and dance. (n.d.). Retrieved from https://www.nordicsounds.info/

Orff, C. (2011). Orff-Schulwerk - Past & Future (M. Murray, Trans.). In B. Haselbach (Ed.), *Texts on theory and practice of Orff-Schulwerk: Basic texts from the years 1932–2010* (pp. 134–156). Mainz: Schott. (Original work published 1964)

PædagogenDK. (n.d.). Astrid Gøssel. Retrieved from https://www.paedagogen.dk/artikler/astrid-goessel-16797/

Telhaug, O. A., Mediås, A. O. og Asen, P. (2006). The Nordic model in education: Education as part of the political system in the last 50 years. *Scandinavian Journal of Educational Research, 50*(3), 245–283.

The University of the Arts Helsinki (n.d.). Retrieved from https://www.uniarts.fi/en/people/soili-perkio/

Thun, H. (n.d.). Nordic voice. Retrieved from https://nordicvoice.dk/

Visit Faroe Islands. Music. (n.d.) Retrieved from https://www.visitfaroeislands.com/about/art-culture-sport/music/

Þorsteinsson, B. (1906–09). *Íslensk þjóðlög.* Siglufjörður: Siglufjarðarprentsmiðja.

Vem är det '93 – Svensk biografisk handbok. (1993). Huddinge: Slams Böcker og Skivor.

Virta, S. (2020, December 2). The living tradition: Kantele in the 21st century. Retrieved from https://musicfinland.com/en/news/kantele-in-the-21st-century

Orff Schulwerk in Russia

Inna Akhremenko, Elena Filimonova, Galina Khokhryakova,
Irina Shestopalova, Natalya Valchenko, Vyacheslav Zhilin

About 50 years have passed since music teachers of our country got to know the Orff Schulwerk. The Russian Orff Schulwerk Association (ROSA) has been existing now for more than 30 years, and it is time to summarize our activity and outline our perspectives.

I. The history of Orff Schulwerk in Russia (earlier—USSR)

Our history starts with the musicologist Oksana Leontyeva. Her monograph *Carl Orff* was published in 1964 as a result of her personal correspondence with and study of the works of the composer. Lev Barenboim published a book about Carl Orff and the Schulwerk after visiting the Orff Institute with a delegation of Russian musicians. He translated Gunild Keetman's *Elemental Music Education* and Wilhelm Keller's *Introduction to Music for Children*. Lev Vinogradov, a teacher and a psychologist, was greatly influenced by Pierre van Hauwe in the 1970s. He created a series of training manuals and presented it throughout the country.

At the same time, Vyacheslav Zhilin's activity had begun. Thanks to his correspondence with Carl Orff (and later with his widow Liselotte Orff) and meeting Leontyeva and Keller, Zhilin began to hold public lessons and seminars concerning improvisation. He also collected and systematized materials and sent them to interested teachers. As a result, a circle of like-minded people was formed, and in 1988 the Russian Orff Schulwerk Association (ROSA) was founded by Zhilin, Safarova, and Kochekov. At the same time, Zhilin began to publish training manuals, as well as an annual magazine, *Vestnik ROSA*, which since 2006 has been edited by Galina Khokhryakova and Rimma Mukhitova.

Since 1992, a series of large international seminars with leading Orff Schulwerk teachers (Manuela and Michel Widmer, Christiane and Ernst Wieblitz, Soili Perkio and Orietta Mattio, Reinhold Wirsching and Holger Maute, etc.) have been held in Russia.

Tatyana Tyutyunnikova made a large contribution to the promotion of Orff's conception in Russia. She has held seminars throughout Russia and in former Soviet republics since 1999 and organized international seminars since 2014. RusFOSA is an association of music teachers founded and held by Tyutyunnikova.

The first levels course (2002–2006) in Russia was held in Shcherbinka, Moscow region (director – Ilya Podkaminsky). It was mainly taught by teachers from the Orff-Institute (Ulrike Jungmair, Leonardo Riveiro, and Barbara Haselbach) because sufficiently trained Russian presenters were not yet available.

The second levels course (2017–2019) took place in Novosibirsk (director – Irina Shestopalova), with three guest teachers (Verena Maschat, Shirley Salmon, and Angelika Wolff) and five Russian teachers. This shows how much more independent and experienced the Russian Orff Schulwerk community had become.

Russian music teachers who studied at the Orff-Institute in Salzburg:

- Vyacheslav Zhilin:1993, one-year internship
- Vadim Kanevsky: 2005, Special Course
- Irina Shestopalova: 2005, Special Course
- Elena Filimonova: 2013, Special Course
- Vera Zolkina: 2015, MA (Elemental Music and Movement Education)
- Natalya Valchenko-Shestopalova: 2015, Baccalaureate
- Nadezhda Svetlichnaya: 2019, Special Course

Other Russian teachers have attended International Summer courses at the Orff Institute in Salzburg as well as the international summer courses organized by Coloman Kallos and other events.

Regional branches of ROSA have been created in 54 of 85 regions of Russia, their number grows every year. In large cities, teachers get together regularly to exchange their experience. The number of subscribers to ROSA pages in social media also grows. The ROSA website has been created and is filled with interesting materials.

One of the main aims of ROSA is to hold seminars in different regions. Among these are the following themes:

- Introduction to Orff Schulwerk pedagogy (Vyacheslav Zhilin, Irina Shestopalova) as well as in-depth study of its particular aspects
- Vocal ensemble. Improvisation. Playing with styles (Elena Filimonova)
- Oral music of 20th century—blues, jazz, rock: history, arrangement, using in work with teenagers (Vadim Kanevsky)
- An orchestra made of nothing (Galina Khokhryakova)
- Correction of psychophysiological development of children by means of elemental music playing (Tatyana Potekhina)
- Communicative games and dances (Iliza Safarova)
- Word—rhythm—movement—music (Elena Zaburdyaeva)
- Russian children's folklore and Orff Schulwerk (Svetlana Zhilinskaya)
- Elemental musical theatre and opera in school. Classical music through the Orff Schulwerk approach (Natalya Valchenko)
- ecently, new projects have emerged in which teachers try to combine the principles of Orff Schulwerk with other learning content:
- In August 2020, a two-year project directed by Olga Dementyeva and Inna Akhremenko (graduates of the second levels course) was started. The project covers 24 historical periods (from the origins of the universe to the present day) from the aspect of the synthesis of different areas of science and arts.
- Irina Baranova's (head of the Moscow regional branch of ROSA) initiative "Orff Schulwerk meetings online" turned out to be timely, inspiring, and useful. Since May 2020 she holds webinars with Russian and foreign presenters on various topics.

II. Russian adaptations of Orff Schulwerk and the characteristics of Russian music culture

The beginning of the application of Orff Schulwerk ideas in Russia made it necessary to explore our own cultural tradition in terms of music, language, dance, children's play.

Russia is a multinational country. More than 150 large and small ethnic groups inhabit its vast area. The majority of them are Russian (80% of the total population); Russian is the official language. The traditional folk music is primarily a tradition of *a cappella* choral singing.

The Russian version of *Music for Children,* based on the traditional music of numerous ethnic groups of Russia, is being created gradually. This opens great opportunities as well as serious problems. We need to select music, lyrics, and dances thoughtfully for editing and publishing, and we try to find a common component that can be understood easily by the children of the whole country, while still preserving the ethnic characteristics.

The diversity of Russian musical scales reflects the genre and the degree of antiquity, as well as the region where they are used. Archaic layers of children's lore in games (counting rhymes, teaser rhymes, ritual songs, etc.) stand out due to their special modes. Their melodies are based on so-called *popevkas*—modal and rhythmic models, typical to one genre or another.

Heterophonic polyphony with melodic variations is typical for the later song tradition. Supporting parts, seconds, and fourths appear in the musical structure. Unlike the tonal system of major and minor, an additional root note appears frequently, thus making a shift from major to minor and vice versa, typical for Russian music. Long lyrical songs are the highest point of the folk singing tradition.

Gusli,[1] *svirel,*[2] *balalaika, domra*[3] are the most well-known Russian folk instruments. Whistles and small percussion instruments like spoons, *treshchotka,*[4] jingle bells, *rubel,*[5] wooden block, etc. are widespread in children's musical life.

Boy with domra   Boys playing flute and domra
Photos: Vyacheslav Zhilin

In the Soviet era, folk choirs, song and dance ensembles, as well as orchestras of Russian folk instruments performed a generalized version of folk music; however, in these performances, the folklore lost its distinctiveness and authenticity. As opposed to these, ensembles, performing local folklore in an authentic manner, appeared in different regions of Russia at the end of the 20th century. These ensembles cooperate closely with our leading folklorists and ethnographic centers.

---

1   Type of zither.
2   Type of end-blown flute.
3   Type of lute with 3 strings.
4   Type of ratchet.
5   A grooved instrument that is scraped.

The centuries-old legacy of the traditional culture remained, largely due to the work of the investigators-collectors who knew the musical tradition firsthand. Scientific studies and anthologies of folklore (including children's lore) are published.

It is not possible to list all the ethnic groups of Russia in this article. But it is worth noting that many of them keep their traditional music in their lives and worldview better than the Russians do. Tatars, Bashkirs, Mari people, Udmurts, Altai people, Yakuts, Khakas people, etc. keep on singing in their mother tongues and playing traditional musical instruments nowadays. Their traditional beliefs and ancient rituals and holidays are still alive.

Nevertheless, in general, **musical life in Russia** is mostly passive these days. Amateur music playing is poorly developed: it is mostly singing to a guitar, karaoke, or a cappella. The repertoire consists of adapted folklore, Russian romance, popular songs, etc. Parents sing with children and for children rarely—they mostly play audio recordings.

But there is also an opposing tendency: lullaby courses for mothers, lessons with groups of parents and children that is based on folklore material, traditional outdoor games and collective singing in parks and yards organized by enthusiasts, summer family camps with broad programs of ensemble music playing. During holidays and festivals, the audience is frequently involved in music, dancing, and games.

The interest in the music of other cultures, including very distant ones (round dances from the whole world, bagpipes, sitar, throat singing, European Medieval, Renaissance, and Baroque music) grows everywhere. Music of different ages and countries is attractive for Russian children as well.

Russian publications connected with the Orff Schulwerk

Many of the leading Russian Orff Schulwerk teachers have published books, offering general information about Orff Schulwerk as well as ideas and examples for working with special groups (see bibliography). Here we would like to mention some projects that are in progress but not yet finished:

- Viktoriya Moytokhonova's project "Orff Schulwerk-Sakha" is aiming to collect, arrange, and publish Yakutian songs of authentic folklore, children's lore, and original songs for children written in the Yakutian language in the style of elemental music.
- On Elena Filimonova's initiative, the material for a large anthology of songs of the multi-ethnic folk music of our country is being collected. We are planning to make the treasures of age-old melodies and lyrics available again to the children of Russia.
- Also, materials from Russian presenters' seminars and training manuals can be considered as Orff Schulwerk adaptations: they include music and dance material, descriptions of didactics, and prescriptive lesson plans.

III. Adaptation of Orff Schulwerk to music education and teacher training

Preschool education is where Orff Schulwerk pedagogy is practiced most frequently. Public kindergartens and comprehensive schools work according to a recognized standard whose general objectives largely correspond to the principles of the Orff Schulwerk. **In kindergartens** these are: individualization of personal development; support of children's initiatives; positive socialization of children taking ethnocultural situations into account; creating situations that require independent decisions and the free choice of activities and materials.

However, in practice the realization of Orff Schulwerk in kindergartens is complicated by a number of factors. Music lessons are mostly dedicated to preparation for calendar festivals. Unfortunately, this often results in only a mechanical study of lyrics and dance movements. Important factors complicating the authentic Orff Schulwerk process are the short duration of lessons (twice a week—from 10 minutes for children aged 1½ to 3 years to 30 minutes for ages 6 to 7) and the large number of children in a group (20–30). But even in these conditions, teachers find possibilities to hold full-fledged Orff Schulwerk lessons. In particular, they use the time reserved for extracurricular activities—30 minutes twice a week with small groups.

In schools, educational standards promote an activity approach and individual initiatives, teamwork and healthy movement training, which is also in tune with Orff Schulwerk pedagogy. Within **general education,** music lessons are held in grades 1 to 7 once a week. Curricula are mostly aimed at studying the classical music legacy and acquiring theoretical knowledge of music. The most common type of practical activity is choral singing with accompaniment by piano or recording. There are no classes equipped for movement (except the sports halls). In music lessons, children mostly sit at desks. Musical instruments in most of the kindergartens and schools are limited to small percussion, pianos, and synthesizers.

The very spirit of Orff Schulwerk is contrary to the traditional authoritativeness of Russian schools, and the bold experiments that introduced Orff Schulwerk into the educational process during the 1990s have been discontinued almost everywhere.

Today, the only case of Orff Schulwerk being supported on the regional level is the curriculum "Music for Everyone" in the Republic of Sakha (Yakutia). Within this curriculum, different modern approaches, including Orff Schulwerk, are used. Schulwerk lessons, using ethnic music material, are held in kindergartens and schools of the republic.

The situation in **private kindergartens and schools** (including Montessori and Waldorf) in large Russian cities, as well as in **non-formal education institutions** is different. Here one finds proper conditions for holding Orff Schulwerk lessons, and qualified teachers work there. Private schools and studios are well equipped with Orff instruments. Teachers strive to have at least several barred instruments in their arsenals. Recorder and ukulele playing is widespread. Boomwhacker[1] sets are acquired more and more often. Ethnic instruments are being collected. Many percussion instruments are used. Longer lessons (from 30 minutes to 1 hour, once or twice a week) and fewer children in a group contribute to deeper immersion into the Orff Schulwerk process.

Nursery rhymes, folk games, dances from the whole world, songs, and counting games in various languages are used actively. Speech and rhythmic exercises from the Russian version of the first volume of Carl Orff's *Music for Children,* as well as models from Orff Schulwerk pedagogy training manuals published in Russian are practiced.

Lessons in **"Mother and child" groups** (children under 2) are very popular. The music is perceived in a special sensory environment, through tactile and movement games, free movement, cooperative dancing, investigation of sounds, etc. **Family lessons**—cooperative lessons for children of different ages and their parents—also occur.

Dissemination of the idea of children's free creativity is a pedagogical credo of Anna Shimkevich (Saratov) and her studio of creative music playing *Orfika,*[2] at which children aged from 1 to 14 create and perform music themselves. They also create video clips, animation films, and stage projects.

---

1   Tuned plastic percussion tubes.
2   Type of accordion.

Lyubov Maramygina (Kurgan) holds Orff Schulwerk group lessons for children aged 5 to 7. In 1995, she developed a curriculum "Elemental Music Playing or an Orff Schulwerk Lesson," the first officially approved "Schulwerk-based" curriculum in Russia. "Tempo primo," an amateur performing ensemble of bayan players of different ages, established in 1989, is a result of her work.

Orchestra with accordions and other traditional instruments
Photo: Private collection

Children's music schools are widely spread in Russia. Children usually learn to play instruments, also take choir, orchestra, and theoretical lessons. Traditional academic and "high level" music education in Russia has a downside—a disregard for amateur music playing, and instead aiming at achievements (competitions, professional career) from an early age. There is a bias towards reading written music and solo performance at the expense of improvisation and ensemble playing.

However, the Orff Schulwerk approach finds its place in this area of education too—mostly in working with preparatory classes.[1] Orff Schulwerk orchestras and ensembles appear in music schools rarely, and their repertoire is sometimes far from the elemental style. Rather, it can be arrangements of popular classic music pieces, learned from sheet music.

There are no state curricula, uniform requirements for the frequency and content in Orff Schulwerk lessons. Teachers can develop their own curricula. In 2010-2020, Irina Shestopalova's "Playful Space of Music: Orff Schulwerk" 72-hour courses for music schoolteachers were held, with the issuance of state certificates. After that, lessons of "Music Playing" for preparatory and elementary grades, held by trained specialists, appeared in many schools.

The subject "Elemental Music Playing with Orff Schulwerk" was included in the curriculum for grades 1 to 4 of a specialized music school for gifted children (Novosibirsk) at the initiative of Natalya Aleksandrova. She believes that using the principles of Orff Schulwerk pedagogy in such schools, as well as in "regular" ones, is essential because elemental music playing prepares children for playing in any ensemble or orchestra. Furthermore, she says that in the specialized school, Orff Schulwerk helps students, with their emotional instability and enormous workload, to solve different psychological problems.

A concept "Orff-ensemble," developed by Vyacheslav Zhilin, is carried out in the children's music and art school of Varna. About 40 students, aged 4 to 16, attend "Music and Movement Education," "Ensemble," "Musical Instruments." Students are offered attractive possibilities for music playing—regardless of their abilities, skills, and even the initial motivation level. The

---

1   Classes in which children prepare for studying in the 1st grade.

lessons also include easy dances and theatre. Thus, an environment for identifying the most capable and motivated children who can later choose a more complex pre-vocational variant of studying, is being created.

Colleges for music and music pedagogy train music teachers for music schools, comprehensive schools, and kindergartens. The subject "Music Pedagogy" is taught in colleges, and within this subject, an acquaintance with Orff Schulwerk is possible if a lecturer has a relevant qualification. Principles of Orff Schulwerk pedagogy make a large part of the subject "Methodology of Working with a Children's Folklore Ensemble" in Sverdlovsk Music College (a certified curriculum by Svetlana Zhilinskaya, an author of training manuals). Nadiya Lobanova, a graduate from the first Russian levels course, has taught an elective course, "Music and Movement Education for Preschoolers," in Tomsk Music College since 1996. The curriculum, developed by her, covers the concept and practice of Orff Schulwerk thoroughly. The students learn the history of Orff Schulwerk, its aesthetic and pedagogical principles, characteristics of an Orff Schulwerk lesson structure, possibilities of using Orff Schulwerk in special education, etc. Sometimes Orff Schulwerk specialists are invited to colleges to offer workshops and courses (for example, "Introduction to Orff Schulwerk Pedagogy," regularly held in Novosibirsk College of Culture and Arts by Irina Shestopalova).

The defenders of the traditions of prescriptive, authoritarian teaching at all stages of education (not only musical) are reluctant to give way to new trends, although the practice of "cooperation pedagogy" is known in our country since the 1980s and is being supported by modern education standards.

Using Orff Schulwerk in Russia is based mostly on individual initiative. Despite the conservativeness of the system of education, there are many talented teachers who discover Orff Schulwerk pedagogy for themselves and try hard to implement and disseminate it. Therefore, Orff Schulwerk pedagogy acquires more and more supporters. The more that teachers turn to the natural, close-to-child pedagogy, the stronger its impact will be, and the more humane, educated, creative, and thus successful the young generation will become.

Translation: Lev Khokhryakov

Bibliography

Barenboym, L. (Ed.). (1978) *Elementarnoe muzykalnoe vospitanie po sisteme Carla Orffa* [Elemental music education in Carl Orff's approach]. Moscow: Sovetskiy kompozitor.

Galyant, I. (2013). *Muzykalnoe razvitie detey 2-7 let: metodicheskoe posobie dlya specialistov doshkolnyh obrazovatelnyh organizatsiy* [Musical development of children aged from 2 to 7: Handbook for the specialists from preschool education institutions]. Moscow: Prosveschenie.

Goodkin, D. (2013). *Poy, igray, tantsuy! Vvedenie v Orff-pedagogiku* [Play, sing, dance! An introduction to Orff pedagogy]. Russian translation by V. Zhilin. Moscow: Klassika XXI.

Haselbach, B. (Ed.). (2019). *Issledovatelskie teksty po teorii i praktike "Orff-Schulwerk," Bazovye teksty 1932–2010 [Texts on theory and practice of Orff-Schulwerk: Basic texts from the years 1932–2010]*. Russian edition co-edited by V. Zhilin & V. Zolkina. St. Petersburg: Kompozitor, 2019. (Original work published 2011)

Kanevsky, V. (2005/2006). Kukhnya Orff-uchitelya [Orff-teachers' kitchen]. *Vestnik ROSA*, (13), 22-29 & (14), 22-31.

Orff, C., & Keetman, G. (2008). *Muzyka dlya detey. Orff-Schulwerk* (Russian version of *Musik für Kinder*, Vol. 1). Compiled and translated by V. Zhilin & O. Leontyeva; (rhymes translated by G. Khokhryakova). Chelyabinsk: MPI; Mainz: Schott.

Potekhina, T. (2006). *Primer terapevticheskogo effecta ritmicheskogo samovyrazheniya* [An example of therapeutic effect of rhythmical self-expression]. Novosibirsk: self-published.

Tyutyunnikova, T. (2003). *Videt muzyku i tancevat stikhi. Tvorcheskoe muzicirovanie, improvizatsiya i zakony bytiya* [To see music and to dance rhymes. Creative music playing, improvisation and the laws of life]. Moscow: URSS.

Ukrainceva, N. (2011). *Shla kukushka mimo lesa* [A cukoo walked past the forest]. Chelyabinsk: MPI.

Zaburdyaeva, E., & Perunova, N. (2008-2012). Posvyaschenie Carlu Orffu / Uchebnoe posobie po elementarnomu muzicirovaniyu I dvizheniyu [Dedication to Carl Orff / A training manual on elemental music playing and movement]. St. Petersburg: *Nevskaya nota*, Issues 1–5.

Zhilin, V. (2004). *Orff-Schulwerk. Russkie narodnye pesni i tancy dlya golosa, blokfleyty I Orff-instrumentov* [Orff-Schulwerk. Russian folk songs and dances for voice, recorder and Orff-instruments]. Mainz: Schott 2000; Chelyabinsk: MPI.

Periodicals

Annual magazine *Orff-focus* of RusFOSA

Annual magazine *Vestnik ROSA*

Orff Schulwerk in Spain

Sofía López-Ibor, Ester Bonal

Introduction

The Spanish Orff Schulwerk initially grew from the important contributions of pedagogues like Elisa Roche and Dolors Bonal, who modeled the new inspiring music and dance education. With their openness to the advanced ideas, curiosity, and determination to succeed, they were effective advocates for innovative teaching and influenced and shaped the lives of many.

A short history

The development of pedagogical movements in Spain have always been tied to the Educational Law that governs the standardization of education and affects not only how schooling is organized, but also how teachers are trained. Although the Schulwerk has not had a similar development throughout the country over the 50 years of its existence, we have seen how it has influenced major reform projects of the national curriculum. In the 1970s music became mandatory in the general school,[1] and we have the first examples of experiences carried out by teachers who had studied at the Orff Institute. At the same time music departments were created in the main education universities in the country.

One of the first Spaniards who learned about the new pedagogy of the Schulwerk was José Peris, a composition student of Orff in Munich who published a book *Música para Niños* in 1965. This first publication was inspiring for music educators who then participated in the first course organized in Pamplona (Navarra) in 1965, taught by Hermann Regner and Barbara Haselbach. In 1967 another introduction to the Orff Schulwerk course took place in Madrid. The organizers were the *Instituto Alemán de Cultura* and the *Centro de Documentación y Orientación Didáctica de Enseñanza Primaria*. Courses in Granada followed in the years 1967 and 1968. After that Orff Schulwerk summer courses took place in the University Menéndez Pelayo in Santander and from this moment a group of pioneers in the field started to be interested in studying at the Orff Institute in Salzburg.

Among other initial contributors to this new pedagogy in our country, Montserrat Sanuy taught many courses, lectured in universities, and brought music education to National Radio with her dynamic program *En Clave de Sol*. A prolific writer, she also authored the adaptation of the first volume of the Schulwerk to Spanish together with Luciano González Sarmiento (1969).

In 1967, María Dolors Bonal, returning from her studies at the Orff Institute, founded the school *L'ARC* in Barcelona, together with Pilar Anglada, the visual artist Esther Boix, and the writer Ricard Creus. *L'ARC* was a pioneer school in its pedagogical ideas, proposing a child centered approach. First the child, then the music and then the instrument has been the school's road map. The interdisciplinary proposals connecting music with poetry, theater, visual arts,

---

1 Ley General de Educación de 1970. Enseñanza General Básica (E.G.B.) and Bachillerato Unificado Polivalente (B.U.P).

and dance constituted the curriculum in which there are no courses or exams. The essence of the Orff Schulwerk has been and still is one of the pedagogical foundations of *L'ARC*. It is present in many aspects and areas of the school, including starting from repertoires of popular roots and oral traditions; using songs and dances to expand cultural references and contexts; improvising and creating; recognizing and representing what surrounds us; connecting artistic expressions; and developing symbolic creativity. Over the years, *L'ARC* became a musical, educational, and pedagogical benchmark and inspired many other schools. *L'ARC* converted into a Foundation in 1992 and has been responsible for the management of the municipal school since then. Meanwhile, María Dolors' vocation of public service led her to the management of the Can Ponsic Municipal School of Music in 2001.

The practical dissemination of the Orff Schulwerk really flourished during Elisa Roche's work at the Royal Conservatory in Madrid. She put into practice the pedagogical principles of Orff and his collaborators for more than 20 years. She created model work in many different types of schools, both public and private, until she became the Professor of Music Pedagogy. From this position she inspired a whole generation of music teachers, many of whom also ventured to study in Salzburg.[1]

Roche also organized a Master's in Music Education program,[2] a revolutionary model in our country at the time. One interesting aspect about that program was the collaborative spirit between teachers and students, generating a new vision that crystallized in performance projects and concerts, publications, TV programs, and courses for other teachers. The group *Ocho por Uno*[3] performed in symposia and conferences modelling a vision of the Schulwerk that was purely Hispanic.

Elisa Roche was also linked to the reform of music education in the 1990s and its legislative development in its dual aspects of compulsory education (preschool to high school) and specialized education (conservatories and music schools).[4] The Orff Schulwerk acquired a predominant role in the training of new music teacher specialists for general education; and a pioneer group of music school directors shaped the new teaching curriculum and model.[5] During this period there was intense activity in the music education field: the teachers showed enthusiasm and adherence to the Orff Schulwerk approach. There was a lot of work for music teachers, who frequently attended seminars, courses, and congresses.

The reform of music education in Spain could not have happened without providing humanistic, pedagogical, and didactic training. From the 1990s to the present the Orff Schulwerk has continued to develop in the country thanks to the efforts and contributions of many teachers and institutions. New questions and challenges were brought up with a new reform of education in 2006.[6] In addition to the impulses already mentioned at the Royal Conservatory in Madrid,[7] Verena Maschat began leading many courses and work groups with secondary school teachers and teaching movement and dance pedagogy in the Dance Conservatory María de Ávila in Madrid. Ester Bonal and Luis García-Vázquez teach music education in E.S.M.U.C.,[8]

1   Leonardo Riveiro, Mariana di Fonzo, Luz Martín León-Tello, Polo Vallejo, Sofía López-Ibor, Luis García Vázquez, Águeda Matute, Ángeles Cuadrado, Alfonso Álvarez, Alfonso Elorriaga, Carlos Chamorro among many.
2   Máster en Pedagogía Musical (1988-1989/1989-1990). Real Conservatorio Superior de Música de Madrid.
3   Javier Benet, Mariana di Fonzo, Sofía López-Ibor, Luz Martín León-Tello, Fernando Palacios, Leonardo Riveiro, Elisa Roche, and Polo Vallejo.
4   Ley Orgánica de Ordenación General del Sistema Educativo en España 1990. L.O.G.S.E.
5   Marisa Santisteban, Marisa Pérez, Eva Gómez Santos, Nuria Sempere, Leopoldo Santos.
6   Ley Orgánica de Educación.2006. L.O.E.
7   R.C.S.M.M. Real Conservatorio Superior de Música de Madrid. (Elisa Roche, Polo Vallejo).
8   Escuela Superior de Música de Barcelona. E.S.M.U.C. (Luis Garcia Vazquez, Ester Bonal).

and over the years Sofía López-Ibor and Wolfgang Hartmann made important contributions in MUSIKENE[1] bringing a strong perspective conveyed in the combination of Orff Schulwerk and general music didactics. Polo Vallejo became the music pedagogy teacher at the Escuela Superior de Música Reina Sofía from the Albéniz Foundation. The departments of music education in several universities in the country have contributed as well, representing the Orff Schulwerk in their teacher training programs.[2]

Asociación Orff España (AOE) / Asociación Orff Catalunya

The Spanish Orff Schulwerk Association (AOE) was founded in 1996 by Elisa Roche, Luz Martín, Mariana di Fonzo, Sofía López-Ibor, and Verena Maschat among others, who worked tirelessly to spread the legacy of Carl Orff and Gunild Keetman. It is worth highlighting the work carried out by Luz Martín as director and manager of the summer courses in Santander in collaboration with the Albéniz Foundation and the International University Menéndez Pelayo. This course was followed by many others organized by the AOE in the regions of Madrid, Barcelona, Valencia, and the Canary Islands and recently in the historical city of El Escorial.

The Spanish Orff Schulwerk Association continues working to develop the Schulwerk in our country by organizing courses and workshops and publishing a yearly magazine.[3] After many years of collaboration with the AOE the Catalan Orff Schulwerk Association was founded in 2020 by a dynamic group of educators who have done exemplary collaborative work and music education projects. Orff Catalunya is leading many workshops to serve not only the music and movement teachers in the municipal music schools but the instrumental teachers as well.

As interest has grown in Orff Schulwerk many Spaniards have studied in Salzburg, both in the regular courses of the Orff Institute and in the Special Course. Many others have completed the American Orff Schulwerk levels in The San Francisco International Orff Course and a young enthusiastic group of teachers is leading the way into the future.

Orff Schulwerk adaptation

Spanish music and dance are vital, dynamic, and distinctive. From the children's games and dances to the wonderful historical music there are many examples that can be explored and learned through the lens of the Orff Schulwerk. Our vocal and instrumental music, dance, literature, and visual arts are essential meaningful elements of our Schulwerk.

Our country is home to five different languages: Aranés, Basque, Catalan, Galician, and Castilian, and Spanish poetry and traditional rhymes are extraordinary in their richness and variety. It is also very interesting to compare our traditional poetry with versions in Latin America. The phonological structures, patterns, and sonorities of these languages are very inviting for exploration with all the possibilities of expression that the Orff Schulwerk suggests—including improvisation and composition.

The form of musical expression most widely used in Spain is singing. We have a vast repertoire of traditional children's songs, work songs, and songs for celebrations. From singing styles with strong "open" voices, to the use of subtle ornaments and rapid text delivery, to the simple melodies of the lullabies, vocal music is powerful in all our communities. We have a vast

---

1 Escuela Superior de Música del País Vasco MUSIKENE (Sofía López-Ibor, Wolfgang Hartmann, Alba Pujol).

2 Universidad Autónoma de Madrid- Luz Martín, Alfonso Elorriaga. Universitat Autònoma de Barcelona - Ester Bonal. Universidad de La Rioja- Carmen Angulo. Universitat de València- Elisabeth Carrascosa.

3 *Orff España*, revista de la AOE.

historical repertoire associated with The Spain of the Three Cultures, consisting of Christians, Jews, and Muslims who for much of the Middle Ages coexisted smoothly in a real multicultural setting until the tolerance ended in the fifteenth century. We can see how the three distinctive cultural, religious, and intellectual communities made important contributions to the arts in a time of coexistence and interculturality.

Spain has a rich tradition of using body percussion, tambourines, hand drums, and square drums to accompany singing and dancing. Each region has a distinctive musical tradition, and some musical styles can be easily adapted and arranged to be played and danced in the Orff Schulwerk style. From traditional *villancicos* accompanied by kitchen utensils, to children's games and dances there is a great variety in the use of modal scales and borduns, and rhythmic accompaniments and improvisation are welcomed as well. Traditional music is very important in the educational field and has gained a space in the primary and secondary curriculum from the hand of Orff Schulwerk teachers who have approached this world with curiosity and responsibility.[1]

The Orff Schulwerk in Spain is not based only on Spanish traditional music and dance. A few decades after the reestablishment of democracy in 1975, our country has been a recipient of migratory flows. During the 2000s the foreign population increased fourfold, and the origins of these immigrants are very diverse. With the increase of diversity in schools, a real call for bringing new interesting repertoires and ways to teach them was needed. Teachers were aware of the difficulty to deal with repertoire and cultures they were unfamiliar with, and they wished to develop sensitivity to the needs of students from different cultural backgrounds.

Spain has the exemplary work of the ethnomusicologist and pedagogue Polo Vallejo, who, after collecting music in many countries in Africa and many other countries, has created numerous materials for the music classroom. He inspired many to represent world music styles with responsibility, creativity, and inventiveness at the same time. He has many compositions in the elemental style that help students approach genres from traditional, to ethnic, to classical and contemporary music styles.

World music repertoire is now practiced in the primary schools in Spain because there is a need for developing curricular and methodological adaptations required for a more inclusive education. Teachers are becoming more and more open and curious about songs and dances from other countries, and the topic becomes one of the healthy staples of the Spanish Orff Schulwerk Association summer courses. AOE organizes master classes and seminars with Schulwerk teachers who have dedicated their research to ethnic music together with Orff Schulwerk teachers, ethnomusicologists, and culture bearers: World Music and Orff Schulwerk courses with Sofía López-Ibor, James Harding and Doug Goodkin; Body Music with Keith Terry; West African Music and Dance with Kofi Gbolonyo; Brazilian Music and Dance with Estêvão Marquez and Deise Alves; Colombian Music with Sandra Salcedo; Venezuelan Music with Jackie Rago; European Folk Dance with Verena Maschat and Andrea Ostertag; Latin Percussion with Alfonso Álvarez; Finnish Music with Soili Perkio; American Gospel Music with Tom Pierre; various Jazz courses with Doug Goodkin; and Spanish Traditional Folk Music with Eliseo Parra.

There is also a great intellectual curiosity for Arts Integration in our Schulwerk, which arose after the many courses of Barbara Haselbach in Madrid and Barcelona. The educator and composer Fernando Palacios, Sofía López-Ibor, Carmen Domínguez, and dance educator Raquel

---

1 Macarena Garesse, Alba Erviti, Pedro Álvarez Sánchez, Marta Santillán, Elia Bernat, Isabel Ortega Oyarzábal, Xavi Manyoses, Jofre Gasol.

Pastor, have modeled examples of how to work with music, poetry, and the visual arts. Students from public and private institutions in Madrid collaborate in an annual project called *Todos Creamos.*[1] Led by Fernando Palacios, this is a clear example how the ideas of the Schulwerk can be applied in a performance in an artistic and interdisciplinary way.

The work in Orff Schulwerk as an inclusive model of education has been fulfilled and carried out in our country in distinct ways by teachers and music therapists working in hospital settings as well as general and music schools. The MAP Institute,[2] directed by Patxi del Campo in Vitoria, is a leading organization for the training of music therapists that always includes the dialogue of the arts as one of the pillars of the specialist's educational experience. Leading work is happening in children's hospitals, oncology departments,[3] and specialized schools.

Another example of multifaceted and inclusive work inspired by the ideas of the Schulwerk is the project of the school Xamfrà in Barcelona. Directed by Ester Bonal, Xamfrà is a center of the *L'ARC* Music Foundation in the neighborhood of Raval, which is characterized by its multiculturalism and diversity. It is a transient neighborhood where one finds conflicts of social class and situations of exclusion in a context in which an array of collectives and communities coexist. This tends to form a map of separated groups that are rarely related, but when they do interact it is in the form of mistrust and sometimes violence. The mission and approach of the school is to fulfill the cultural and socio-economic rights of people, and it offers meeting times and spaces in which to share music, dance, and theater. Xamfrà encourages the participation of groups at risk of exclusion, together with those who do not struggle with it. They have created a network of connections with other institutions in the city, and they pay special attention to the participation of groups that do not feel so inclined to engage in cultural or artistic activities.

Why do they do this through music and the scenic arts? The performing arts facilitate the simultaneous expression of the diverse arts that appeal directly to our emotions. Music, dance, and theater are richer when they are done collectively and cooperatively and allow different people, with various skills and knowledge, to express themselves together in an ensemble, and the result is harmonious, balanced, and beautiful. The purpose of the project is to contribute to forming more reflective societies in which the paradigms that are taken for granted are questioned, people are capable of imagining other ways of living and relating to each other, and they move towards scenarios of coexistence.

Preschool class at Xamfrà   From a masque play
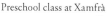
Photos: From the Xamfrà archive

---

1   Todos Creamos [we all create] – CNDM - Centro Nacional de la Difusión de la Música. Fernando Palacios.
2   M.A.P- Música, Arte y Proceso.
3   Hospital Monteprincipe- Camino Bengoechea. Hospital Gregorio Marañón/ Hospital Doce de Octubre- Isabel Ortega Oyarzábal.

Artistic and cultural practices are facilitators of social climates; they are common languages; they are generators of beauty perceived individually and collectively; they are opportunities for expression and listening; they are the raw material with which to build new joint artistic proposals. And it is this creative work—which starts from the essential, from the elemental of each of the artistic languages with which we work—that connects and reconnects the Xamfrà processes with the principles of Orff Schulwerk.

A future drummer exploring sounds
with small percussion instruments
Photo: Sebastián Raffo

Music and dance in the family class
with Leire Amonarriz and Vesna Stegnar
Photo: Mache Figini

Choral dance for children and parents with Leire Amonarriz and Vesna Stegnar.
Photo: Sebastián Raffo

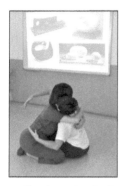

Creative exploration in movement with ideas from Barbara Hepworth's sculptures.
Master's Degree students, Universidad Autónoma de Madrid.
Photo: Raquel Pastor

Movement exploration
in self-built spaces.
Photo: Carmen Domínguez

Inventing melodies for their fan dance.
Photo: Laura Miret

OEB Music School (Madrid)

Orff Schulwerk in Spain is practiced by many teachers who are inspired by the aesthetic qualities, the benefits of intercommunication values, and the depth of its pedagogy. From examples of inclusive education and work in music therapy, to educational concerts, to the work of the teachers in general and music schools we can see how the approach has influenced our education system. We see new generations of teachers inspired by the approach, interacting with visual arts, creating body percussion pieces, composing and designing new materials—a whole world of richness and joy. While some Schulwerk teachers are making serious efforts to improve the quality of music, dance, and arts education in general, many areas of the country still need to improve their existing programs. We hope teachers in those areas can be motivated by our new team of inspiring leaders and educators that keep innovating and facilitating projects in schools, universities, and other institutions. We are now seeing a bright future for the further development of the Schulwerk in Spain.

Selected Bibliography

Haselbach, B., Maschat, V., & Sastre, F. (Eds.). (2013). *Textos sobre Teoría y Práctica del Orff-Schulwerk. Textos Básicos de los Años 1932–2010* [Texts on theory and practice of Orff-Schulwerk: Basic texts from the years 1932–2010]. Vitoria-Gasteiz: Agruparte. (Original work published 2011)

Instituto Alemán. (1979). *Música y Danza para el Niño* [Music and dance for the child]. Madrid: Instituto Alemán.

López-Ibor, S. (2011). *Blue is the sea. Music, dance and visual arts.* San Francisco: Pentatonic Press.

López-Ibor, S. (2007). Carl Orff. In M. Díaz (Ed.), *Aportaciones teóricas y metodológicas a la educación musical* [Theoretical and methodological contributions to music education] (pp. 71–76). Barcelona: Graó.

Palacios, F. (1985). *Piezas Gráficas para la Educación Musical* [Graphic pieces for music education]. https://fernandopalacios.es/piezas-graficas-para-la-educacion-musical-2/

Palacios, F., & Riveiro, L. (1990). *Artilugios e instrumentos para hacer música* [Objects and instruments for music making]. Madrid: Opera tres.

Peris, J. (1965). *Música para Niños* [Music for children]. Madrid: Doncel.

Riveiro, L., & Schinca, M. (1992). *Expresión corporal: Optativas* [Body expression: Electives]. Madrid: Ministerio de Educación y Ciencias.

Roche, E. (1990). Orff-Schulwerk en España [Orff-Schulwerk in Spain]. In H. Regner (Ed.), *Begegungen: Reports about the acceptance and development of stimuli from Orff-Schulwerk* (pp. 149–150). Orff-Schulwerk Forum Salzburg.

Roche, E. (1998, Summer). Auswirkungen des Orff-Schulwerks auf die Musik-, Tanz- und Bewegungserziehung in Spanien [The effects of Orff-Schulwerk on music, dance and movement education in Spain (English summary, p. 55)]. *Orff-Schulwerk Informationen,* (60), 53–55.

Roche, E. (2000/2001, Winter). Einige Gedanken zur sozialen Dimension des Orff-Schulwerks [Some reflections about the social dimension of Orff-Schulwerk (English summary, p. 16)]. *Orff-Schulwerk Informationen,* (65), 13–16.

Roche, E. (2010). *El secreto es la pasión. Reflexiones sobre educación musical.* [Passion is the secret. Reflections about music education]. Barcelona: Clivis.

Sanuy, M., & González Sarmiento, L. (1969). *Orff Schulwerk, Música para Niños I* (adaptation of C. Orff & G. Keetman Music for Children). Madrid: Unión Musical Española.

Sanuy, M., & González Sarmiento, L. (1969). *Orff Schulwerk, Introducción* (adaptation of C. Orff & G. Keetman Music for Children). Madrid: Unión Musical Española.

Vallejo, P. (2000). *19 cánones circulares y 15 miniaturas corales.* [19 circular canons and 15 choral miniatures]. Madrid: Mundimúsica.

Periodical

Orff España, revista de la AOE [Orff Spain, magazine of the Spanish Orff Schulwerk Association]. 17 Volumes.

Orff Schulwerk in Turkey

Editor's comment: This article is composed of the reports of three institutions that work successfully with the Orff Schulwerk in Turkey, each of them in their own way. We begin this article by the contributions of ORFF SCHULWERK EĞITIM VE DANIŞMANLIK MERKEZI TÜRKYE, who is the oldest Turkish Orff Schulwerk Association, followed by the PEKINEL PROJECT TO IMPROVE MUSICAL EDUCATION IN ANATOLIA and finally the youngest Turkish Orff Schulwerk Association, ANADOLOU ORFF-SCHULWERK DERNEĞI (ORFFDER).

ORFF MERKEZI – Orff Schulwerk Education Center Turkey

Banu Özevin, Bilgehan Eren, Fatoş Cümbüş Auernig, Işık Sabırlı

It has already been more than eighty years since the seeds of Orff Schulwerk in Turkey were planted. Year after year, it grows and blossoms with the expertise of many precious educators from Turkey and abroad and spreads all over Turkey through lifelong-learner Turkish teachers who set their hearts to the Orff Schulwerk approach.

To salute the efforts of Muzaffer Arkan as the first Turkish composer and pedagogue who realized the importance of bringing Orff Schulwerk principles and Turkish music together, we want to start with an overview of music and dance culture of Turkey.

General characteristics of traditional music and dance in Turkey

The rule of many different civilizations throughout the region's history like Sumerians, Hittites, and Phrygians, the Byzantines, Seljuks, and the Ottomans has generated a cultural richness and diversity that in turn has given rise to variations in traditional music and dance.

Folk music in Turkey has vast variations in different regions of the country due to geographic, economic, historical, ethnical, and cultural factors. Consequently, folk dances in Turkey offer a rich formative and figurative variety. For example, the dance *zeybek*, which is usually slow, in nine-beat rhythms, and dominant in the western regions (Aegean) where the climate is relatively milder, reflects the individuality, courage, and heroism of the western people and it is performed one-by-one. In contrast, the dance *horon*, which is fast, in seven-beat rhythms, and common in the Black Sea region with its harsh winds and rains, and *halay* dances of the eastern regions are chain dances performed hand-in-hand, symbolizing collective living and working traditions.

Classical Turkish music is a product of Central Asia, Seljuks, and Ottoman Empire. It is mostly complex in terms of *makam*,[1] rhythm, form, and execution. Turkish folk music and classical Turkish music differ significantly from Western music in terms of musical structure.

---

1   *Makam* is a system of melody. It provides a complex set of rules for composing and performance. Each *makam* specifies a unique scale and melodic development.

The whole tone is divided into nine equal parts; each part is called a *koma*. The use of *komas* characterizes the microtonal structure of Turkish music that separates it from the Western equal temperament system. This is the reason why playing some Turkish music pieces exactly on fretted, keyed, or barred instruments is not possible. However, there are some *makams* that are similar to Western modes. For example: Ionian mode can be associated with *Rast makam*, Dorian mode with *Hüseyni makam*, Phrygian mode with *Kürdi makam*, and Aeolian mode with *Nihavend makam*. *Re Hüseyni makam*, which is frequently used in Turkish children's songs, is given as an example below:

Re Hüseyni Scale

Regarding rhythmic structure, irregular rhythms, such as 9/8, 7/8, 5/8 meters and also 4/4, 2/4 meters are frequently used in Turkish folk music and also in Turkish school songs.

Traditional musical instruments are primarily plucked (such as *bağlama, ud, kanun, cümbüş*) or bowed (such as *kemençe, kabak kemane, yaylı tambur*) strings, flute-type winds (*ney, kaval,* etc.), and a variety of drums (*darbuka, bendir,* etc.) and small percussion (wooden spoons, hand-cymbals, etc.).

Children playing instruments: kemençe, kaşık, and davul, with the teacher Birgül Berna Uysal
Photo: Private collection

The history of Orff Schulwerk in Turkey

In 1936 Edward Zuckmayer came from Germany to Turkey upon Hindemith's suggestion and, with the official invitation from the government of the Republic of Turkey, he was asked to reform the training of music teachers and general music education. He also introduced ideas of Orff Schulwerk at Gazi Education Institute in Ankara. Later Muzaffer Arkan came into personal contact with Carl Orff and wanted to implement the basic ideas of the Schulwerk.

During the 1950s, Arkan opened courses to teachers in Turkey on playing techniques of Orff instruments that he had brought from Germany (Jungmair, 2015; Uçan, 2003).

In 1991, Ulrike Jungmair was invited to present Orff Schulwerk at Gazi University. There she met Liz Sey, who in 1997 started to organize regular seminars on Orff Schulwerk for kindergarten teachers, music teachers, and also for professors from conservatories and universities. Financial assistance for the seminars came from the Austrian Cultural Institute in Istanbul.

Based on a suggestion by Jungmair, Katja Ojala Koçak, a graduate of the Orff-Institute, came to the ALEV school, Istanbul in 1999. She not only taught children but also introduced her colleagues to the Orff Schulwerk, which then became influential in all teaching at the school. In 2001, the ALEV School was awarded the title "Carl Orff School" and recognized as a model school.

Also in 2001, **Orff Schulwerk Eğitim ve Danışmanlık Merkezi Türkye** (Orff Schulwerk Education and Consulting Center) was founded by the Austrian High School Alumni Foundation with the approval of Carl Orff's widow Liselotte Orff and with the support of the Carl Orff Institute Salzburg, the Carl Orff Foundation, and the Austrian Cultural Office Istanbul. Since then, it has become a member of the International Orff-Schulwerk Forum Salzburg and participates regularly in all of its international events.

In 2003, the International Symposium "Orff Schulwerk Elementary Music and Dance Pedagogy" was organized by Orff Merkezi in Istanbul with national and international lecturers. In addition to conveying theoretical knowledge of elementary music and dance pedagogy, it was also questioning to what extent the principles of Orff Schulwerk could be realized on the basis of Turkish culture.

Since its foundation, Orff Merkezi organizes seminars for teachers. In addition to seminars on general topics related to Orff Schulwerk in kindergarten and primary school, there have also been seminars with various focus points like the use of Orff Schulwerk in secondary language education, music therapy, and inclusive education.

In 2010 the piano duo Güher and Süher Pekinel started a project to improve music education in all Anatolia. This happened over several years in co-operation with the Orff Merkezi and the Ministry of National Education (MEB). After 2019 it continued in independent form in co-operation with MEB (see detailed description in the article below).

Beginning in 2013, Orff Merkezi also offers levels courses in Turkey given by Orff Schulwerk instructors resident in Turkey as well as teachers from the Orff Institute, Mozarteum University, Salzburg. The aim here is that the pedagogical content of Orff Schulwerk is conceptualized and internalized. Those students who complete the three-year levels course with distinct success according to the examination committee's assessments are invited to attend the "Train the Trainer" program, a further 1-1.5 year-long intensive program. In this program, the candidates are trained to teach in teacher education courses, to give the participant teachers the guidance they need to communicate to their respective target groups; in other words, to be role models.

The *Orff Info* magazine published by the Orff Merkezi Turkey with its 25 issues to date since 2002 has played a pioneer and major role in promoting Orff Schulwerk in Turkey. Its content is comprised of Turkish and translated scholarly articles, insights from local and international seminars and projects, and practical examples.

In September 2019 the **Anatolian Orff-Schulwerk Association** was founded as a new Orff Schulwerk initiative in Turkey (see report below).

The following is a selection of significant projects of Orff Merkezi, also in collaboration with other institutions:

- Between 2010–2015, a cooperative project was initiated and financed by the renowned pianist twins Güher and Süher Pekinel. Thirty teachers from different cities of Turkey participated in a series of seminars throughout the year, mainly with Ulrike Jungmair.
- From 2015–2018 it was named "Pekinel's Orff Schulwerk in Anatolia" (see also the report: Pekinel Project: Orff Schulwerk in Anatolia below) and was financed by Finansbank. During two project periods, six Turkish teachers were accepted to take part as scholarship holders. In their first year, they attended an English language course in their hometown. In the second year, they participated in the Special Course (Advanced Studies in Music and Dance Education) at the Orff Institute in Salzburg. In the third year, they offered a series of Orff Schulwerk seminars in six different cities of Turkey. Orff Merkezi contributed a great deal to this (organization, instruments, program design, lecturers, etc.).
- Since 2013, weekend workshops for children ages 5–8 years have been held in Istanbul at Mimar Sinan University and University State Conservatories, in Izmir at Dokuz Eylül University, initiated by Orff Merkezi and conducted by its lecturers.
- "Dancing Notes Project" was another project for children, financed by the pharmaceutical company Eczacıbaşı in 2015. For three years, 120 preschool teachers from Istanbul, Samsun, Konya, and Hatay participated for 12 months in courses given by instructors of Orff Merkezi.
- TOBAV (Fraternal Foundation of Opera and Ballet Employees of State Theater) in Izmir has organized Orff Schulwerk seminars/workshops together with Orff Merkezi for children and adults (mainly teachers) regularly.
- There have also been seminars and summer schools organized by individual initiatives and Regional Directories of Ministry of National Education in various cities of Turkey in cooperation with Orff Merkezi.

Music and dance in the national education system of Turkey

Because private schools may have variable visions, missions, material, and human resources, this discussion refers to more consistently resourced public schools. Music lessons are given by a music teacher generally after the fourth grade. Before that, music lessons are to be taught by the classroom teacher. However, as a matter of fact, many of them choose not to do the music lessons for the sake of other academic areas like math, science, and language, or they include merely "singing" together due to the fact that the musical competences of an average classroom teacher are generally limited.

In middle school (5th through 8th grades), students receive a compulsory music lesson for one hour per week (if not offered more as elective), and it is completely elective during high school (if the school employs a music teacher at all).

In lower grades, there are rhymes from Turkish culture (mostly used 3 notes: la–sol–fa), songs adapted to Turkish that are mainly of European and American origin, and Turkish school songs, usually in simpler *makams*. Through the upper grades, the musical, rhythmic, formal structural and historical information of Turkish folk music is taught along with simple songs from classical Turkish music. Instead of the traditional Turkish musical instruments, recorder and melodica are commonly used in schools. As of today, movement and dance education are not part of the Turkish education curriculum.

In university teacher training programs, there has been more interest in Orff Schulwerk. In 2018, in addition to the "Music Teaching Methods," a course called "Orff Instruments" was added to the Music Teacher Training program. In the preschool teacher programs "Rhythm, Dance, and Orff in Early Childhood" was introduced as an elective course in some universities.[1]

Publications about Orff Schulwerk in Turkey

Orff Schulwerk has been the subject of many postgraduate theses, research articles published in national and international academical journals, and papers presented in national and international congresses, symposia, and conferences by Turkish scholars. In addition to academic studies, many books that include both the theoretical foundations and the original application examples are ready for the use of educators, families, and children.

A total of 31 master's theses and 8 doctoral dissertations examining Orff Schulwerk have been issued so far in Turkey Higher Education Thesis Center (1998–2020). The focus of these studies is mainly on preschool and primary education. Research topics in both theses and journal articles have been diverse and interdisciplinary, for example, attempts for establishing a theoretical background, effects on developmental domains (cognitive, socio-emotional, language, physical), attitudes and perceptions of teachers and teacher candidates, children with special needs, and the applicability of Orff Schulwerk in different settings.

Conclusion

There are promising endeavors by teaching professionals regarding the use of Orff Schulwerk in Turkey. However, there is still a long way to be able to say that the philosophy of Orff Schulwerk is understood and being applied correctly. For exactly this reason, all efforts to improve and intensify teacher education are of utmost importance. Orff Merkezi for more than 20 years has assumed a pioneer role to build a solid infrastructure of Orff Schulwerk in Turkey that considers both theoretical and practical aspects. So, it would not be wrong to say that Orff Merkezi and all those who are devoted to Orff Schulwerk in Turkey are ready to take further responsibility to ensure sustainable progress toward an accurate direction.

---

1 Undergraduate teacher training programs can be reached through the web page of Council of Higher Education (www.yok.gov.tr)

THE PEKINEL PROJECT
to Improve Musical Education in Anatolia

Güher Pekinel, Süher Pekinel [1]

Our system for the promotion of music education in Anatolia supports music education in state preschools and primary schools in Anatolia through the Orff Schulwerk. We firmly believe that every child must have a right to adequate free music education and this vision is implemented as a principle of the system.

The Orff Schulwerk is an approach that has been recognized and implemented worldwide. Having lived overseas in different countries for long periods of time and being familiar with the Orff Schulwerk, we decided to start an initiative to improve the state of music education in Turkey with its help. Its purpose is to utilize all branches of art in order to uncover the creative power and develop important social, cognitive, and emotional skills within us all by utilizing rhythm, motion, and speech. It approaches human values as a whole.

Therefore, we contacted the Orff Merkezi in Istanbul in order to research the state of music education in Turkey. In line with the data that we summarized and in close cooperation with the Merkezi and years of pre-work, we started our system, the "Pekinel Project to Improve Musical Education in Anatolia," in 2010 in order to ensure that Orff Schulwerk could be implemented as part of music courses in all of the schools in Turkey. We applied to the Ministry of National Education (MEB) with this project and signed a protocol with them on 10 September 2010 in order to realize the project. We assumed the project's fundamental configuration, implementation, and sponsorship ourselves.

The education in question was first implemented in 10 preschool and elementary school classes in 9 pilot cities (Istanbul, Ankara, Antalya, Izmir, Mersin, Bursa, Trabzon, Gaziantep, Mardin). 30 of the 60 teachers recommended by the ministries of the 9 pilot cities were selected and provided with training at Bosphorus University's facilities for 10 full days, and then subsequently at the private ALEV elementary school and home of Orff Merkezi. The MEB undertook the accommodation services so that participants could return for the 2nd and 3rd stages of the project. This was significant help for the continuation of the Project.

In cooperation with the team of the Orff Merkezi, Istanbul, and with Ulrike Jungmair, from the Orff Institute (former vice-president of the Austrian Orff-Schulwerk Association and long-time consultant and lecturer for Orff Merkezi), who personally led this seminar, a great program was put together and carried out.

In the first stages, the music lessons in schools were increased by two hours a week, parents were informed, their participation was encouraged, and teachers began to receive additional training, as mentioned above. The principals of the schools of the 30 teachers who received training as part of the pilot project, were also tasked with opening music classrooms. Music education, which had been halted for 18 years, found its place in classrooms once again due

---

1 Güher Pekinel and Süher Pekinel, are duo pianists. After extended studies in Paris, Frankfurt, and Philadelphia they completed their master's degree at the Juilliard School with honors. In 1984 Karajan invited them to the Salzburg Festival. Krzysztof Penderecki, Leonard Bernstein, and Jacques Loussier composed for them, and they performed with distinguished orchestras and conductors all over Europe, the Far East, and the USA. Their extensive discography includes all the major works for piano duo. They have also pioneered three significant music education systems in international standards in Turkey and have been honored with many high awards: Honorary Doctorate and "Honorary Award" for their lifetime achievements in Turkey, "Order of Merit" in Germany among others.

to the enthusiastic response from students. Arising problems were solved in collaboration with teachers and by personally contacting principals. The MEB inspected the courses and announced that they would appoint more music teachers as part of the project. 10,000 children had been reached by the end of the first year.

Preschool music education in Turkey

In Turkey under the title "Preschool Education" children are generally provided with chorus, individual instrument, and rhythmic dance training only in private schools and daycares. While this is encouraging, by being solely open to private education this development is not enough to meet current needs. Realizing the implementation of the Orff Schulwerk approach, especially in state preschools and elementary schools, will open new doors in music as well as in overall education by supporting the development of future generations' aesthetic and artistic foundations. As it is in Europe, the most important topic in music education is that music lessons are taught by preschool teachers with knowledge and experience, who have been specifically trained for this.

It is important to note that such a training should contain courses not only in basic music education and preschool education, but also in child development and psychology, aesthetic education for children, children's literature, drama, children's choir conducting, music-play-movement, and music and dance. In Turkey, however, such highly equipped institutions, departments, or even programs that train preschool music educators are only newly forming. Furthermore, in departments, conservatories, or other music schools training music teachers, the major area course offerings in music education and courses covering cognitive development are still insufficient.

Today's stage of the system

Six carefully selected music teachers received scholarships to study at the one-year post-graduate program "Advanced Studies in Music and Dance Education – Orff Schulwerk" at the Orff Institute, University Mozarteum in Salzburg. After having completed their studies, they returned to our country and started to train preschool and music teachers from provinces within the scope of local trainings in line with our protocol, which we signed as a result of long negotiations with the Ministry of National Education.

The project has developed itself into the existing and recognized system with results never seen before. In this way, Orff Schulwerk was presented all over Anatolia to teachers, parents, and students by our teachers and initiative. In addition, it was also the first Orff Schulwerk formation that was recognized by MEB as an official vocational training.

Lately, the system expanded itself to all cities in Anatolia. This is a future-oriented innovation, and an explosion.

Finally, we would once again like to highlight how important it is that music education should be offered again at all schools and be implemented in curriculum to raise a generation with dialogue, global vision, harmony, and peace.

ORFFDER – Anatolian Orff-Schulwerk Association

Ali Öztürk, Atilla Coşkun Toksoy, Didem Karşıyakalı Doğan, Evrim Onay, Senem Özyoğurtcu, Emine Yaprak Kotzian

In September 2019, ORFFDER—Anadolu Orff-Schulwerk Derneği (Anatolian Orff-Schulwerk Association)—was founded by music educators and scholars who have many years of experience in learning and teaching the Orff Schulwerk approach and licensed by the Carl Orff Foundation. Since then, ORFFDER has rapidly entered the educational field through courses, projects, and publications.

The spirit of solidarity, working, and producing together are the principles ORFFDER has developed. All members can exchange ideas, express opinions, produce, and implement projects and actively participate in various working groups.

ORFFDER education and training programs

ORFFDER has designed various programs to contribute to a conscious implementation of the basic pedagogical, didactic, and methodological principles of the Orff Schulwerk in teaching practice, as well as to gain experience, repertoire, and at least minimal expertise in various areas of the arts.

Chain Course:
This is a series of courses that are complementary to each other in relation to the learning areas of the Orff Schulwerk. The purpose of the Chain Course, which consists of three modules, is to provide participants with knowledge and understanding of Orff Schulwerk pedagogy, both theoretically and practically.

Model courses: These courses come in two variants.
a) Orff Schulwerk Teaching Models: These courses are designed to enable participants to learn about different teaching styles of experienced Orff Schulwerk teachers as well as to get ideas for their own lesson planning by expanding their repertoire of music, movement, and dance material.
b) Additional Interdisciplinary Courses: Considering the interdisciplinary and comprehensive aspect of the Orff Schulwerk, the combination of materials, methods, and techniques from different arts disciplines and different areas of competence allows for the discovery of a variety of expressive possibilities. In these courses, participants will gain experience and repertoire in different areas such as dance, acting, puppet theatre, painting, staging techniques, storytelling, juggling, magic, mime, origami, puppet, and marionette design. The main aim of these courses is to acquire extra-musical ideas and skills that help develop more aesthetic and artistic qualities and create thematic diversity that can be integrated into creative teaching processes.

Teaching Practice—Mentoring Program:
This course is designed for small groups so that the mentor can guide participants individually in lesson planning and in putting the prepared lessons into practice with different teaching groups, especially with children of different ages. This training is an adaptation of the teaching practice subjects taught in graduate and undergraduate programs in Elementary Music Education at European universities and at the Orff Institute.

Three-Level Teacher Education Certificate Program—Levels Courses:
In addition to carefully following the guidelines of the Carl Orff Foundation, the content of this program has been revised and adapted to the current needs of the education system in Turkey. This program has developed a very comprehensive scope to train Orff Schulwerk teachers according to European standards.

Sharing days:
In these 90-minute sharing sessions, members are invited to present theoretical lectures and teaching models or small teaching ideas, games, songs, music pieces, etc. prepared by them.

ORFFDER publications

Orffdergi is a bi-annual digital journal on Orff Schulwerk - Elementary Music and Movement Pedagogy. It includes basic Orff Schulwerk literature, current research studies, articles, interviews, model curricula, songs written by members of ORFFDER, and current news such as training opportunities, publications, etc. The main aim of *Orffdergi* is to at least partially compensate for the need for relevant literature in Turkish.

ORFFDER projects

CROSA—ORFFDER Cultural and Musical Project
This project was created as a result of the meetings between CROSA (Croatian Orff-Schulwerk Association) and ORFFDER in 2019. The aim of the project is to contribute to cultural exchange as well as to create a space where music educators interact with each other in the area of music therapy based on the Orff Schulwerk approach. Two Turkish and four Croatian educators will meet in Zagreb for the first training. The language of instruction is English, and the event is open to everybody, but especially from Turkey and Croatia. The continuation of the project will take place in Turkey.

ORFFDER ORCHESTRA—elemental music and dance ensemble
Every member of ORFFDER is also an equal member of the ORFFDER Orchestra and can contribute to the ensemble with his or her instrument, voice, and body. The basic working principles of the ORFFDER Orchestra include the exchange of ideas, participation in joint improvisation processes, the shaping and fixing of individual ideas of the orchestra members through group decisions, and thus the creation of group compositions in both music and dance. The aim is to develop the ORFFDER Orchestra into a semi-professional ensemble that can perform and give concerts as well as present ORFFDER at festivals, symposia, or other national and international organizations.

Project on revisiting Anatolian music and dance elements through microtonal xylophone - Bağlafon within Orff Schulwerk pedagogical framework
Although Turkish folk music and Turkish classical music present themselves as different domains, the phenomenon of *maqam* is the common structure for both. The other significant commonality between these two musical genres is the fact that both are based on a master-apprentice relationship, in other words, "playing by ear." The experience of "playing by ear" through pitches and exemplary melodic motifs plays an important role in the perception of *maqam* music to facilitate the learning and transmission of folkways to the next generations. in which İTÜ (Istanbul Technical University) and ORFFDER are collaborating, aims to realize such an experience. As part of the project, a xylophone with microtonal pitches (B♭2,

F♯3) of the traditional Turkish musical instrument *Bağlama* was developed. For the microtonal xylophone, we call it *Bağlafon* (baglaphone), the pitches *Segâh* and *eviç*, which are the third and seventh steps of *Rast maqam*, were made according to the frequency values of *Kanun* (or *Qanun*, a traditional Turkish musical instrument that is a kind of large zither). The additional pitches enable the instrument to play some of the scales of Turkish folk music, such as *Kerem-Yahyalı Kerem* (*Hüseyni* scale), *Garip* (*Hicaz* scale), *Bozlak* scale (*Kürdi* scale) and *Rast* scale, which are tuned to the Kanun chord system. The project intends to explore different ways of performing Turkish folk music through elementary teaching processes as well as ear training and differentiation of maqams through *Bağlafon*. It will also investigate how this instrument can be integrated into literature as a school instrument.

Set of bars for alto xylophone. These bars are used to create the three most commonly used maqams, Rast, Hüseyni, and Hicaz. The bars are marked with "sun" and "moon" symbols in order to assist non-professionals to distinguish the maqams that contain pitches with comma (microtones).
Photo: ©Zen Müzik / Zen Instruments

European and Anatolian sounds

This project, coordinated by ORFFDER, will be realized in partnership with at least three European countries. The aim of the project is to organize all the components of folk culture (folk songs, ballads, lullabies, rhymes, riddles, stories, fairy tales, folk dance, etc.) that are peculiar to the participating countries and suitable for music teaching into a model based on the Orff Schulwerk approach. In the first step of the project, each participating country will conduct a thorough literature review and identify the cultural components that can be used in music lessons. In the next step, these components will be adapted into teaching processes based on Orff Schulwerk principles. These prepared teaching processes will be carried out with sample groups of different ages, and after a review and revision process, a valid and reliable teaching model will be developed. In the end, each country will have a new musical teaching model based on this new paradigm and all its content components, which will be composed of their own cultural components in their respective education systems. In addition, all lesson plans and audiovisual materials will be published on the project website and a music album and e-book will be prepared for access from all over the world, which should be seen as a cultural exchange on a global scale.

Academics Association—a platform for discussion and exchange of ideas

ORFFDER is working hard to create various platforms where interested academics can meet periodically to stimulate academic debates and the exchange of ideas that can guide the development and implementation of Orff Schulwerk in our cultural and educational system. In this way, ORFFDER hopes to increase the quantity and quality of new academic research studies and expand the literature in Turkish, as well as unite academics to work together in the long term to establish music education departments in elementary music and movement education at Turkish universities.

Since its foundation, ORFFDER has placed great emphasis on experience-based and intellectual exchange between its founders, board, and members in order to create and maintain a common ground where all can come together with a community spirit that grows in a democratic, independent, transparent, cooperative, solidary, respectful, and loving atmosphere. This character of ORFFDER, unfolds the potential that still exists in our country in the field of Orff Schulwerk. Likewise, it drives ORFFDER to work and produce collectively and to organize a variety of projects in a short time, some of which have been mentioned here. ORFFDER is determined to continue working, learning, and growing without losing that special quality.

BIBLIOGRAPHY

Andante, Turkey's classical music magazine, Special Issue. (2015, June). Türkiye'de Müzik Eğitimi ve Orff Yaklaşımı [Music education and Orff approach in Turkey]. Contributions by G. Amus, T. Başar, F. Cümbüş Auernig, M. Emeç Birol, D. Goodkin, B. Haselbach, U. Jungmair, B. Özevin, G. Pekinel, & S. Pekinel.

Bilen, S., Özevin, B., & Canakay, E. (2009). *Orff Destekli Etkinliklerle Müzik Eğitimi* [Music education with Orff Schulwerk supported activities]. Ankara: Müzik Eğitimi Yayınları.

Eren, B. (2017). *Önüm Arkam Taşım Topum- Özel Eğitimde Müzikli Etkinlik Örnekleri* [Musical activity samples in special education]. Ankara: Eğiten Kitap.

Eren, B. (2018). Orff as a music therapy approach: Who, with whom, where, when and how? In B. U. Çifdalöz & E. F. Türkmen (Eds.), *Music therapy in Turkey*. UK: Cambridge Scholar Publishing.

Erol, O., & Ojala-Koçak, K. (2017). *Karamela Sepeti* [Caramel basket]. Ankara: Eğiten Kitap.

Jungmair, U. (2015, June). Hindemith'den bugüne Türkiye'de Orff Schulwerk uygulamaları [Orff Schulwerk applications in Turkiye since Hindemith]. *Andante Magazine Special Issue*, 6–7.

Karşıyakalı-Doğan, D. M. (2020). *Orff Yaklaşımı Ile Birlikte Sunulan Sosyal Öykü Uygulamalarının Gelişimsel Yetersizliği Olan Çocuklara Müzikal Beceri Kazandırmada Etkililiği* [The Effectiveness of social story applications presented through Orff approach in teaching musical skills to children with developmental disabilities] [Doctoral dissertation]. Istanbul: Marmara Üniveristesi Eğitim Bilimleri Enstitüsü.

Koçak, K. O., & Laslo, N. (Eds.). (2013). *Türkiye'de Orff Schulwerk, Müzik, Oyun ve Dans Üzerine Makaleler* [Orff Schulwerk in Turkey, articles on music, play and dance]. Ankara: Müzik Eğitimi Yayınları.

Laslo, N., (Ed.). (2003). *International Symposium on Orff Schulwerk Music and Dance Pedagogy* (January 16–18, Istanbul). Symposium book published by Orff Schulwerk Eğitim ve Danışmanlık Merkezi (ORFF Merkezi).

Özevin, B. (2020). Orff Schulwerk Müzik ve Hareket Eğitimi [Orff Schulwerk music and dance education]. In E. Mübeccel & S. Gönen (Eds.), *Erken Çocuklukta Ritim, Dans ve Orff Eğitimi*. Ankara: Pegem Akademi.

Özevin, B., & Bilen, S. (2011). *Yaratıcı Dans* [Creative dance]. Ankara: Müzik Eğitimi Yayınları.

Öziskender, G. (2011). *Orff Yaklaşımı ile Yapılan Okul Öncesi Müzik Eğitiminin Öğrencilerin Sosyal Becerilerinin Gelişimine Etkisi* [The effect of preschool music education through Orff approach on the development of students' social skills] [Unpublished master's thesis]. Ondokuz Mayıs Üniversitesi Eğitim Bilimleri Enstitüsü, Samsun.

Öztürk, A. (2006). Türkiye'de Orff- Schulwerk Yaklaşımının Dünü Bugünü [The past and present of Orff Schulwerk approach in Turkey]. *Yaratıcı Drama Dergisi, 1* (2), 79–88.

Özyoğurtcu, S., & Milli, M. (2017). *Türk Müziği ile Orff Schulwerk Uygulamaları* [Orff Schulwerk applications with Turkish music]. Ankara: Eğiten Kitap.

Toksoy, A. (2014). *Orff Yaklaşımı, Elementer Müzik ve Hareket Eğitimine Giriş* [Orff approach, introduction to elemental music and movement education]. İTÜ Vakfı Yayınları.

Uçan, A. (2003). *Türkiye'de müzik eğitiminin gelişimi, Orff okulöğretisi'nin tanımı, uygulanımı-uyarlanımı ve Orff anlayışıyla temel müzik eğitiminin genel durumu* [The development of music education in Turkey, the definition of Orff Schulwerk, its implementation-adaptation and the general situation of basic music education with Orff's understanding]. In N. Laslo (Ed.), International symposium on Orff Schulwerk music and dance pedagogy (January 16-18, Istanbul). Symposium book published by Orff Schulwerk Eğitim ve Danışmanlık Merkezi.

Yaprak Kotzian, E. (2018). *Elementer Müzik ve Hareket Pedagojisinin Temelleri*. Istanbul: Pan Yayıncılık. [Published in English in 2019: *Orff-Schulwerk handbook. Principles of elemental music and movement pedagogy*. Mainz: Schott Music.]

Periodicals

Orff Info Magazine (April 2002–) (25 issues). Issued by Orff Schulwerk Eğitim ve Danışmanlık Merkezi (ORFF Merkezi), Istanbul.

Orffdergi: Digital magazine. (2020–). Orffder – Anadolu Orff-Schulwerk Derneği (www.orffder.org).

Orff Schulwerk in Ukraine: Traditions and Innovations

Svetlana Fir, Tatiana Chernous [1]

Our Ukrainian folk-art tradition, expressed in poetry, music, dance, and theater, is a fundamental part of the cultural tradition of Ukraine. Its origins are found deep in antiquity, and their development is connected with the history and unique geographical location of our country. Our traditions are a source for creative ideas that are very close to Orff Schulwerk, and they can be adapted and used in the modern educational process with people of all ages.

How it all began: The history of the Orff Schulwerk in Ukraine

The first acquaintance for Ukrainian teachers with Orff Schulwerk happened in Russia in 2009. Because of contacts with the Russian Orff Schulwerk Association, our teachers were able to participate in workshops presented by foreign educators such as Jos Wuytack, Soili Perkio, and Vyacheslav Zhilin. In 2010 Svetlana Fir and Katerina Zavalko attended the International Summer Course in Salzburg. It was the first educational experience for Ukrainian teachers in Europe. That visit played an essential role in the future organization of the Orff Schulwerk Association in Ukraine (OSAU).

Since then, the authors of this article have started to study and experiment independently with Orff Schulwerk in the field of music pedagogy and preschool education. They have been actively developing this area, learning from the experience of foreign colleagues, and integrating their new knowledge in the context of Ukrainian cultural traditions. Gradually, they were joined not only by musicians, but also by colleagues from different professional areas. These ideas have been spread to adjacent areas of psychology and child development and have been used in both educational and scientific spheres.

The fundamental and purposefully planned work with the adaptation of Orff Schulwerk in Ukraine began with the day of the founding of the Orff Schulwerk Association of Ukraine and its official acceptance as a member of the International Orff-Schulwerk Forum Salzburg during the 2018 convention.

There was a most helpful contribution from Katerina Zavalko (National Pedagogical Dragomanov University), who helped to organize the first three international Orff Schulwerk conferences in Ukraine. The first one called "Orff-Pedagogy: Modern Aspects of the Implementation" was held in 2018 in Kiev and hosted by the National Pedagogical Dragomanov University. In 2019 the second convention, "Orff Schulwerk Approach in the Development of Creativity: Ways of Integration into Modern Arts Education," took place at the same location. T. H. Shevchenko National University "Chernihiv Colehium" in Chernihiv supported the third conference in 2020. It was dedicated to the theme "Elemental Music Making with the Orff Schulwerk: From the Development of Musical Abilities to Professional Instrumental Education," and it gathered specialists from different regions of the country. Colleagues from

1 We are so grateful to Katerina Zavalko and Yevhenia Shulga, who professionally and patiently supported the writing of this article.

European countries—Poland, Austria, Slovakia—were invited to each convention. We are proud of the participation of the special guests Joanna Tomkowska (Poland), Angelika Wolf (England, Austria), and Tomas Borosh (Slovakia).

During the summer of 2019 the 22nd International Orff Schulwerk Summer Course "Encounters," initiated and led by Coloman Kallós, took place at the National University "Ostrog Academy" (Ostrog) and has become an important event[1] in the process of developing the Orff Schulwerk movement in Ukraine. It has great resonance among specialists in the sphere of music pedagogy. More than 100 people from Ukraine, Turkey, South Korea, the Czech Republic, Slovakia, and Russia have become participants in this annual course.

In the early years of the Ukrainian Association, music teachers working with preschoolers had the greatest interest in the concept of Orff Schulwerk. Shortly after, due to the educational activities and some reforms in music education, teachers in music schools also became interested in the Orff Schulwerk approach, trying to find ways for integrating it into the teaching of instruments. With the emergence of a large number of private general education schools, we could observe in them the necessity for new ways and principles of teaching music. The popularity of Orff Schulwerk in primary and middle schools has increased significantly for a few years.

At the present time the adaptation of Orff Schulwerk ideas in the educational system in Ukraine is an area of active research, both pedagogical and psychological. We can see it now, for instance, in the area of inclusive education, where the idea of using the Orff Schulwerk approach is actively developed.

Ukrainian folk music tradition

Ukraine is located in the center of Europe. That fact undoubtedly has an enormous impact on its culture and traditions in general. When we talk about folklore, the reason for its great diversity is not only in the historical characteristics, but also in the interaction with different ethnic cultures. We can find elements of Hungarian, Romanian, Polish, and Russian folklore, particularly in the song and dance genres of Ukrainian folk music.

Every region of Ukraine, in accordance with its dialect, climate, territory, and customs, has its own characteristics, similarities, and differences. And most important, each region has a unique flavor of Ukrainian music and dance that is recognizable all over the world.

Examples of the ancient culture that is deep-rooted in pre-Christian beliefs have survived until today in the singing tradition. There we can find children's folklore, created by adults for children and by the children themselves. The folklore heritage for children is traditionally divided into two categories: calendar folklore, which is connected with the seasons and the most important natural phenomena, and non-calendar. These songs can be used in music lessons. The playful nature, simplicity, and brevity of text are very typical for them. In the songs you can find diverse combinations of singing and speaking, onomatopoeia, shouts, and rhymes. In most of the songs, tunes are based on two-tone calls or tree-tone melodic formulas. Scales are simple and without semitones. Tunes have a range within a fourth or a fifth and they are melodies with variations. The songs include a variety of genres, including lullabies (*kolyskovi*), nursery rhymes (*zabavlyanki*), Christmas carols (*kolyadki, shchedrivki*), counting rhymes (*lichilki*), teasers (*draznilki*), and calls (*zaklichki*).

---

1   "Encounters" is an annual international summer course organized in Europe. Ukraine was the first non-EU country to host the course.

Ukrainian folk songs of the later period are well-known for their beautiful, long, lyrical melodies and for the predominance of minor or alternating scales (major and relative minor with a shifting tonal center). They are also characterized by the simplicity of the structure (verse-chorus) and the alternation of different measures that comes from features of speech and the manner of the performance. Variations and improvisations are often included. A particular feature of Ukrainian songs is the variety of singing traditions in different regions. There is also a tradition of multi-part singing (3–4 voices) in Ukrainian folklore, and you can often find canons.

We are very proud that the bearers of the traditions of folk singing are still alive today and that they are passing along this important aspect of our culture to the younger generation.

Ukrainian folk-dance tradition

Our dance traditions have a long and rich history. Ukrainian folk dances are characterized by improvisation, a playful character, the presence of "a story," and an interaction of partners. There is a wide variety of circle dances of historic origin. In the later dances such as *Balamut* and *Grechaniki* you can see more choreography, the interaction of musicians and dancers in a common space, and more typical movements (for instance, there are many types of stomping and movements with squats for the male dancers in *Hopak* and *Kazachok*). Dances are often accompanied by shouts, body percussion, or a sung improvisation.

Instruments

Ukrainian folk dance is performed with instrumental accompaniment. It was traditionally accompanied by three or more (as in the western regions) musicians: a violin played a melody, a tambourine part was rhythmical, and a *tsymbaly* (a type of the hammer dulcimer) or a bass played a drone. In some regions, musicians used a large side drum called a *baraban* with a large cymbal.

Some wind instruments—*tylynka* (an overtone flute), *sopilka* (a fife made of a variety of materials), and others—were used both in the shepherd's culture and also for making music generally. Many of these instruments can be effectively adapted to musical activities with children. Wooden percussion instruments—*kalatalo* (a wooden plate with a handle and a movable hammer played with a quick wrist movement to get a sound), *trischata* (a rattle), and *rubel* (a board with notches played with a spoon or a rolling-pin like a guiro)—are especially suitable for use with children.

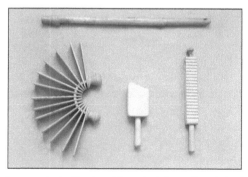

Across the top: tylynka (flute); and from the left: trischata, kalatalo, rubel
Photo: Tetiana Lushchenko

Folk music and dance have been the guides to the heart of the Ukrainian people, the keepers of the nation's spirituality and culture for many centuries. Historically, Ukraine was often deprived of independence and the national culture did not have the opportunity to develop freely.

Ukrainian nation has been experiencing a national revival, and the state has been standing for its independence for the last several years. In that historical context, the application of Orff Schulwerk ideas is very timely and current.

Unlike well-established music education, which unfortunately for many decades has not been interested in the popularization of Ukrainian folklore, the philosophy of Orff Schulwerk can give new life to the traditions of music-making at home, in amateur collective music-making, and it can help to spread these traditions in different areas of the general education.

On the other hand, Orff Schulwerk has potential in the development of Ukrainian music pedagogy in the future. From the time of the Soviet Union to the present day, declarative, directive, and authoritarian approaches have remained in the system of general and music education. These approaches are characterized by a lack of creativity in lessons and cannot support children in the development of their individuality. The Orff Schulwerk approach, where the creativity of a teacher and students is an essential aspect of the music education process, might be considered as a necessary "key" not only for music schools, but also for actual demands and needs of kindergartens and general education schools.

Orff Schulwerk in teacher training

Today an interesting tendency can be observed among Ukrainian universities and institutions. Some of them take an active interest in introducing the Orff Schulwerk concept and include its ideas in their programs. At the moment of writing this article, the National University "Ostrog Academy" offers as an additional subject the course, "Using the elements of the Orff Schulwerk approach in inclusive education." Vinnytsia State Kotsyubinsky Pedagogical University has an additional course with the name "Orff pedagogy in preschool education." We can say confidently now that the ideas of Orff Schulwerk are not only interesting for teachers of kindergartens and private studios, as it was a few years ago when the Orff Schulwerk Association of Ukraine was created, but it also gains the popularity among teachers of music in general education and universities. Students in different humanitarian departments, psychologists, social workers, and professionals working with the special needs population show their sincere interest in it.

OSAU actively participates in the development of educational programs for training specialists who could use Orff Schulwerk ideas in their practice. Katerina Zavalko, Tatiana Chernous, and Svetlana Fir have developed several introductory courses for specialists in the field of the creative pedagogy. A course for psychologists, special education teachers, and specialists in the field of inclusive education is also presented. The Association regularly organizes workshops with foreign teachers to train Ukrainian specialists and actively facilitates the implementation of various public projects that contribute to the integration of Orff Schulwerk ideas in the field of inclusive education. This gives a powerful impulse for the development of Orff Schulwerk ideas in Ukraine. A collection of recommendations, "Inclusive Practices for Cultural Workers," has been recently released as a result of a project. It includes articles by members of the Orff Schulwerk Association. Katerina Zavalko and Svetlana Fir published the guide, "The Basis of Orff Pedagogy." Members of the Association regularly publish their materials in periodical music magazines in Ukraine. OSAU publishes a collection of conference materials every year, which is interesting for practitioners in different fields as well as those in the research environment.

Plans for the future

Until now, our work has concentrated on using material from our own culture and history.

There are many modern artists (Mariya Prijmachenko, Anatolij Krivolap), composers (Igor Skorik, Lesya Dichko, Lyudmila Shukajlo), children's authors, dancers, choreographers, and poets in Ukraine—many of them well-known in the world—whose works can inspire teachers and students to do interesting experiments in music lessons with Orff Schulwerk. It is essential for us to find a way to use the idea of emphasizing creativity and individuality in leading our students to create their own compositions and choreographies or scenic creations and also to love and understand the modern arts.

The members of the Ukrainian Association are planning to extend our work in various directions. At the present time there are a number of initiatives to set up a few local Orff Schulwerk clubs in different Ukrainian cities. The idea of the creation of a Ukrainian adaptation of Orff Schulwerk is actively discussed by members of the Association. We plan to organize levels courses for teachers who are practicing in the field of Orff Schulwerk. There are also plans to expand the target audience, realizing not only pedagogical projects with children, but also with adults. We also see prerequisites to organize creative interdisciplinary projects. Another necessary aspect of our work will be to open our teaching to the music of other cultures and countries.

Translation: Nadya Svetlichnaya

Publications

Chernous T. (2019). Orf-muzyka ta rukh. Shcho, yak i dlia choho. Muzychnyi kerivnyk. No. 4 [Orff-music and movement. What, how and what for. *Musical Educator, 4*].

Chernous T. (2020). Orf-pidkhid v roboti z liudmy z invalidnistiu. In *Inkliuzyvni praktyky dlia pratsivnykiv kultury: metod posibnyk,* ukladachi: I. M. Brushevska, V. V. Kolodiazhna, & O. M. Halapchuk-Tarnavska [Orff-approach in working with people with disabilities. In *Inclusive practices for cultural workers: a methodological guide*, compiled by I. M. Brushevskaya, V. V. Kolodyazhnaya, & O. M. Galapchuk-Tarnavskaya]. Lutsk: Veja-Druk.

Zavalko, K., & Fir, S. (2013). Osnovy Orf-pedahohiky. In K. Zavalko (Ed.), navchalno-metodychnyi posibnyk [The basis of Orff Pedagogy. In K. Zavalko (Ed.), educational and methodological guide]. Cherkasy.

Proceedings of international scientific-practical conferences

Zavalko, K. (Ed.). (2018). Orf-pedahohika: suchasni vymiry vprovadzhennia [Orff-pedagogy: modern aspects of the implementation]. Kyiv (Ukraina).

Zavalko, K. (Ed.). (2019). Orf-podkhid v razvytku kreatyvnosti: shliakhy intehratsii v suchasnu osvitu u sferi mystetstva [Orff-approach in the development of creativity: ways of integration into the modern art education]. Chernihiv (Ukraina).

Zavalko, K. (Ed.). (2020). Elementarne muzykuvannia Karla Orfa: vid rozvytku muzychniykh zdibnostei do navchannia hri na muzychnomu instrumenti [Elementary music making of Carl Orff: from the development of musical abilities to the professional instrumental education]. Chernihiv (Ukraina).

The Orff Approach in the United Kingdom

Kate Buchanan, Sarah Hennessy, Caroline McCluskey

Beginnings and early development

In the first half of the 20th century music education for young children in school was largely focused on singing and sometimes percussion band. Ideas about child-centered teaching, creativity, and learning through play had been introduced in the early decades with Montessori, Froebel (early childhood education), and later by Marion Richardson (art education) and others. But very little of this permeated the music classroom.[1] It was not until the beginning of the 1960s that these ideas were effectively introduced into music teaching through Margaret Murray's work with Orff Schulwerk (more commonly referred to in the UK as the Orff approach).

The development of Orff Schulwerk in the UK grew out of a collaboration between Margaret Murray, Carl Orff, and Gunild Keetman. Although Doreen Hall, a Canadian, had created the first version of the *Music for Children* volumes in English (Orff & Keetman, 1956–1961), Orff was keen for Murray to collaborate on another version. She dedicated herself to finding English equivalents from folk song, children's songs, and folklore. The English recordings of Volumes I and II took place in London six months after this first contact with the Schulwerk in June 1957. It should be noted that the natural speech rhythms of German and English are rather closer than many other languages, so it was perhaps easier to adapt to English without disrupting the material of the musical models composed by Orff and Keetman in the original volumes (1950-1954).

> *No attempt has been made in this English version to keep rigidly to the original German texts or to traditional English tunes… because a way has been sought to follow the principle of Carl Orff's theories. (Jellineck, 1957)*

The first Orff Schulwerk UK teachers' course took place in 1958 led by Margaret Murray and involved singing, body percussion, rhythmic work, improvisation, and group composition. It was well received and later that year, Murray was asked to send Orff Schulwerk materials to Her Majesty's Inspectors with responsibility for music. At the 1958 Music Advisers' National Conference Murray gave a presentation that sparked interest amongst many leading music educators who helped establish the Orff approach across the UK. These included Kate Baxter (1978, 1985, 1994) who applied many of its principles in designing innovative resources and materials for children and adults with special educational needs, and Michael Lane (1984) whose practice and writing were strongly influenced by the approach.

In the early 1960s the number of courses grew and in 1964 the Orff Society UK was founded by Margaret Murray with a group of like-minded music educators. A network of local organizers was established, and members were encouraged to contact each other for mutual support. By 1965, membership had increased to 250 and communication was maintained through

---

1 Dalcroze Eurythmics was introduced in 1912 but made little impact on music teaching in general.

regular bulletins. Whilst members were encouraged to contribute articles, the bulletins were dominated by articles written by Murray, some of which articulate her frustration when Orff Schulwerk principles were not understood or applied appropriately in classrooms. A series of six articles (1967) by Marjorie Blackburn (later Ayling) provided a concise description of Orff Schulwerk in order to dispel the "rather confused and frequently suspicious attitude" that some people had towards it. Blackburn was a powerful advocate of the approach and worked closely with Margaret Murray to develop the content of the summer courses and provide opportunities for training. She taught on many courses, wrote articles, and was President of the Orff Society (2007-2017). Here she describes how elements of Orff Schulwerk were used in BBC programs (although unacknowledged):

> John Hosier (1928–2000), senior music producer for educational programmes for the BBC from 1953 to 1973, … pioneered an extensive range of schools' music programmes, drawing on the work of Carl Orff and Zoltán Kodály and skillfully adapting their continental practices to suit the British school system. With extensive guidance notes, these imaginative programmes gave children opportunities to develop their own creative ideas, whilst also supporting non-specialist primary school teachers who often lacked the confidence to conduct their own music lessons. (Ayling, 2013, p. 65)

Through the 1970s and early 1980s the Orff approach continued to be disseminated through teachers' courses and publications but also, and perhaps much more widely through teachers sharing activities and the principles by a kind of osmosis. In the 1970s ideas about creativity in education generally, and arts education particularly, abounded.[1] There were many different sources of ideas flowing into schools through professional development courses and initial teacher education. While the Orff approach was perhaps the only creative pedagogy in music education focused on primary education, what was happening in secondary arts education resonated strongly also.

New challenges: 1980s to now

Through the past 50 years there has been a growing consensus within the music teaching profession (in the UK) that young people should learn through practical engagement and should develop knowledge and skills to make their own music through exploring and experimenting, improvising, and composing. Writers such as Paynter (1970, 1990), Swanwick (1988, 1999), and Small (1987, 1998) argued for this as a central aim in music education. Much of the focus of these writers was on children in secondary school rather than younger learners, and while creativity in music remained a central element of the curriculum for all ages, the numbers of primary teachers teaching music dwindled, as did the time and support for music in the curriculum. In response to loss of funding for specialist staff in the late 1970s class teachers were encouraged to teach music to their own class. This coincided with a growing belief that music should be a "normal" part of every teacher's practice, and that music teaching should adopt a more inclusive, less elitist stance. It was not just about different materials but about a different way of teaching, especially regarding teaching for creativity, and if general class teachers were teaching music, then they needed support and resources. Thus, the specialist as consultant emerged: a class teacher with music training who could lead the subject and support colleagues while continuing to do the more specialist tasks of running choirs and ensembles. This role was developed through the 1980s and 1990s and was endorsed by government policy. Many

---

1 By the 1970s both drama education and contemporary dance education had joined the school curriculum.

leading educators wrote materials and books in support of this new focus (see for example Mills (1991), Hennessy (1995), Glover & Ward (1993)) It is clear, when looking at this material, that the influence of the Orff approach alongside other sources is strong despite some lack of acknowledgement. The pedagogical theories of social constructivism, teaching for creativity (Jeffery & Craft, 2004), learning through play, and collaborative learning were (and still are) widely promoted and the pedagogy of Orff Schulwerk reflects these.

While Orff Schulwerk was never intended for generalist teachers, the content of this new ("non-elitist") approach was an amalgam of its more accessible aspects (working with rhythmic speech, rhymes and chants, body percussion, rhythmic and expressive movement, and singing) and composition ideas drawn from Orff Schulwerk and also from Paynter and other composer/educators mentioned earlier.[1] These involved found sounds, invented notations, experimenting with and exploring sounds in the world around, playground games, poems and stories, drama and movement, still and moving visual images. It is difficult to unpack the origins of these ideas, but they are clearly focused on the principle that children are naturally musical and need diverse opportunities and sensitive guidance to grow skills and understanding.

Orff Society workshops and summer schools attracted many teachers who were working as consultants in their own and other schools, as well as generalist teachers. In the hands of those with musical expertise the Orff approach sparked and nourished their practice and gave them greater insight into a pedagogy which encourages adaptation and creativity and is fundamentally inclusive. Through the 1970s, 1980s, and 1990s, practitioners (many introduced to Orff Schulwerk by Margaret Murray) wrote books and led workshops and training for teachers in their own institutions. Their influence was wide reaching and their legacy accounts for the embedding of Orff Schulwerk principles in mainstream "good" practice. Perhaps the least developed aspect remains that of using dance and expressive movement. This is perhaps a cultural resistance, but also a result of the limited time and space teachers often have to work with. The Orff approach in the UK is predominantly associated with music education, but interdisciplinary practices are very relevant in all creative contexts.

In 1992 music became part of the National Curriculum.[2] The "orders" gave equal status to composing, performing, and listening, and primary teachers were supported (initially) to gain skills and confidence through professional development and through the now established model of consultants. How individual schools chose to provide for music was not prescribed and not all schools had equal access to support. Although for some years things improved, as other priorities emerged, the gap between schools in relation to both quantity and quality of music teaching has widened. To some extent the informal sector (community music and the outreach work of professional ensembles) has grown to partially fill the gaps. Practitioners working in these settings as well as in the preschool[3] and special needs sectors are a growing audience for Orff Schulwerk.

The increasing focus on literacy and mathematics, testing and inspections through the 1990s and up to now has meant a further fall in time and resources for music. This has also affected teacher training, and most primary teachers qualify with very little knowledge of music teaching. The loss of music education courses in higher education means that there are few opportunities for advanced study in music pedagogy.

The Orff Society UK offers free introductory workshops to teacher training courses and a course for experienced music teachers. We also hold workshops focusing on different aspects

---

1   See for example: McNichol (1992), McGregor (1995), Adams (1997), Buchanan & Chadwick (1995).
2   All 4 nations had their own version and music was included in all of them.
3   Children start school in the UK in the year they are 5, and many attend nursery prior to this.

(e.g., inclusion, early years, dance) and often led by internationally renowned practitioners, and a biennial summer school in different venues around the UK.

Scottish Orff Schulwerk Association (SOSA)

In 2011 SOSA was established as the association for Scotland. Previously, the Orff Society UK had served the whole of the UK but, as the education systems in each of the four nations[1] have become increasingly distinct, it became more relevant for Scotland to have its own association. This was established by Moira Jakobsson. SOSA has a growing community of teachers, music specialists, arts educators, and students who attend workshops and courses in Scotland, the UK, and beyond. In partnership with Beatroute Arts[2] SOSA hosts training courses at their venue where they keep instruments and maintain a resources library. SOSA invites international teachers to lead weekend courses which take place in Glasgow, Edinburgh, or in the Scottish Highlands where there is an enthusiastic community.

The Orff approach to music, dance, and speech education complements the Scottish Curriculum as exploratory, creative learning across the arts. Interdisciplinary learning is a key aspect of the Scottish *Curriculum for Excellence* (Education Scotland, 2021).

Cultural adaptations

Alongside popular music in all its forms, the musical traditions of many cultures are now enjoyed in and out of classrooms, reflecting both the main minority cultures of the UK (originating in Africa, China, South Asia, and the Caribbean), and those of the Americas. Because the Orff approach is more about how we teach than what we teach, teachers can embrace any repertoires they find musically engaging for their children. Paradoxically this "multi- and intercultural" trend has made the traditions of the British Isles less familiar.

In the 1950s it could be argued that there was more apparent cultural cohesion in the UK, but in the past 20 years each nation has gained varying degrees of political autonomy and their own education system (although Scotland has always had educational independence). There has been a resurgence of interest in local cultures and identities with Welsh and Gaelic taught in schools.[3]

Peter Sidaway (a founding member of the UK association) published songs in Welsh (1993) and there is renewed interest in traditional, local songs and dances across the UK. While in today's practice such traditional sources no longer predominate, they are a valuable source of often neglected repertoire.

The Orff Society UK and SOSA continue to offer professional development that goes beyond the limits of the school curriculum. Creative music education is intrinsically important and valuable and, while the formal education system rarely broadens its focus beyond the core subjects, many teachers and musicians working in educational settings seek us out.

---

1   England, Scotland, Wales, and Northern Ireland.

2   www.beatroutearts.com

3   Note from author McCluskey: In traditional Scottish songs there is often a strong connection with the landscape, nature and agriculture. These themes are as relevant for today as they were historically and are richly valuable in music education. When sourcing repertoire, I have found myself creating music inspired by the farm and animals like the cow, our special highland coo, the sea and fishing and traditional foods like porridge.

References

Adams, P. (1997). *Sounds musical.* Oxford: Oxford University Press.

Ayling, M. (2013). Orff-Schulwerk in the UK over the past 50 years – a personal perspective. In S. Hennessy (Ed.), *Reflections on Orff-Schulwerk: Essays in celebration of Margaret Murray* (pp. 64–71). London: Schott.

Baxter, K. (1978). *Jazzylophone.* London: Schott.

Baxter, K., & Thompson, D. (1989). *Pompaleerie jig.* Walton-on-Thames, Surrey: Nelson.

Baxter, K. (1994). *Fundamental activities.* Nottingham, England: Fundamental Activities.

Blackburn, M. (1967). *Orff Schulwerk teachers' world.* Orff Society UK.

Buchanan, K., & Chadwick, S. (1995). *Music connections.* London: Cramer.

Education Scotland. (2021). *What is curriculum for excellence?* https://education.gov.scot/education-scotland/scottish-education-system/policy-for-scottish-education/policy-drivers/cfe-building-from-the-statement-appendix-incl-btc1-5/what-is-curriculum-for-excellence

Glover, J., & Ward, S. (1993). *Teaching music in the primary school.* London: Cassel.

Hennessy, S. (1995). Music 7–11, *Developing primary teaching skills.* Abingdon, UK: Falmer.

Hennessy, S. (2000). Overcoming the red feeling. *British Journal of Music Education,* 17(2), 183–196.

Jeffery, B., & Craft A. (2004). Teaching creatively and teaching for creativity: Distinctions and relationships. *Educational Studies* 30(1), 77–87.

Jellineck, W. (1957). *Introduction to Carl Orff and Gunild Keetman: Music for Children* [2 LPs]. London: EMI/Columbia.

Jones, E. (1973). *Chwe Cân Werin Gymreig.* London: Schott.

Lane, M. (1984). *Music in action: An interpretation of Carl Orff's Music for Children.* St. Louis, MO: MMB Music.

McGregor, G. (1995) *Listening to music.* London: A&C Black.

McNichol, R. (1992). *Sound inventions.* Oxford: Oxford University Press.

Mills, J. (1992). *Music in the primary school.* Cambridge: Cambridge Univ. Press.

Orff, C., & Keetman, G. (1950-1954). *Orff-Schulwerk. Musik für Kinder* (Vols. 1–5). Mainz: Schott.

Orff, C., & Keetman, G. (1956-1961). *Orff-Schulwerk. Music for children* (Vols. 1–5) (English adaptation by D. Hall & A. Walter). Mainz: Schott.

Orff, C., & Keetman, G. (1957-1966). *Orff-Schulwerk. Music for children* (Vols. 1–5) (English adaptation by M. Murray). London: Schott.

Paynter, J. (1970). *Sound and silence.* Cambridge: Cambridge Univ. Press.

Paynter, J. (1990). *Sound and structure.* Cambridge: Cambridge Univ. Press.

Sidaway, P. (1993). *Rhigymau plant.* Llandysul: Gwasg Gomer.

Small, C. (1977). *Music, society, education.* Schirmer.

Small, C. (1998). *Musicking: The meanings of performing and listening.* Middletown, CT: Wesleyan University Press.

Swanwick, K. (1988). *Music mind and education.* London: Routledge.

Swanwick, K. (1999). *Teaching music musically.* London: Routledge.

Periodical

Orff Times. Publication of the Orff Society UK.

OCEANA

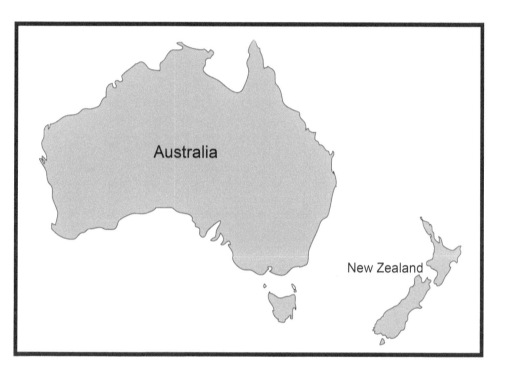

Orff Schulwerk in Australia

Compiled and edited by Peta Harper and Sarah Powell [1]

Introduction

Australia is a melting pot of different cultural traditions and, subsequently, Australian music, song, and dance draw from a range of musical traditions, representative of its British colonial history, growing multiculturalism and cultural diversity, and Indigenous traditions. Western pedagogical approaches, such as Orff Schulwerk, Kodály, and Dalcroze, have been embraced by the music education profession of Australia over a number of years. For those who have undergone training in Orff Schulwerk, there is a recognition that Orff Schulwerk could easily be the basis of all music education strategies, where teachers facilitate the active participation of children within a positive social environment and provide opportunities for children to experiment and develop their musical skills and understanding.

A short history

In the late 1960s, the Kodály method was considered the ideal approach to primary music education. However, Orff Schulwerk began to appear as the more adventurous music teachers attended courses at the Orff Institute and returned home to present workshops and courses. Inspired by this, in 1971 the tertiary music education lecturer Keith Smith was sponsored by the Australian Council for the Arts to conduct a six-month world tour to study Orff Schulwerk, and this took him to the Orff Institute as a guest student for two months. International connections were made, materials and ideas were shared and brought back to Australia where workshops and courses were conducted.

In 1967 the first Orff Schulwerk association of Australia was established in Queensland (QLD) followed by the New South Wales (NSW) Association in 1972. Over the next few years, Orff Schulwerk associations were established in the other states, and in 1976, the Australian National Council of Orff Schulwerk Association (ANCOSA) was founded, with the aim of promoting Orff Schulwerk in state education. In 1991, the Australian National Council of Orff Schulwerk (ANCOS), as it is known today, was established and now consists of two representatives from each of the six state associations. Since 1978 ANCOS has hosted a national conference every two years, boasting some of the most influential and well-regarded international and local Orff Schulwerk presenters.

Australia is a culturally diverse nation made up of Indigenous Australians, descendants of the first White settlers, and immigrants from many cultures. It has developed from its Western, English-speaking heritage. However, the significant growth of multiculturalism has seen an

1   We would like to thank everyone who has generously contributed, without which this chapter would not have been possible. We would especially like to thank Nikki Cox, Susie Davies-Splitter, Audrey Fine, Diana Humphries, Kirabelle Lovell, Heather McLaughlin, Margie Moore OAM, Lorna Parker, Michelle Rollins, Biddy Seymour, Robyn Staveley, and Helen Wilson.

increase in European, Asian, and African cultural influence. More recently, the incorporation of Aboriginal and Torres Strait Islander culture means that music education is increasingly incorporating material from a range of traditions.

The music and traditions of Indigenous Australians are highly valued, and commitment to integrating traditional music and dance in educational and community settings is growing. This is not a simple task and in order to understand the complexity of such circumstances, it is important to know that the Aboriginal and Torres Strait Islander population is made up of hundreds of different countries, each with its own culture, customs, language, and laws. This means that every people or language group has its own strict protocols surrounding the appropriate use (and non-use) of traditional materials, songs, dances, instruments, and occasions. Respect for these ancient traditions is demonstrated by seeking permission from local elders to use their materials. More recently, Aboriginal and Torres Strait Islander artists have created, sometimes commissioned, contemporary music and dance for use in the public domain, circumventing the difficulties associated with using traditional Indigenous material. These endeavors provide valuable and culturally appropriate opportunities for all Australians to appreciate and engage with First Nations music, dance, language, and ways of being and knowing.

The multicultural nature of Australian society means there is a wealth of songs, dances, and traditions that teachers can use. Embracing such diversity is a challenge and, consequently, a typical Australian style is almost impossible to define. The sharing of musical cultures builds acceptance, embraces diversity, and broadens cultural awareness. Australia is a colonized nation, with a musical history based on British settlement. There are traditional bush dances, derived from English, Irish, and Scottish dances, and the use of nursery rhymes and Western tonalites is commonplace. The growing interest and commitment to integrating aspects of Indigenous culture into education, particularly arts education, is an acknowledgment of its significance and valued place in Australia's history as well as in its future.

Educational adaptations

Since their inception, state Orff Schulwerk associations have made significant contributions to the promotion and implementation of quality music education across educational sectors. Many Orff Schulwerk practitioners were engaged in developing a music curriculum that incorporated Orff Schulwerk approaches, such as speech, body percussion, non-melodic instruments, and movement, which could be developed by teachers, or for teachers, depending on their varying levels of music and dance experience and skill. The curriculum designed in this process was well received and it survived for many years. In the new Australian Curriculum vestiges of the Orff Schulwerk approach can be seen, although without recognition. These include exploring sound through singing, playing, chanting, moving, and body percussion; using simple songs, chants, and nursery rhymes; imitating, composing, and performing. Whilst Orff Schulwerk is not a mandated part of teacher education, the associations provide many opportunities for members and non-members to learn, including four national Levels Courses taught by accredited presenters and overseen by ANCOS. Although a license is not required to use Orff Schulwerk in Australia, activity is monitored by the Orff Schulwerk community, and it is left to the educator, center, school, or university to decide whether Orff Schulwerk training is included. Adapting an approach to music and movement education is not without its issues, and many educators in schools, early childhood centers, private studios, and universities, constantly work to adjust resources and ideas to fit unique contexts.

Australia consists of six states and two territories. Each is responsible for funding and regulating its own education system, with some support from the federal government. Recently, the Australian National Curriculum was introduced to ensure an approach to education that is consistent across the country. In this curriculum, The Arts is one of eight distinct learning areas, which includes Dance, Drama, Media Arts, Music, and Visual Arts. The way The Arts is implemented in schools varies across states, educational sectors (public, independent, and Catholic systems), and from school to school. In some schools the five arts areas are taught as separate entities and in others they are integrated across curriculum areas. In most circumstances it is left to the class teacher (generalist) to provide arts experiences; however, in many schools this is the role of specialist teachers.

Creativity is a valued principle in the Australian system. The National Curriculum has seven General Capabilities (GC), one of which is *Critical and Creative Thinking*. These are "addressed through the content of the learning areas" and "offer opportunities to add depth and richness to student learning" (https://www.australiancurriculum.edu.au/f-10-curriculum/general-capabilities/, n.d.). *Critical and Creative Thinking* encompasses a range of skills and dispositions related to inquiry, reflection, generating ideas, evaluating, and analyzing knowledge. Teachers are expected to teach and assess the GC across all subject areas, but they are finding it increasingly difficult to address all that is required, largely as a result of time constraints and the growing focus on mandated, standardized testing. Creativity in the form of composition, choreography, and improvisation is fundamental to the music and dance curricula Music and dance are not often integrated—except in early childhood settings—and they remain discrete arts areas. The national Music curriculum explores music of other cultures, including Indigenous music. Despite this requirement, resources are often very difficult to access due to the oral nature of Indigenous traditions and the associated cultural conventions and sensitivities. To address this, many organizations, such as Musica Viva, Sydney Symphony Orchestra, Bangarra Dance Company, Gondwana Voices, and Moorambilla have produced online modules, resources, and teaching kits, which feature songs and commissioned works written in local Indigenous language or by Aboriginal and culturally diverse performing artists, composers, and choreographers.

Class playing with paper
Photo: Jane Nicholas

A significant barrier for arts education is government support. The government has consistently cut funding to organizations and schools due to the focus on literacy, numeracy, and science. The pressure on schools to perform in standardized testing regimes means that resources devoted to music and dance have declined substantially. Tertiary institutions reflect these priorities, with diminishing time allocated to arts education in initial teacher education programs, particularly in early childhood and primary school preservice teacher education. Arts academics in universities are faced with having to cover the entire arts curriculum, with sometimes as little as six hours on each art form, leaving new teachers ill-equipped and lacking confidence to integrate arts into their daily practice. As a result, music and dance education is left to specialist teachers or avoided altogether. There are many tertiary educators across the country, however, who are incorporating Orff Schulwerk pedagogy into their initial teacher education courses, equipping them with the basics of the approach, providing them with an embodied experience of music and movement, and introducing them to accessible resources.

In response to this situation, the prominent Orff Schulwerk educator Richard Gill AO[1] championed creating a school based upon the Orff Schulwerk principles. This dream has come to fruition, and in January 2021 the Richard Gill School opened in rural NSW. All subjects in this school are taught using movement and music as their starting point to enable students to embody and explore their learning and make concrete connections to the world around them. Mary Walton returned from the Special Course in 2015 inspired to start a school with the main focus on Orff approach and Art at the family farm. In 2019 Eton Farm Education was registered and the dream became a reality and now around 30 students from the age of 2 years enjoy learning at the Farm.

Australia has a large community of skilled Orff Schulwerk educators who are teaching in preschools, primary and secondary schools, special needs settings, universities, and even private instrumental studios. There are those who adhere to a traditional application of Orff Schulwerk and those who practice what they think that is. However, many practitioners are exploring how to use this approach more effectively, develop their practice, and generate new ideas. Across Australia, teachers collaborate to enhance their skills and understanding of Orff Schulwerk, and their commitment to ongoing professional development can be seen from the many who complete the International Summer Course at the Orff Institute. ANCOS is also committed to providing professional development and encouraging collaboration. It serves the Australian Orff Schulwerk community by inviting international presenters to national conferences, maintaining contact with Orff Schulwerk communities overseas, and helping members to experience the range of adaptations and possibilities that Orff Schulwerk offers.

Access to musical instruments varies across Australia, and often depends on the geographical location of a school. Some schools have access to Orff Instruments, and many use a range of more traditional instruments, including recorder, piano, guitar, ukulele, orchestral instruments, and ethnic instruments from the school's cultural community. Traditional Aboriginal instruments are sometimes used in school contexts with the permission of local Aboriginal elders. In secondary or high schools there can be a heavy emphasis on music technology. This is especially evident in various rural and regional areas, where access to instruments can be limited. In some schools, students have been inspired by artists, groups, and music educators to build their own marimbas or make instruments from found objects.

---

1 Richard Gill AO (1941–2018) received the Order of Australia medal in 1994.

Playing marimbas
Photo: Michele Rollins

Materials, resources, and adaptations

There is a large variety of publications used in Australia that are adaptations of Orff Schulwerk. Any resources developed that support the Orff Schulwerk pedagogical approach must be regarded as adaptations, because they offer an interpretation. Adaptations have been made that cater to the specific needs of groups, such as those with physical or intellectual disabilities and those in remote schools where lack of resources is a significant issue. Unfortunately, there are various commercially published resources that purport to be based on Orff Schulwerk pedagogy but that cannot be considered accurate. Rather, they simply use the Orff Schulwerk name to bolster the credibility of the publication.

Fundamental publications, such as the Murray adaptation of the Music for Children volumes (Orff & Keetman, 1957–1966) are broadly used, but there are no published Australian adaptations of the original German volumes. Australian Orff Schulwerk associations and individual teachers are constantly adapting material to fit the different contexts in which they work. These contexts are many and varied—ranging from socio-demographic environments, ethnic backgrounds, Indigenous cultures, educational, therapeutic or community settings—and related publications address specific needs. Locally, some of these teachers have published their compositions and teaching ideas and many teachers get material from Levels Courses, local workshops, and the biennial ANCOS National Conference. Music for Children continues to be used in various contexts and still forms the basis of the Levels Courses. Material from these books is often adapted and arranged by individual teachers to suit their students' needs and educational contexts. Other adaptations designed for classroom use include resources related to contemporary styles of music (such as pop and jazz), simplified classical music, folk music from around the world, and Schulwerk-based instrumental music written for recorder, ukulele, marimba, and small percussion instruments. New arrangements or compositions often use traditional Western music conventions, such as 2/4 and 4/4 meter, major or minor pentatonic or diatonic scales, as well as rondo, binary, and ternary forms.

Other publications have been significant in Australia for many years. Keith Smith's comprehensive *Questions and Answers on Orff Schulwerk* (1979) and The New South Wales *Music for Children* series (Aggett et al., 1992–96), have been popular; the latter could be considered an Australian adaptation of the English volumes. Australian Ways with Orff (https://www.ancos.org.au/pages/resources, n.d.) showcases many Australian artists who use Orff Schulwerk approaches in their practice. A number of years ago the NSW Department of Education produced a popular teacher resource, *Music and Dance for the Regular and Special Classroom: Games and Activities for Speech and Singing* (1985), consisting of two books and supporting recordings, written by Lorna Parker and Diana Humphries. The ABC *Sing* book series has been used by many teachers for many years, and Shenanigans have produced a number of CDs with a variety of bush dances and folk dances from around the world. A video about the Orff Schulwerk approach in Australia was made, featuring Richard Gill AO (OSANSW, 1995). Significant people who have produced quality resources and contributed to Orff Schulwerk publications in Australia over many years include Jon Madin, Susie Davies-Splitter, Carolyn Royal, and Margaret McGowan-Jackson to name but a few. In addition, many arts organizations such as Musica Viva, the Sydney, Melbourne, and Tasmanian Symphony Orchestras, Bangarra Dance Company, Gondwana Voices, and Moorambilla have created resources for teachers that embrace the principles of Orff Schulwerk.

In addition to supporting artists and associations and producing quality resources from across the country, ANCOS distributes the music education journal, *Musicworks: Journal of the Australian National Council of Orff Schulwerk*. *Musicworks* is a publication of peer-reviewed research and practice-related articles that consider the application and implementation of Orff Schulwerk pedagogy across many different educational contexts.

Orff Schulwerk in community music and dance

Community participation in music, particularly singing, is largely seen at special cultural events, such as sporting fixtures, government events, or community Christmas carol celebrations. In recent years, these events commence with a Welcome to Country, delivered by a local Aboriginal or Torres Strait Islander person, or an Acknowledgment of Country, which can be presented by a non-indigenous person or a person who does not belong to the traditional land upon which the event is being held. The Welcome is often followed by a performance of the National Anthem, *Advance Australia Fair*, which remains controversial for many because of its colonial history.

Examples of active community music-making from Orff Schulwerk practitioners and those facilitated by arts organizations include Jon Madin hosting community projects where participants build marimbas as part of a group. These marimbas have grown in popularity over the years and can be purchased ready-made, providing a significant addition to some school collections. Members of the Victorian Association (VOSA) have made major contributions in early childhood music education, the use of marimbas in schools, and community music activity. For more than 20 years they have built an awareness of the Orff Schulwerk approach more widely in the community through events such as the national Early Childhood Conference of Performing Arts and Family Marimba Camps.

Dance in Australia is not strong in the Western culture but is practiced within the multicultural and Indigenous groups that make up our society. Prior to his death, Andre van de Plas ran many folk-dance workshops around the country each year for the wider community.

Supporting and maintaining the richness of Indigenous culture has become a priority for a number of organizations across Australia. For example, there are hundreds of different Aboriginal languages, many of which are seriously endangered. In response, efforts are being made by arts organizations and educational institutions to address this by commissioning musical works in imperiled languages and embedding the teaching of these languages into the curriculum. *Moorambilla Voices* (see https://moorambilla.com) is a music education organization that operates in the northwest area of New South Wales, actively supporting the recovery of Indigenous languages. *Moorambilla* works with local Aboriginal elders, artists, and composers, encouraging them to tell their stories and write about their world in the native language/s of the geographical area/s. These stories are expressed through music, song, and dance. *Moorambilla* employs composers and Indigenous and non-indigenous dance teachers who use creativity and improvisation to devise movement works with young participants. *Moorambilla* programs are underpinned by the Orff Schulwerk pedagogy and understanding and are supported by the Australian National Council of Orff Schulwerk (ANCOS).

Conclusion

Australian Orff Schulwerk Associations and educators have made significant contributions to the promotion and implementation of quality music and dance education across a wide range of sectors. Despite the complexities surrounding the use of Indigenous music, the lack of government support, and the diminishing time given to the arts in initial teacher education programs, Orff Schulwerk practitioners across Australia continue to deliver high quality music and dance education experiences and maintain their commitment to professional development in Orff Schulwerk pedagogy, all the while supported by state Orff Schulwerk Associations and ANCOS.

Children with masks   Developing a dialogue between the cuddly toys
Photo: Jane Nicholas   Photo: Jane Nicholas

References

Australian Broadcasting Commission. (1975-2014). ABC Sing! Australian Broadcasting Commission, Sydney, NSW.

Aggett, C., Ash, M., Birrell, J., Christie, H., & Hoare, M. (1992-1996). New South Wales *Music for Children* series (Vols. 1–3): Reprints from the Bulletin of the OSANSW (Inc.), OSANSW.

Australian Ways with Orff. (2001). https://www.ancos.org.au/pages/resources.

King, G., & Maubach, C. (1986–2003). *Shenanigans*. Dance Music and Instruction Booklets. Victoria, Australia: Shenanigans Music.

New South Wales. Department of Education. Resource Services (1985). Music and dance: *Activities for the regular and special classroom.* Resource Services, Division of Services, N.S.W. Dept. of Education, Sydney.

Orff, C., & Keetman, G. (1950–1954). *Orff-Schulwerk. Musik für Kinder* (Vols. 1-5). Mainz: Schott.

Orff, C., & Keetman, G. (1957-1966). *Orff-Schulwerk. Music for children* (Vols. 1–5). (English adaptation by M. Murray). London: Schott.

Orff Schulwerk Association of New South Wales. (1995). *Creative music education in Australia: The Orff Approach* [Film]. OSANSW.

Smith, K. (1979). *Questions and answers on Orff Schulwerk*. Kedron Park, Q.: K. Smith.

Periodical

Musicworks. Journal of the Australian National Council of Orff Schulwerk.

Orff Schulwerk in Aotearoa New Zealand

Linda M. Locke

A brief overview of the human history of our country will help to identify features of our cultural context that are unique to New Zealand and therefore of relevance to our music education setting.

In the twenty-first century, Aotearoa New Zealand society is characterized by diversity of every kind. Our unique environment and acoustic soundscape (Schafer, 2012) and an increasing understanding of the need to act as kaitiaki (caretakers) of ngā whenua (the land) have inspired a wealth of artistic expression in music and other art forms. In turn there is a focus in music education on the study, performance, and composition of music that is recognizably related to our physical landscape, and native flora and fauna.

Human history in New Zealand began around A.D. 1200, when Polynesian ancestors of the indigenous Māori navigated the Pacific and began settling here. Pre-European Māori culture was oral and based around small, autonomous sub-tribes living in valleys and coastal settlements. Indigenous music, intricately connected with everyday life and ritual, comprised sung forms (*waiata*, *mōteatea*, and *karanga*) and *taonga pūoru* (wind, percussion, and whirled instruments[1]). While versions of such traditional material may still be performed at specific Māori occasions, such material is neither available nor appropriate for general educational use.

Taonga pūoru (wind, percussion, and whirled instruments)
Photo: Private collection

However, a wealth of 'folk' material derived from traditional Māori sources and influenced by western art and popular music conventions is available for general use in educational settings. In addition, the work of Hirini Melbourne, Richard Nunns, and Brian Flintoff in exploring and presenting in performance the rich tradition of *taonga pūoru* has led to a revival

---

1 A whirled instrument is a device attached to a cord and spun. –Ed.

of interest in this art form, which features in contemporary art music and popular compo-sition (Flintoff, 2004). A wide range of educational resources and opportunities, including instrument-making workshops to support the appropriate inclusion of these instruments in educational settings, are now available.

European colonization began in the 18th century following a visit by British explorer, Cap-tain James Cook. During the latter part of the 18th century and early part of the 19th century, whalers, sealers, miners, and others drew on musical traditions from their homelands and their new experiences in New Zealand to compose songs in English that told stories of these early times.

In 1840 Great Britain established New Zealand as a British colony. The country's founding document, *Te Tiriti o Waitangi*, is an agreement between the British Crown and Māori signed on February 6, 1840. The subsequent colonization of this country by British and other groups from Scandinavia, Germany, Dalmatia, and China led to a complex historical and psycholog-ical relationship between Māori and the colonizing power. In the early days of the colony, the cultural lives of new settlers reflected their countries of origin, especially Great Britain.

After the Second World War people from all parts of the world chose to call New Zealand home. Their musical traditions (including song repertoires) established themselves in the mu-sical life of Aotearoa communities and educational settings. Changing immigration patterns, the identification of Aotearoa as a Pacific nation, and an increased determination to right the wrongs of colonization have contributed to the creation of an education system and music ed-ucation curriculum considerably less oriented to Britain and other English-speaking countries.

Today, the character of musical expression in Aotearoa is inextricably connected to its natural and social history and to its ever-increasing connectivity to the "global village." A homogeneous Aotearoa/New Zealand musical identity cannot be identified.

The dissemination of Orff Schulwerk in Aotearoa New Zealand

Orff Schulwerk arrived in New Zealand as a result of a 1961 encounter in England between Auckland-based music educator, Lindo Francis and Margaret Murray, whose seminal En-glish-language version of *Musik für Kinder* (Orff & Keetman, 1950–1954) was produced in 1959. Francis was clearly impressed by the repertoire of *Music for Children* (Orff & Keetman, 1959), and interest in the Orff Schulwerk was subsequently aroused in the music education community here.

At this time, New Zealand was blessed with its own innovators in the creative arts. Building on ideals of progressive education that had taken root in the 1930s, Clarence Beeby, Director of Education between 1940 and 1960, not only initiated curriculum reforms, but also appointed key advisers in music and 'arts and crafts.' Innovative classroom-based projects were under-taken by educators such as Sylvia Ashton Warner, Elwyn Richardson, and Alan and Bebe Simpson, who explored the role of creative expression in programs that responded to the needs of all students, in particular rural Māori students.

Working closely during the 1950s with the Māori school community at Ngataki School in Northland, the Simpsons "developed their own version of an elemental music program that was based on movement, rhythmic and melodic improvisation in body percussion and non-technical instruments and playing by ear" (Gain, 2018, p. 16).

> *To develop musicality, a variety of experiences in sound and rhythm were built up through melodic improvisation. So, body instruments (stamp, clap, snap and patschen) were used to prepare rhythm patterns. Then non-pitched percussion instruments such as drums,*

tambourines, rattles, maracas, claves and wood blocks were made in large numbers with great care and attention to detail by children of more senior classes...To give a variety of tone, color and sound duration that would encourage worthwhile composition, melody instruments such as recorders, ukuleles, guitars and bits of old iron were added. Later, before the advent of chime-bars, bottles were carefully filled, corked, tuned, and played by now competent explorers of sound. (Gerlich, 2016, cited by Gain, 2018, p. 16)

The use of such words as "stamp," "clap," "snap," and "patschen" suggests that the Simpsons had access to Orff and Keetman's *Music for Children* and were already engaged in its adaptation to the local context.

From the sixties onwards Orff Schulwerk principles began to be reflected in teacher education, especially in Auckland campuses. Work with rhythm began to incorporate language and percussion in various forms. The use of the pentatonic scale as a basis for exploration and improvisation introduced many students to the joy of realizing their own music-making potential, sometimes for the first time.

From the early eighties onwards various American music educators visited New Zealand. As interest in the approach grew, New Zealand teachers travelled to Australia and the USA to attend conferences and study Orff Schulwerk.

The recognition of the importance of local contextualization as a principle of the approach led to a desire for closer collaboration with ANCOS (Australian National Council of Orff Schulwerk). Subsequent visits from Australian Orff practitioners followed. In 2004, after several years of informal gatherings of music teachers with an interest in the Orff approach, ONZA (Orff New Zealand Aotearoa) was formed. ONZA became affiliated with IOSFS (International Orff-Schulwerk Forum Salzburg) and several visits from Barbara Haselbach[1] ensued.

By 2008 ONZA had committed itself to the need for local contextualization by developing local 'expert teachers' based in schools, early childhood centers, and communities. From 2006 to 2013, a Memorandum of Agreement between ONZA and the University of Waikato enabled workshops and courses of study in Orff Schulwerk that took careful account of how Orff Schulwerk principles could be incorporated in New Zealand educational settings. When this Memorandum lapsed, formal tertiary study in the Orff Schulwerk approach relocated to the School of Music at the University of Auckland, where the program continues to be developed by David Lines and Millie Locke.

The New Zealand curriculum and music education

Most teachers attending Orff Schulwerk workshops are primary or early childhood teachers. The Arts, as one of eight designated curriculum areas of the New Zealand curriculum (Ministry of Education, 2007), specifies four arts disciplines: Music, Dance, Drama, and Visual Art. Each discipline is framed by four topic strands, each accompanied by sets of 'achievement objectives' at eight levels of achievement (covering years 1 to 13 of schooling):

- Understanding (Music, Dance, Drama, or Visual Art) in context
- Developing ideas in (Music, Dance, Drama, or Visual Art)
- Practical knowledge (Music, Dance, Drama, or Visual Art)
- Communicating and interpreting ideas (Music, Dance, Drama, or Visual Art).

---

1   President of the International Orff-Schulwerk Forum, 1994 to 2018

Despite the satisfactory nature of the arts curriculum, an emphasis on literacy and numer-acy in recent years, a relentless focus on standards-based assessment, and an ongoing lack of resourcing for the arts have led to inadequacies in the provision of quality arts education programs for all New Zealand children (Centre for Arts and Social Transformation, 2020). Moreover, there has been a continuing shrinkage in the provision of teacher education in the arts disciplines, including music.

Of the six, broad, guiding principles mandated in the curriculum, three are particularly relevant to the challenges of contextualization and adaptation of the Orff Schulwerk approach.

Treaty of Waitangi

This principle reflects the ideal of partnership embodied (but not always practiced) in the Treaty of Waitangi and a commitment to build a bi-cultural (Māori and Pākehā) Aotearoa New Zealand. ONZA is committed to developing a bicultural framework for both its organi-zation and its classroom pedagogy (Gain, 2018), where "Māori and Tauiwi (non-Māori) work together to learn about and incorporate mātauranga Māori (Māori knowledge), recognizing that the cultural wisdom embedded in Māori spiritual and philosophical beliefs can generate solutions for our bi-cultural context." [1]

Cultural diversity and inclusion

The Orff Schulwerk approach, as a person-centered approach with an emphasis on the facil-itation of participation in music and movement for all students, resonates with the two New Zealand curriculum principles of cultural diversity and inclusion. Locke (2016) states that "a teacher of music in the New Zealand school context not only needs to address differences in cultural backgrounds, learning styles, and aptitude but, as well, the huge variations in students' prior musical experience" (p. 274).

> *The person-centered emphasis of the Orff approach, as manifested in 21st-century Aotearoa New Zealand, is not only embraced for the way music-making is viewed as yielding ben-efits to the development of creativity, expressiveness and artistry in each child, but also for the way it enables the strong endorsement of the unique and diverse funds of knowledge that each student brings to the learning situation. This inevitably leads to an acceptance and embrace of the inherent and all-pervasive diversity found in Aotearoa New Zealand classroom settings. (2016, p. 274)*

Speech/Language

English is the most widely spoken language in New Zealand, while Māori and New Zealand Sign Language also have status as official languages. In honoring the Orff Schulwerk principle of "language as the source of music" (Shamrock, 2020, p. 2), New Zealand teachers draw on models from other English-speaking parts of the world. However, sources such as playground rhymes, locally written poetry for and by children, musical genres that include the spoken word, and New Zealand stories including Māori myths, also provide a rich source of material.

Te reo Māori (Māori language) is spoken proficiently by a small number of people (around 3%) and a few teachers practiced in the Orff Schulwerk approach have sophisticated knowl-edge of *te reo* Māori. However, paying close attention to the readily available models of correct pronunciation of *te reo* Māori words and phrases, and the language's rhythmic implications, enables the use of Māori texts as a starting point for music-making.

---

1 Personal communication with Anaru Kapa, adviser for ONZA on Māori tikanga, personal email, March 17, 2018.

Songs for children accompanied by New Zealand Sign Language such as the New Zealand National Anthem[1] and "Paradise," a student-composed song, are available on YouTube. These examples provide models for the incorporation of the gestural vocabulary of New Zealand Sign Language, which can be imitated and adapted to music and movement projects in the elemental style.

Movement and dance

The inclusion of "dance" in the arts curriculum document attests to the value 'in the total educational process' (Shamrock, 2020, p. 2) placed upon dance, at least aspirationally. However, delivery of this learning area remains problematic and highly inconsistent. Melchior (2013) noted: "In theory, dance is firmly established in the curriculum, but in practice the ideal of dance as an integral part of every child's learning is still a long way off" (p. 100). She noted inadequate funding, emphasis on numeracy and literacy, and poor teacher education as obstacles to its implementation.

ONZA includes dance/movement as an essential subject in Orff Schulwerk courses. Renée Morin, graduate of the postgraduate course Advanced Studies in Elemental Music and Dance - Orff Schulwerk (Orff Institute, Mozarteum University, Salzburg) collaborates with Rozy Winstone, a South-Island-based arts educator, to teach and develop the ONZA dance curriculum. The integration of movement and music in Māori *kapahaka*[2] and other Polynesian dance/music forms provides ongoing inspiration and opportunities for future collaboration.

Tonal material and development

As Cain (2001) asserts, school-based music education needs to establish a progression of learning that is congruent with the nature of music-making in authentic contexts. 'Sensitivity to and delight in sound and its expressive qualities' (Paynter, 1982, p. 59) are the goals in progressions of learning derived from the musical experience itself. A wide range of melodic material derived from local and contemporary contexts including Hirini Melbourne's original compositions of *waiata* (songs) inspired by the natural world and characteristically set within the hemitonic, pentatonic, or hexatonic scale, provide a suitable basis for elemental music-making. Teachers frequently include 'local' sounds such as *taonga pūoru*, locally crafted instruments, and sounds produced by environmental objects that evoke the mood or subject matter of these simple melodies.

Singing

In recent times the state-owned enterprise Learning Media produced an annual *Kiwi Kidsongs* album, which comprised approximately ten songs, each with a notated score, chord chart, arrangement suggestions, and a karaoke-style recording. The songs, written in English, Māori, Samoan, and other Pasifika languages, covered all musical genres and referenced distinctly Kiwi brands, places, and things. This singable "Kiwi" repertoire provides culturally relevant material that can be used in playful ways for singing, playing, and moving activities in the classroom.

---

1   See https://www.youtube.com/watch?v=mlHyZyUR4EA&ab_channel=nzsignsinging and https://www.youtube. com/watch?v=CbDf0YG2xnA&list=RDBwKpTbWemQw&index=4&ab_channel=DeafAotearoa.

2   The term for Māori performing arts, which involves a combination of song, dance, and chant.

Instruments

Several local music stores import xylophones in order to cater for their growing demand. A Marimba Festival, which has been described as a joyous celebration of Schulwerk-inspired music-making occurs annually.[1] Adaptation of elemental repertoire from sources around the world as well as locally composed items often feature improvisatory breaks in music and/or movement, and include innovative, home-crafted, and traditional instruments (such as recorder and ukulele).

Marimba Festival
Photo: Jo Charman

Improvisation

The opportunity for creativity inherent in the emphasis on improvisation in the Orff Schulwerk approach finds a fertile ground in the musical and pedagogical imagination of teachers in Aotearoa. This is evidenced in the pedagogical research of Baker (2014), Locke (2016), and Stewart (2013). Schulwerk-based pedagogy inspired two significant composition projects at Henderson Valley Primary School, where students who had experienced Schulwerk-based music classes for six years engaged successfully in composition projects that led to integrated arts performances featuring the students' original work (Locke, L., & Locke, T., 2011; Locke, M., & Locke, T., 2012).

Traditional sources for activity development

Finding "representative material for each culture" (Shamrock, 2020, p. 2) involves ongoing investigation and critical reflection by music teachers in Aotearoa New Zealand (Gain, 2018; Locke, 2016). ONZA's professional development courses encourage the use of New Zealand material as a basis for exploration and development in music and movement activities. Workshop leaders offer as examples elemental arrangements of folksongs (including waiata) and New Zealand poetry. Stories celebrating the landscape and culture of Aotearoa New Zealand are also incorporated. At the same time ONZA teacher educators emphasize the scope that exists for the artistic teacher to identify material that is culturally appropriate to their particular context and develop it using Orff Schulwerk pedagogical principles.

---

1 See https://onza.nz/media/

Conclusion

Over the 60 years since the music pedagogy of Orff and Keetman arrived in Aotearoa New Zealand, music educators in schools and teacher education institutions have explored and adapted this approach to our unique context. The recognition in 2018 by the Ministry of Education of ONZA as a network of expertise has enabled the organization to expand its in-service professional development work. The current collaboration with the University of Auckland School of Music provides an opportunity for young musicians to encounter Orff Schulwerk and consider the role this pedagogical approach might play in what are likely to be portfolio careers.[1] ONZA is sustained by dedicated music teachers whose enthusiasm for and commitment to principles of equity and access in music education is being actualized as classroom, community, and studio practice.

References

Baker, D. L. (2014). *Improving student motivation and engagement in high school music composition through Orff Schulwerk pedagogy* [Master's thesis, University of Waikato, Hamilton, New Zealand]. University of Waikato Research Commons. https://hdl.handle.net/10289/8694

Centre for Arts and Social Transformation (2020, October). *Replanting creativity during post-normal times* (Research report). Auckland, NZ: University of Auckland.

Faherty, A. (January 18, 2018). *Sausages and custard: An ode to the weird and wonderful Kiwi Kidsongs albums.* The Spinoff. https://thespinoff.co.nz/music/18–01–2018/sausages-and-custard-an-ode-to-the-weird-and-wonderful-kiwi-kidsongs-albums/

Flintoff, B. (2004). *Taonga Pūoro – Singing Treasures.* Nelson, New Zealand: Craig Potton.

Gain, P. (2018). *A study investigating how five experienced New Zealand Orff teachers responded to a six-day bi-culturally framed Orff course* [Unpublished master's thesis], University of Waikato. https://onza.nz/orff-teachers-responding-to-biculturalism/

Gerlich, R. (2016). *The importance of music at school: Lessons from Ngataki.* https://reneejg.net.

Ministry of Education. (2007). *The New Zealand curriculum for English-medium teaching and learning in years 1–13.* Wellington, NZ: Learning Media.

Locke, L. M. (2016). *The Orff approach in the professional lives and practices of teachers in the Aotearoa/New Zealand school context* [Doctoral dissertation, University of Waikato, Hamilton, New Zealand]. University of Waikato Research Commons. https://hdl.handle.net/10289/9990

Locke, L., & Locke, T. (2011). Sounds of Waitakere. Using practitioner research to explore how year 6 recorder players compose responses to visual representations of a natural environment. *British Journal of Music Education, 28*(3), 263–284.

Locke, M., & Locke, T. (2012). Introducing a mentor into a children's composition project: Reflections on a process. *Thinking Skills and Creativity, 7* (1), 8–20.

Melchior, L. (2013). Looking back: Considering thirty years of growth in dance education in New Zealand schools. *Dance Research Aotearoa, 1,* 92–101.

Orff, C., & Keetman, G. (1950-1954). *Orff-Schulwerk. Musik für Kinder.* (Vols. 1–5). Mainz: Schott.

Orff, C., & Keetman, G. (1959). *Orff-Schulwerk. Music for children: Vol. I. Pentatonic* (M. Murray, Trans.). London: Schott.

Paynter, J. (1982). *Music in the secondary school curriculum.* Cambridge: Cambridge University Press.

---

1   Combining multiple sources of income; creating a mix of employment e.g., parttime, fulltime, freelance. --Ed.

Schafer, R. M. (2012). The soundscape. In J. Sterne (Ed.), *The sound studies reader* (pp. 95–103). New York: Routledge.

Shamrock, M. (2020). A consideration of cross-cultural adaptation of the Schulwerk pedagogical model. Unpublished handout provided by Barbara Haselbach.

Stewart, C. A. (2013). *Facilitating elemental composition in an Orff classroom* [Master's thesis, University of Waikato, Hamilton, New Zealand]. University of Waikato Research Commons. https://hdl.handle.net/10289/7575

Periodical

Sounding Orff. Newsletter of Orff New Zealand Aotearoa

Appendix

Selected Bibliography and Discography

Important works on the subject in German and English language. Publications in other languages can be found in the bibliographies listed at the end of each of the articles.

Beegle, A., & Bond, J. (2016). Releasing and developing the musical imagination. In C. Abril & B. M. Gault (Eds.), *Teaching general music: Approaches, issues, and viewpoints* (pp. 25–48). New York: Oxford University Press.

Campbell, P. S. (2004). *Teaching music globally. Experiencing music, expressing culture.* New York: Oxford University Press.

Campbell, P. S., & Wiggins, T. (2014). *The Oxford handbook of children's musical cultures.* New York: Oxford University Press.

Choksy, L., Abramson, R. M., Gillespie, A. E., Woods, D., & York, F. (2001). *Teaching music in the twenty-first century.* New Jersey: Prentice-Hall.

de Quadros, A. (Ed.). (2000). *Many seeds, different flowers: The music education legacy of Carl Orff.* Perth: Callaway International Resource Centre for Music Education.

Erion, C., & O'Hehir, M. (Coordinators). (2005, Spring). Keetman Centenary [Special issue]. *The Orff Echo, 37* (3).

Fischer, C. (2009). *Gunild Keetman und das Orff-Schulwerk. Elementare Musik zwischen künstlerischem und didaktischem Anspruch* [Gunild Keetman and the Orff-Schulwerk. Elemental music between artistic and didactic demands]. Mainz: Schott.

Frazee, J. (1998). *Discovering Keetman.* New York: Schott.

Frazee, J. (2006). *s today: Nurturing musical expression and understanding.* New York: Schott.

Gersdorf, L. (1986). *Carl Orff.* Reinbek bei Hamburg: Rowohlt.

Goodkin, D. (2002). *Play, sing and dance: An introduction to Orff Schulwerk.* New York: Schott.

Grüner, M. (2016). *Orff instruments and how to play them* (Y. Douthat Hartinger, Trans.). Mainz: Schott. (Original work published in 2011 as *Orff-Instrumente und wie man sie spielt*, Mainz: Schott)

Grüner, M., & Haselbach, B. (Eds.). (2011). 50 Jahre Orff-Institut / 50 Years Orff Institute 1961-2011 [Special edition]. *Orff-Schulwerk Informationen*, 85. https://www.orff-schulwerk-forum-salzburg.org/magazine-osh

Grüner, M., & Haselbach, B. (Eds.). (2015/2016). Interkulturalität in der Elementaren Musik- und Tanzerziehung I und II / Interculturality in the elemental music and dance pedagogy I and II. *Orff-Schulwerk Heute*, 93 & 94. https://www.orff-schulwerk-forum-salzburg.org/magazine-osh

Harding, J. (2015, Winter). HOW? Models of intercultural teaching and learning. *Orff-Schulwerk Heute*, 93, 28–33. https://www.orff-schulwerk-forum-salzburg.org/magazine-osh

Hartmann, W. (forthcoming). *Roots and branches: A guide to understanding Orff Schulwerk.* San Francisco: Pentatonic Press.

Hartmann, W., Maschat, V., & Regner, H. (2000). Orff-Schulwerk im Bayerischen Rundfunk [Orff-Schulwerk in the Bavarian Broadcasting Company]. *Orff-Schulwerk Informationen*, 64, 24–28. https://www.orff-schulwerk-forum-salzburg.org/magazine-osh

Haselbach, B. (1979). *Dance education: Basic principles and models for nursery and primary school* (M. Murray, Trans.). London: Schott. (Original work published 1971)

Haselbach, B. (1994). *Improvisation, dance, movement* (M. Murray, Trans.). St. Louis, MO: Magnamusic-Baton. (Original work published 1976)

Haselbach, B. (Ed.). (2011). *Studientexte zu Theorie und Praxis des Orff-Schulwerks: Basistexte aus den Jahren 1932–2010 / Texts on theory and practice of Orff-Schulwerk: Basic texts from the years 1932–2010*. Mainz: Schott.

Haselbach, B. (2018, Winter). Orff Schulwerk dissemination: Background and commentary from the International Orff-Schulwerk Forum Salzburg. *The Orff Echo, 50*(2), 10–15.

Haselbach, B., Grüner, M., & Salmon, S. (Eds.). (2007). *Im Dialog. Elementare Musik- und Tanzerziehung im Interdisziplinären Kontext / In dialogue. Elemental music and dance education in interdisciplinary contexts*. Mainz: Schott.

Haselbach, B., & Bacher, E. (Eds.). (2010, February). Index (1961-2009) Orff-Schulwerk Informationen, Year-Books of the Orff Institute, Documentation of Orff-Schulwerk Symposia [Special Edition]. *Orff-Schulwerk Informationen*. https://www.orff-schulwerk-forum-salzburg.org/magazine-osh

Jungmair, U. (1992). *Das Elementare. Zur Musik- und Bewegungserziehung im Sinne Carl Orffs. Theorie und Praxis* [The Elemental: On music and movement education in the spirit of Carl Orff. Theory and practice.]. Mainz: Schott.

Keetman, G. (1974). *Elementaria. First acquaintance with Orff-Schulwerk* (M. Murray, Trans.) London: Schott. (Original work published in 1970 as Elementaria. Erster Umgang mit dem Orff-Schulwerk, Stuttgart: Klett)

Keetman, G. (1991) *Gunild Keetman Collection. Orff-Schulwerk—Musik für Kinder* [Album: CD]. Deutsche Harmonia Mundi (1013-2). Selection and compilation by Hermann Regner on behalf of the Orff-Schulwerk Forum Salzburg.

Keller, W. (1974). *Introduction to Music for Children* (S. Kennedy, Trans.). Schott, Mainz. (Original work published in 1954 as *Einführung in Musik für Kinder*, Mainz: Schott)

Keller, W. (1996). *Musikalische Lebenshilfe. Ausgewählte Berichte über sozial- und heilpädagogische Versuche mit dem Orff-Schulwerk* [Musical help in life. Selected reports on social and curative educational experiments with the Orff-Schulwerk]. Mainz: Schott.

Kotzian, R. (2018). *Orff-Schulwerk rediscovered: Music and teaching models*. Mainz: Schott.

Kugler, M. (2000). *Die Methode Jaques-Dalcroze und das Orff-Schulwerk "Elementare Musikübung." Bewegungsorientierte Konzeptionen der Musikpädagogik* [The Jaques-Dalcroze method and the Orff-Schulwerk "elemental music practice." Movement-oriented conceptions of music education]. Frankfurt am Main: Lang.

Kugler, M. (Ed.). (2013). *Elemental dance—elemental music: The Munich Günther School 1924–1944* (M. Murray, Trans.). New York: Schott. (Original work published in 2002 as Elementarer Tanz – Elementare Musik. Die Günther-Schule München 1924–1944, Mainz: Schott)

Lex, M., & Padilla, G. (1988). *Elementarer Tanz:* Bände 1–3 [Elemental Dance: Volumes 1-3]. Wilhelmshaven: Noetzel.

López-Ibor, S., & Maschat, V. (2002/2003, Winter). Adaptación total oder Vielfalt und Anpassung / Total adaptation or variation and suitability. *Orff-Schulwerk Informationen, 69*, 36–42. https://www.orff-schulwerk-forum-salzburg.org/magazine-osh

Niessen, A., & Lehmann-Wermser, A. (Eds.). (2012). *Aspekte Interkultureller Musikpädagogik. Ein Studienbuch* [Aspects of Intercultural Music Education. A study book]. Augsburg: Wißner.

Nykrin, R. (2001/2002, Winter). Konzept und Methode – Ein Beitrag zur Klärung des Selbstverständnisses von Musik- und Bewegungserziehung [Concept and method: A contribution clarifying the self evidence of music and movement education]. *Orff-Schulwerk Informationen, 67*, 6–12. https://www.orff-schulwerk-forum-salzburg.org/magazine-osh

Orff, C. (1978). *The Schulwerk* (M. Murray, Trans.). New York: Schott. (Original work published 1976 as *Carl Orff und sein Werk: Dokumentation, Vol. 3, Schulwerk - Elementare Musik*, Tutzing: Hans Schneider)

Orff, C., & Keetman, G. (1950-1954) *Orff-Schulwerk. Musik für Kinder*, 5 Volumes. Mainz: Schott.

Orff, C., & Keetman, G. (1990). Orff-Schulwerk: Music for children [Album: CD]. London: Schott (ED 12380).

Orff, C., & Keetman, G. (1994). *Musica Poetica. Orff-Schulwerk* [Album: 6 CDs]. Berlin: BMG.

Orff, C. & Keetman, G. (1995-1996). Orff-Schulwerk: Vol. 1: Musica Poetica [Album: CD 13104-2]; Orff-Schulwerk: Vol. 2: Musik für Kinder [Album: CD 13105-2]; Orff-Schulwerk: Vol. 3: Piano Music [Album: CD 13106-2]. Tucson, Arizona: Celestial Harmonies.

Padilla, G. (1990). Inhalte und Lehre des Elementaren Tanzes [Contents and teaching of elemental dance]. In E. Bannmüller & P. Röthig (Eds.), *Grundlagen und Perspektiven ästhetischer und rhythmischer Bewegungserziehung* [Foundations and perspectives of aesthetic and rhythmic movement education] (pp. 245–271). Stuttgart: Klett.

Preussner, E. (1962). The ABC of musical perception: An attempt to locate Orff's "Schulwerk" (R. Holburn, Trans.). In W. Thomas & W. Götze (Eds.), *Orff-Institute Year-Book 1962* (pp. 7–13). Mainz: Schott.

Regner, H. (Ed.). (1990). *Begegnungen. Berichte über die Aufnahme und Entwicklung von Anregungen des Orff-Schulwerks / Encounters. Reports about the acceptance and development of stimuli from Orff-Schulwerk*. Salzburg: Orff-Schulwerk Forum Salzburg.

Regner, H. (1995). Vom Wandel, der Erneuerung und den Grundideen des Orff-Schulwerks. In *Das Eigene – das Fremde—das Gemeinsame. Dokumentation des Internationalen Symposions Orff-Schulwerk, Musik- und Tanzerziehung als Beitrag zu einer interkulturellen Pädagogik* (pp. 14–15) [English publication in 1996: Change, renewal and basic ideas of Orff-Schulwerk (M. Samuelson, Trans.). In *The inherent—The foreign—In common. Documentation of the International Symposium Orff-Schulwerk, music and dance education as a contribution to intercultural pedagogy* (pp. 16–17)]. Orff Institute and the Orff-Schulwerk Forum Salzburg.

Regner, H., & Ronnefeld, M. (Eds.). (2004). *Gunild Keetman. Ein Leben für Musik und Bewegung /A life given to music and movement* (M. Murray, Trans.). Mainz: Schott.

Reily, S. A. (1993/1994, Winter). An approach to world music in Orff-Schulwerk. *Orff-Schulwerk Informationen*, 52, 4–10. https://www.orff-schulwerk-forum-salzburg.org/magazine-osh

Salmon, S. (2010, June). Inclusion and Orff-Schulwerk. *Musicworks*, 15, 27–33. http://bidok.uibk.ac.at/library/salmon-orff-e.html

Salmon, S. (2012, Winter). MUSICA HUMANA—Thoughts on humanistic aspects of Orff-Schulwerk. *Orff-Schulwerk Informationen*, 87, 13–22. https://www.orff-schulwerk-forum-salzburg.org/magazine-osh

Shamrock, M. (1995). *Orff Schulwerk: Brief history, description and issues in global dispersal*. Cleveland: American Orff-Schulwerk Association.

Stibi, S. (2016, Summer). Der Beitrag der Elementaren Musik- und Tanzpädagogik zur Interkulturalität – eine kritisch-konstruktive Bestandsaufnahme / The contribution of elemental music and dance education to interculturalism: A critical and constructive survey. *Orff-Schulwerk Heute*, 94, 20–31. https://www.orff-schulwerk-forum-salzburg.org/magazine-osh

Thomas, W. (1988). *Carl Orff: A concise biography* (V. Maschat, Trans.). London: Schott.

Thomas, W. (1990). *Das Rad der Fortuna* [The Wheel of Fortune]. Mainz: Schott.

Vallejo, P. (2015, Winter). WHAT to use? The importance of the material in its cultural context. *Orff-Schulwerk Heute*, 93, 21–27. https://www.orff-schulwerk-forum-salzburg.org/magazine-osh

Wang, C. C. (Ed.). (2013). *Orff Schulwerk: Reflections and directions*. Chicago: GIA Publications.

Warner, B. (1991). *Orff-Schulwerk: Applications for the classroom*. Hoboken, New Jersey: Prentice Hall.

Widmer, M. (2011). *Die Pädagogik des Orff-Instituts in Salzburg. Entwicklung und Bedeutung einer einzigartigen kunstpädagogischen Ausbildung als Impuls für eine allgemeinpädagogische Diskussion* [The pedagogy of the Orff Institute in Salzburg. Development and significance of a unique education through the arts as an impulse for a general pedagogical discussion]. Mainz: Schott.

Widmer, M. (2015, Winter). WARUM? Interkulturelle Pädagogik im Rahmen von Orff-Schulwerk- Aktivitäten [WHY? Intercultural pedagogy in the context of Orff-Schulwerk]. *Orff-Schulwerk Heute*, 93, 16–20. https://www.orff-schulwerk-forum-salzburg.org/magazine-osh

Yaprak Kotzian, E. (2019). *Orff-Schulwerk handbook. Principles of elemental music and movement pedagogy.* Mainz: Schott.

Authors

Akhremenko, Inna (Russia). Levels course graduate; OSA Russia website editor; music teacher.

An, Sung-Sil (South Korea). Vice Chairperson of OSA South Korea; master's in musicology; lecturer in Early Childhood Education at Songgok University.

Beheshtian, Shahrzad (Iran). Board member of OSA Iran; graduate of the Orff Institute Special Course; performer, teacher, composer, singer, and songwriter.

Bonal, Ester (Spain). Educator, promotor of educational and artistic projects; director of Xamfrá (Barcelona), a center for social inclusion through music and theatre.

Boonprakong, Krongtong (Thailand). Studied at the Orff Institute and Orff Schulwerk Certification Program levels 1–3 in USA; founder and executive of Jittamett Kindergarten; current president of OSA Thailand.

Brooke, Sarah (Australia, China). PhD; Australian creative arts educator who has spent considerable time as a music and movement education consultant in China.

Buchanan, Kate (United Kingdom). Freelance music education consultant and Deputy Chair of the Orff Society UK. She worked at the Royal Northern College of Music and Trinity Laban.

Chernous, Tatiana (Ukraine). Music teacher at the music center for children; art educator of the National University Ostrog Academy; leader of the art-psychological project for people with disabilities; Vice President of OSA Ukraine.

Correa Lopera, Catherine (Colombia). Master's in music education, violinist and lecturer; graduate of the Orff Institute Special Course and the San Francisco Orff Internship Program; member of the Board of directors of OSA Colombia; music and movement teacher.

Coşkun Toksoy, Atilla (Turkey). PhD; teaches music history and music pedagogy at ITU Turkish Music State Conservatory Musicology Department; author.

Cümbüş Auernig, Fatoş (Turkey). Coordinator for Orff Merkezi (OSA Turkey) and editor of their magazine *Orffinfo*.

Eren, Bilgehan (Turkey). PhD; Associate Professor, Ankara Music and Fine Arts University, Music Education Department; author.

Evans, Janice Klette (South Africa). Bachelor of Arts Honours; Orff Schulwerk Levels 1-3 (San Francisco); music teacher for 30 years at pre-primary, primary, secondary, and tertiary education levels; OSA South Africa committee member since 2003.

Farnia, Farzan (Iran). Graduate of the Orff Institute Special Course; Board member of OSA Iran; works as a music and movement instructor, author, lecturer, and composer.

Filianou, Maria (Greece). Music educator; master's in Special Education; PhD nominee in Special Pedagogy and Psychology; former president of OSA Greece (1998-2002); teaches at the Orff Schulwerk Course in the Moraiti School and the University of the Aegean.

Filimonova, Elena (Russia). Graduate of the Orff Institute Special Course; college lecturer.

Fir, Svetlana (Ukraine). Teacher of theory and history of music; founder and director of a private music studio; more than 10 years practice with the Orff Schulwerk approach; President of OSA Ukraine.

Gbolonyo, Kofi (Ghana, Canada). PhD; Professor of Ethnomusicology and African Studies at the University of British Columbia, Canada; founder & director of Nunya Academy and the Orff-Afrique Courses in Ghana.

Ghabrai, Kamran (Iran). Researcher at OSA Iran, has been working as fellow and senior researcher and lecturer in different educational institutes.

Goodkin, Doug (USA). Orff Schulwerk music educator: preschool/primary/middle school/adults/elders; created and developed music program at The San Francisco School (45 years); director of SF International Orff Course; author of many publications.

Grenier, Françoise (Canada). Master's in Music Education; graduate of the Orff Institute in Salzburg; director of the levels courses for the Québec Chapter of OSA Canada and COC Francophone Liaison.

Grosse, Paul (Singapore). MA; graduate of the Orff Institute Special Course; attended levels training in San Francisco; presently Vice President of OSA Singapore.

Hakimi, Mastaneh (Iran). Board member of OSA Iran; graduate of the Orff Institute Special Course; teacher trainer, composer, lecturer, percussionist, and singer.

Harper, Peta (Australia). Music educator for over 20 years; graduate of the Orff Institute Special Course; Vice President of OSA New South Wales and Board member of the Australian national OSA.

Hartmann, Wolfgang (Germany, Spain). Experience teaching Orff Schulwerk in primary school, conservatory, and university of music (Vienna, Salzburg, and San Sebastián-Donostia). Former Board Member of the Carl Orff Foundation and the IOSFS. Orff Schulwerk workshops in more than 30 countries.

Haselbach, Barbara (Austria). Prof. for dance; for many years director of the Orff Institute, its Special Course, and the IOSFS; editor of *Orff-Schulwerk Informationen/Heute;* dance teacher, choreographer; OS teachers' teacher in more than 35 countries; author of several books and articles; editor.

Hennessy, Sarah (United Kingdom). Chair of the Orff Society UK. She worked at the University of Exeter as a teacher educator and researcher, and is a Board Member of the IOSFS.

Hosoda, Junko (Japan). Professor of Early Childhood Education at Tokyo Kasei University; studied at the Orff Institute; former representative and Honorary Advisor to OSA Japan.

Iguchi, Tohru (Japan). Emeritus Professor of Kindergarten Education at Tokyo Gakugei University; master's in Education; graduate of the Orff Institute; Honorary Advisor to OSA Japan.

Jackson, James (Canada). Graduate of the Orff Institute Special Course; teaches primary to grade 6 students and acts as a Music Teacher Coach in Halifax, Nova Scotia; levels course director and instructor in Nova Scotia; Past President of OSA Canada.

Jantarawirote, Amanut (Thailand). Bachelor's degree in Music Education; master's in Composition; teacher of music at Triphat School; pursuing a doctorate in curriculum and teaching.

Jiřičková, Jiřina (Czech Republic). PhD; Asst. Prof. Dept. of Music Education, Charles University, Prague; teaches at the Prague Conservatory; choirmaster of a children's choir; lecturer and Executive Committee of the OSA Czech Republic.

Karşıyakalı Doğan, Didem (Turkey). PhD; music teacher at Ministry of Education; teaches Orff Schulwerk with autistic children; editor of *Orffdergi.*

Kawaguchi, Junko (Japan). Associate Professor of Music Education at Shirayuri University; master's in Pedagogy; graduate of the Orff Institute; deputy representative of OSA Japan.

Khokhryakova, Galina (Russia). Graduate of the Russian levels course; *Vestnik* editor; music teacher.

Kim, Hye-Young (South Korea). PhD in Early Childhood Education; Chairperson of OSA South Korea; lecturer at Gachon University & Osan University.

Kim, Yeni (South Korea). Master's in Music Pedagogy; Director of Seoul Institute of Music Education; Orff Schulwerk instructor at Unhyun Elementary School.

Kimiavi, Nastaran (Iran). President of OSA Iran; graduate of the Orff Institute Special Course; Orff Schulwerk teacher trainer, lecturer, composer, and music teacher.

Kugler, Michael (Germany). PhD; retired professor for music education at the Ludwig-Maximilians-Universität Munich; research on early instrumental music, the Jaques-Dalcroze method, Orff Schulwerk, and the pedagogical reception of African American vocal music; honorary member of OSA Germany.

Kuo, Fang-Ling (Taiwan). Assistant Professor at National Taipei University of Education and Music Department of Taipei Municipal University; Past President of OSA Taiwan and PhD candidate at National Taipei University of Education.

Kweon, Hyeon-Kyeong (Sr. Johannita, South Korea). Studied Music and Dance Pedagogy at the Orff Institute; master's in Integrated Arts Therapy; Deputy Director of Notre Dame Orff Schulwerk Education Institute.

Kwon, Oh-Sun (South Korea). PhD in Early Childhood Education; lecturer at Kyungin University of Education; director of the Korean Association for Early Childhood Music Education.

Laithong, Wittaya (Thailand). Attended a summer course at the Orff Institute and the Orff Schulwerk Certification Training Program Levels 1–3, Mills College, USA; currently special lecturer at Chulalongkorn University.

Locke, Linda M. (New Zealand). PhD; music educator (early childhood, studio, primary, pre-service, and in-service) for many years; co-founder and inaugural president of OSA New Zealand; lecturer in Music Education, Faculty for Creative Arts and Industries at the University of Auckland.

López-Ibor, Sofía (Spain, USA). Music educator, researcher, and performer; graduate of and teacher at the Orff Institute; presenter of OS workshops around the world; teacher at The San Francisco School and its International Orff Schulwerk teacher training program; author; former IOSFS Board Member.

Maubach, Christoph (Germany, New Zealand). M.Ed.; DIPT Waikato University and Orff Institute; former senior lecturer in New Zealand; teaches hybrid and live sessions for participants of all ages; frequent consultant and presenter in Taiwan. IOSFS Board Member.

McCluskey, Caroline (Scotland). Freelance musician and educator based in Glasgow; graduate of the Orff Institute Special Course; currently secretary of OSA Scotland.

Mongeon-Ferré, Julie (Canada). B.Ed. in Music Education; 29 years of music teaching experience in Manitoba; currently an Arts Education Consultant with Manitoba Education; OSA Canada Francophone Liaison.

Mosca, Maristela (Brazil). PhD in Education: curriculum, interdisciplinarity, and inclusion; certified Orff Schulwerk teacher; current president of OSA Brazil.

Nagaoka, Wakako (Japan). PhD; Professor of Music Education at Hamamatsu Gakuin University, Junior College; Mag. art. (Orff Institute, Mozarteum University Salzburg); deputy representative of OSA Japan.

Nakaji, Masayuki (Japan). PhD; Professor of Music Education at Tokyo Gakugei University; Mag. art. (Music Pedagogy, Mozarteum University Salzburg); representative of OSA Japan.

Onay, Evrim (Turkey). PhD; teaching flute and general music to children and adults; lecturer at TED University, Faculty of Education, Early Childhood and Primary Education Departments; author.

Özevin, Banu (Turkey). PhD; Associate Professor at Dokuz Eylül University, Music Education Department, Izmir; author.

Öztürk, Ali (Turkey). PhD; teaching at the Faculty of Education of Anadolu University, Eskisehir; chairman of the master's program in Drama in Education; graduate of the Orff Institute Special Course; author.

Özyoğurtcu, Senem (Turkey). Music educator; currently studying for a master's degree at the Orff Institute (Mozarteum University Salzburg); editor of *Orffdergi*.

Pekinel, Güher and Pekinel, Süher (Turkey). International duo pianists, performed with most distinguished orchestras and conductors all over Europe, the Far East, and the USA; pioneered three significant music education systems that follow international standards in Turkey.

Powell, Sarah (Australia). Committee member of the OSA New South Wales since 2011 and editor of *The Bulli*; lecturer in Creative Arts at Macquarie University teaching pre-service teachers.

Propato, Nacho (Argentina). Music teacher in different areas and levels of music education in Buenos Aires for over 25 years; current President of OSA Argentina; Orff Schulwerk Certification levels 1-3 in San Francisco.

Pucci, Magda (Brazil). PhD in Artistic Research; musician, anthropologist; researcher of world music and Brazilian Indigenous cultures; member of the Board of the ICTM Study Group in Music and Dance in Latin America and the Caribbean.

Purmpul, Geeta (Thailand). Bachelor's degree and a master's degree in Music Education; professor of Art in Music and Dance at Chulalongkorn University Demonstration School, Primary Division.

Raktaprajit, Sakrapee (Thailand). Bachelor of Music in Jazz; master's degree in Music Education; currently a researcher at the Galyani Vadhana Institute of Music and a special lecturer at Banditpatanasilpa Institute.

Regner, Hermann (Austria, 1928–2008). PhD; composer, conductor; Prof. at the Mozarteum University, Salzburg. He was director of the Orff Institute, the Orff-Schulwerk Forum, and the Special Course as well as editor of *Orff-Schulwerk Informationen* for many years. Author of numerous publications.

Rosensteiner, In-Hye (South Korea). Studied Music & Movement Education at the University of Music Vienna and Music & Dance Pedagogy at the Orff Institute; Orff Schulwerk lecturer at various educational institutions.

Sabırlı, Işık (Turkey). PhD candidate in Adult Education, Boğaziçi University.

Serna Mejía, Beatriz (Colombia). Master's in Music Education; certified in the San Francisco International Orff Course program; co-founder and current president of the OSA Colombia; music and movement teacher.

Shamrock, Mary (USA). PhD; Professor Emerita, California State University Northridge, music education and world music; Past President, OSA USA; former editor, *The Orff Echo;* Schulwerk teacher education course instructor, levels 1–3.

Shestopalova, Irina (Russia). Graduate of the Orff Institute Special Course; President of OSA Russia; music teacher; director of the Russian levels courses.

Silva, Lucilene (Brazil). Holds a master and is a doctoral candidate in music at UNICAMP, researcher of childhood music; member of the Board of the ICTM Study Group in Music and Dance in Latin America and the Caribbean.

Stewart, Carolee (USA). PhD; retired Dean—Peabody Preparatory, Johns Hopkins Univ.; middle and high school teacher; teacher educator; conference chair, editorial board, past president of OSA USA; graduate of the Orff Institute Special Course; editor of American Edition supplements; IOSFS Board 2010-2021.

Valchenko, Natalya (Russia). Orff Institute graduate (baccalaureate degree); music teacher.

Valsdottir, Kristín (Iceland). PhD; graduate of the Orff Institute; Dean of Department of Arts Education and Program Director for Music Teacher Education at the Iceland University of the Arts.

West, Catherine (Canada). Former editor of the national journal and Honorary Lifetime Member of OSA Canada; director of Orff Teacher Education at the Royal Conservatory of Music in Toronto.

Xu, Mai (China). Completed studies at the Shanghai Conservatory of Music and the University of Melbourne. She provides professional development in music education in a variety of settings in China.

Yaprak Kotzian, Emine (Turkey). University lecturer for Elemental Music Education at the Hochschule für Musik Nürnberg, Germany; studied at the Orff Institute; author; editor in chief of *Orffdergi.*

Yun, Young-Bae (South Korea). PhD in Child Studies (children's music education); Professor of Child Studies at Eulji University; executive conductor of the Rainbow Choir.

Zhilin, Vyacheslav (Russia). Founder of OSA Russia; music teacher; author and editor of Russian Orff Schulwerk publications.

Information about the
International Orff-Schulwerk Forum Salzburg

History

The Seminar and Information Centre for Orff-Schulwerk "Orff-Institut" was founded in 1961 at the then Mozarteum Academy in Salzburg by Carl Orff and Dr. Eberhard Preussner with the support from the Austrian Ministry of Education. In 1983, the Information Centre was re-named Orff-Schulwerk Centre Salzburg by Dr. Hermann Regner and became an independent institution. In 1984 it was registered as an independent non-profit association in Austria. When the Orff Centre Munich was created in 1988, the name was changed to Orff-Schulwerk Forum Salzburg. Finally, in 2014 the organization's name changed to International Orff-Schulwerk Forum Salzburg, assuming an increased area of responsibility.

The directors of the organization were Wilhelm Keller (1966–1982), Hermann Regner (1983–1994), Barbara Haselbach (1994–2018), and Shirley Salmon (2018-present).

The Forum

(Latin: market, marketplace) was placed in the city center in ancient times. It was a place where people could meet, gain information, execute business, listen to, and be heard by others. Today "forum" also means a meeting place for specialist discussion, for the exchange of experiences and opinions.

Structure

The IOSFS is a network of national Orff-Schulwerk Associations, Associated Schools and Institutions and individual members around the world. Its mission is to collect, to document and to publish international information about the work with Orff-Schulwerk, to further communication between institutions or individuals, to be an advisor for pedagogical questions and to initiate events or support them.

Forms of membership

• Orff-Schulwerk Association

- Associated School or Institution
- Individual member
- Honorary member

Tasks

As the center of an international network, it is the task of the International Orff-Schulwerk Forum Salzburg to collect and make available information about working with Orff-Schulwerk and to encourage exchange of information. In fulfilling this function, it works in close contact with the Orff Institute, the Orff Centre in Munich and all international Orff-Schulwerk associations.

The activities of the International Orff-Schulwerk Forum Salzburg include:

I. Contact and Exchange

- with and among national Orff-Schulwerk Associations
- with and among Associated Schools and Institutions
- with graduates with advanced studies in Orff-Schulwerk
- with interested teachers, researchers, artists, and institutions

II. Information

- about Orff-Schulwerk in the past and present
- about projects and developments in different countries
- about courses and publications
- about current themes with regard to contents and organizational questions

III. Publications

- Magazine: *Orff-Schulwerk Informationen / Orff-Schulwerk Heute* (OSH) Issues 1–100
- *Texts about the Theory and Practice of Orff-Schulwerk* (Vol. 2 is in preparation)
- Reports about international Orff-Schulwerk work
- Documentations of symposia (Book/DVD)
- Other publications

IV. Advice

- on publications of new adaptations of the Schulwerk
- on academic work, publications, new editions
- on syllabi, curricula and for lecturers in various educational and social institutions
- on future projects
- on the introduction of Orff-Schulwerk to an institution or country
- on the founding of a new Orff-Schulwerk Association or Associated School/Institution

V. Events

- Annual conventions for IOSFS members
- Meetings with editors of Orff-Schulwerk association newsletters and magazines
- Orff-Schulwerk symposia and other events

VI. Recommendations and Guidelines of the International Orff-Schulwerk Forum Salzburg

- Recommendations and guidelines for organizing Teacher education courses
- Recommendations for the founding of a national Orff-Schulwerk Association
- Recommendations for the founding of an Associated School/Institution

Contact:
www.orff-Schulwerk-forum-salzburg.org
info.iosfs@gmail.com

Orff Schulwerk Associations around the World

COUNTRY	ASSOCIATION	FOUNDED
ARGENTINA	Asociación Orff-Schulwerk Argentina (AAOrff)	2009
	http://www.aaorff.com	
AUSTRALIA	Australian National Council of Orff Schulwerk (ANCOS)	1976
	http://www.ancos.org.au	
AUSTRALIA	Victorian Orff-Schulwerk Association (VOSA)	1977
	http://www.vosa.org	
AUSTRALIA	West Australian Orff-Schulwerk Association (WAOSA)	1994
	http://www.waosa.org.au	
AUSTRALIA	Queensland Orff-Schulwerk Association (QOSA)	1967
	http://qosa.org.au	
AUSTRALIA	Tasmanian Orff-Schulwerk Association (TOSA)	1983
	http://www.ancos.org.au/pages/state-associations/tasmania	
AUSTRALIA	Orff-Schulwerk Association of South Australia Inc. (OSASA)	1987
	http://www.osasa.net	
AUSTRALIA	New South Wales Orff-Schulwerk Association Inc. (NSWOSA)	1972
	http://www.orffnsw.org.au	
AUSTRIA	Orff-Schulwerk Gesellschaft Österreich	1961
	https://orff-schulwerk.at/	
BRAZIL	Associação ORFF Brasil - "Música e Movimento na Educação" (ABRAORFF)	2004
	http://www.abraorff.org.br	
BULGARIA	Bulgarische Assoziation Orff-Schulwerk	2004
CANADA	Carl Orff Canada - Music for Children / Musique pour Enfants	1974
	https://www.orffcanada.ca/	
CHINA	Orff Association of the Chinese Musicians Association (COSA)	1991
	http://www.chinaorff.com	
COLOMBIA	Asociación Orff Colombia (ACOLORFF)	2014
	http://www.acolorff.org	
CROATIA	Croatian Orff Schulwerk Association - CROSA - Hrvatska Orff Schulwerk Udruga – HOSU	2002
	http://www.hosu.hr/	
CZECH REPUBLIC	Česká Orffova společnost (COS)	1995
	http://www.orff.cz/	

COUNTRY	ASSOCIATION	FOUNDED
ESTONIA	Estonian Society for Music Education (EMÕL)	1992
	http://www.emol.ee	
FINLAND	JaSeSoi ry, Orff-Schulwerk Association of Finland	1985
	http://www.jasesoi.com	
FRANCE	Association Carl Orff France	2001
	http://orff.fr/	
GEORGIA	Georgian Orff-Schulwerk Association (Georff)	2015
GERMANY	Orff-Schulwerk Gesellschaft Deutschland e.V., Musik+Tanz+Erziehung	1962
	http://www.orff-schulwerk.de	
GREECE	Hellenic Association of Music & Movement Education (ESMA)	1990
	http://www.orffesma.gr	
HONG KONG	Hong Kong Orff-Schulwerk Association	2016
	http://www.hosa.org.hk	
ICELAND	Samtök Orff Tónmennta Íslandi (SOTI)	2007
IRAN	Association Orff-Schulwerk Iran (ADAMAK)	2015
	http://www.iranorff.com	
ITALY	Orff-Schulwerk Italiano (OSI)	2001
	http://www.orffitaliano.com	
ITALY	Società Italiana di Musica Elementare Orff-Schulwerk (SIMEOS)	1978
	http://www.simeos.it	
JAPAN	Japanese Orff-Schulwerk Association	1988
	http://www.orff-schulwerk-japan.com	
MACAO	Macau Orff Schulwerk Association (MOSA)	2018
	https://www.macauorff.org	
NEW ZEALAND	Orff New Zealand Aotearoa (ONZA)	2005
	http://www.orffnz.org	
POLAND	Polskie Towarzystwo Carla Orffa (PTCO)	1994
	http://www.orff.pl	
RUSSIA	Orff-Schulwerk Association Russia (ROSA)	1988
	http://rusorff.ru	
SCOTLAND	Scottish Orff Schulwerk Association (SOSA)	2010
	http://www.orffscotland.org	
SINGAPORE	Orff-Schulwerk Association Singapore	2002
	https://www.singorff.com	
SLOVAKIA	Slovenská Orffova spoločnost	1998
SLOVENIA	Slovensko Društvo Carla Orffa (SDCO)	2001
	http://slorff.weebly.com	

COUNTRY	ASSOCIATION	FOUNDED
SOUTH AFRICA	Orff-Schulwerk Society of South Africa	1972
	http://www.orff.co.za	
SOUTH KOREA	Korean Orff Schulwerk Association (KOSA)	2004
	http://www.korff.or.kr	
SPAIN	Asociación Orff España (AOE)	1996
	http://www.orff-spain.org	
SPAIN	ASSOCIACIÓ ORFF CATALUNYA	2020
	https://www.orff.cat/	
SWITZERLAND	Orff-Schulwerk Schweiz - Gesellschaft für Musik- und Tanzerziehung	1979
	http://www.orff-schulwerk.ch	
TAIWAN	Taiwan Orff-Schulwerk Association (TOSA)	1992
	http://www.orff.org.tw	
THAILAND	Thai Orff-Schulwerk Association (THOSA)	2008
	http://www.thaiorff.org	
TURKEY	Orff-Schulwerk Egitim ve Danismanlik Merkezi Türkiye - Orff Merkezi	2001
	http://www.orffmerkezi.org	
TURKEY	Anadolu Orff-Schulwerk Dernengi (ORFFDER)	2021
	http://www.orffder.org	
UKRAINE	Orff Schulwerk Association Ukraine	2018
UNITED KINGDOM	Orff Society UK http://www.orff.org.uk	1964
USA	American Orff-Schulwerk Association (AOSA)	1968
	http://www.aosa.org	

Network of Associated Schools and Institutions

COUNTRY	NAME OF SCHOOL OR INSTITUTION
ARGENTINA	Escuela de Artes Pestalozzi
	http://www.pestalozzi.edu.ar
CHINA	IMMEA - Institute for Music and Movement Education Advancement
	http://www.immeachina.cn
CZECH REPUBLIC	Grundschule der deutsch-tschechischen Verständigung
	http://www.gtmskola.cz
FINLAND	Taidepäiväkoti Konsti Kindergarten
	http://www.taidepaivakotikonsti.fi
GERMANY	Carl-Orff-Grundschule Traunwalchen
	https://www.carl-orff-gs-traunwalchen.de
GERMANY	Carl-Orff-Grundschule Andechs
	https://carlorffschule.de
GERMANY	DOrff-Werkstatt e.V.
	http://www.dorffwerkstatt.de
GERMANY	Carl Orff-Grundschule Altenerding
	http://www.carl-orff-gs-altenerding.de
GERMANY	Carl-Orff-Schule (Grund- und Musikmittelschule) Dießen a.A.
	http://www.c-o-v.de
GERMANY	Elementare Musikpädagogik. Künstlerisch-pädagogischer Studiengang innerhalb der Hochschule für Musik und Theater München
	http://emp.hmtm.de/
GREECE	The Moraitis School
	http://www.orff.gr
ITALY	CDM Centro Didattico Musicale
	http://www.centrodidatticomusicale.it
ITALY	Musicanto - Centro per la Ricerca e la Didattica Musicale
	http://www.musicanto.org
ITALY	Scuola Popolare di Musica Donna Olimpia
	http://www.donnaolimpia.it
ITALY	International School of Bergamo
	http://www.isbergamo.com
THAILAND	Jittamett Kindergarten
	http://www.jittamett.ac.th/jittamett.ac.th_public_html/About.html

COUNTRY	NAME OF SCHOOL OR INSTITUTION
TURKEY	ALEV Schule
	https://alev.k12.tr
USA	Alliance for Active Music Making (AAMM)
	https://www.allianceamm.org
USA	American Center for Elemental Music and Movement (ACEMM)
	http://www.acemm.us
USA	The San Francisco School
	http://www.sfschool.org

OTHER PENTATONIC PRESS PUBLICATIONS

LOOKING TO THE ROOTS: A Guide to Understanding Orff Schulwerk
—Wolfgang Hartmann

A look at how the history of Orff Schulwerk's development and its guiding principles can inform the practice of the present and the possibilities of the future. (2021)

TEACH LIKE IT'S MUSIC: An Artful Approach to Education
—Doug Goodkin

A look at some of the details behind inspired teaching, with emphasis on creating a musical flow in one's classes with enticing beginnings, connected middles and satisfying endings. A seamless blend of philosophy, pedagogy and practical ideas useful for teachers of all subjects. (2019)

FROM WIBBLETON TO WOBBLETON:
Adventures in the Elements of Music and Movement
—James Harding

Integrated arts lessons with graphic illustrations. Includes arrangements of nursery rhymes for Orff instruments. (2013)

ALL BLUES: Jazz for the Orff Ensemble
—Doug Goodkin

36 pieces including roots, vocal blues and jazz blues scored for Orff Instruments, with accompanying CD of children playing the arrangements. The first of several supplements to Now's the Time. (2012)

BLUE IS THE SEA: Music, Dance & Visual Arts
—Sofía López-Ibor

Integrated arts and activities for preschool, elementary and middle school that includes poetry, dance, drama, artwork in various media and music arranged for Orff Ensemble. Many examples of student art and photos of children, all in full vibrant color. (2011)

INTERY MINTERY: Nursery Rhymes for Body, Voice and Orff Ensemble
—Doug Goodkin

48 activities connecting music and poetry, with musical scores and suggested lesson plans. (2008)

THE ABC'S OF EDUCATION: A Primer for Schools to Come
—Doug Goodkin

26 essays imagining ways in which schools could be refreshed by including Arts, Beauty, Character and more. (2006)

NOW'S THE TIME: Teaching Jazz to All Ages
—Doug Goodkin

A unique approach to jazz education via Orff practice. 64 activities that move from speech, movement, body percussion and roots music to blues, jazz standards and compositions arranged for Orff instruments. (2004)